TRIUMPHS and

YOUNG PEOPLE, MARKETS and the TRANSITION from SCHOOL to WORK

Phil Hodkinson, Andrew C. Sparkes and
Heather Hodkinson

David Fulton Publishers

London

David Fulton Publishers Ltd
2 Barbon Close, London WC1N 3JX

First published in Great Britain by
David Fulton Publishers 1996

British Library Cataloguing in Publication Data

A catalogue record for this book is available from the British Library

ISBN 1–85346-442-2

Typeset by The Harrington Consultancy Ltd.
Printed in Great Britain by the Cromwell Press Ltd, Melksham

Contents

Acknowledgements

Far too many people have contributed to the writing of this book for us to include them all. We hope that those not mentioned will forgive us if we highlight just a few significant contributions. The first is the Economic and Social Research Council (ESRC). Without their funding of the research nothing could have been written, and we are grateful for their support. As significant was the Training and Enterprise Council (TEC), who ran the pilot scheme which was the focus of this investigation. They gave us access to people and information, and were positive and helpful when we made requests of them, even though our requests must have added to already demanding work loads. They have always been open with us, and never attempted to influence what we discovered or chose to say. We were impressed by the professionalism, dedication and commitment with which the TEC personnel we met were working to improve the training of young people for the benefit of the local economy. They have continued to do that long after the fieldwork for our study was completed, and the Youth Credits scheme they are operating today will be different in many respects from the one we analysed. This book, in that sense, is already a piece of history.

Above all, we wish to thank all the people, from different walks of life, who gave up their time to be interviewed, and answered our questions so helpfully. Of all these, 10 young people stand out, for it is about part of their lives that this book is written. To Alison, Becky, Clive, David, Elaine, Frances, Helen, Laura, Peter and Sam, we owe the greatest debt of all.

Tables 1.1 and 8.1 and Figure 9.2 were first published in P. Hodkinson and A.C. Sparkes, 'Markets and Vouchers: the inadequacy of individualist policies for vocational education and training in England and Wales', *The Journal of Educational Policy*, **10(2)**, 189–207. They are reproduced here with the kind permission of Taylor & Francis.

The Purpose and Structure of the Book

The transition from school to work has always been a crucial time in the lives of young people. How and when this transition is made can have a major impact upon the sense of identity they develop, the importance they feel they have in the eyes of others, the kind of person they want to be and their view of the world in general. This book is about the nature of that transition for one small group of young people, making the journey in the new policy environment of post-Thatcherite Britain. These young people were the focus of a major research study, funded by the Economic and Social Research Council (ESRC), whose support is gratefully acknowledged. Our main purpose is to tell their stories and to explore issues of policy and social theory that have significance far beyond the immediate contexts of their lives.

Many of the issues raised have implications beyond Britain. There is an extensive literature addressing the transition from education to work and the provision of Vocational Education and Training (VET) [1] in the late twentieth century in a wide range of countries. No attempt has been made in this book to summarise this literature, or to analyse the extent of commonality and difference between national contexts and approaches. Readers wishing to explore these issues should consult other sources (Bynner and Roberts, 1991; Green and Steedman, 1993; Ryan, 1991; Skilbeck *et al.*, 1994; Springhall, 1993). Rather, this British example is a case study. In some respects, Britain is a worst-case/best-case exemplar of a global shift towards individualism and market forces as key policy imperatives in this area. The lessons drawn here have implications for any society where such approaches are being considered or developed.

Our investigation focused on the career decision making of young people, together with the development of their careers through the first 18 months or so of their time on a government funded training scheme. In what we call the new paradigm for VET in Britain, the choices of young people in a training market are supposedly central to policy and practice. However, there has been surprisingly little research done into how such choices are actually made.

Partly because of our teaching experiences, we share a concern to help young people, perhaps especially those against whom society appears to stack the odds. We wanted to give voice to some of those young people who choose to leave full-time education at the ages of 16+ or 17+. For this group, the rhetoric of the new policy approach was of empowerment. The issuing of vouchers, called Training Credits, supposedly gave them more control over their own training and made training providers more responsive to 'customer' demand. We were curious about how well such approaches would work. We hoped that something could indeed be done to help and support such young people, without waiting for some future utopia where the deep-seated inequalities of society magically disappear.

However, we were also aware of overwhelming evidence that life chances in Britain are unequal, and structured by factors such as social class, gender, ethnicity and geographical location. We wished to explore the middle ground, between such broad structural patterns of inequality and the individualist idealism of current policy approaches.

We approached the research from the starting assumption that the operation of the new Training Credits pilot scheme (explained in Chapter 1) would depend upon the perceptions of and interactions between a diverse range of stakeholders. By stakeholders, we mean groups and individuals who had a legitimate personal or professional interest in the operation of the scheme. These included the young people themselves, their parents, careers teachers, employers, training providers and officials of the Training and Enterprise Councils (TECs), who were responsible for operating the schemes in England and Wales.

Our previous research interests, together with the broader aims of the intended research, caused us to focus on a small case study. One of the advantages of this is that the data produced is rich and multi-dimensional. In making sense of this data, we focused on the lives and experiences of 10 young people, through their perceptions and those of the other stakeholders they came into contact with. In presenting some of our findings here we have retained that focus. One of our hopes is that what follows will allow you, the reader, to experience aspects of the training careers of these young people, and through their stories, make your own sense of the complexity that was Training Credits in action. As Wolcott (1994:17) writes,

> Qualitative researchers need to be storytellers. That, rather than any disdain for number crunching, ought to be one of their distinguishing attributes. To be able to tell ... a story well is crucial to the enterprise. When we cannot engage others to read our stories – our completed and complete accounts – then our efforts at descriptive research are for naught.

We do not believe that there is one correct interpretation of these stories that we researchers should reveal. Part of our purpose in writing these stories is to allow readers to make their own interpretations of what we were told. However, we also believe that part of our job, as researchers and authors, is to share with others our own interpretation of what we discovered based, as it is, on access to far more data than can be presented here, and to wider reading than some others will have time or interest in doing. Our analysis and interpretation of the data resulted in a new theoretical model of career decision making and career progression, which we call 'careership'. This is fully explained in the final two chapters, but a brief summary is given here so that readers can see why we have told the stories in the ways we have and understand where the narrative is leading.

We see career decision making as consisting of three completely inter-locked dimensions. Firstly, the ways in which young people made actual choices about which job placement to take were *pragmatically rational*. They were neither irrational, nor did they follow a completely *technically rational* decision making process, such as that which is often assumed within recent policy literature. These pragmatically rational decisions were both constrained and enabled by their *horizons for action*. There are two parts to this. No one can choose a placement that does not exist or for which they would not be considered. Horizons for action, therefore, are partly determined by external opportunities in the training market. Equally, no one can choose a placement that they do not perceive as suitable or appropriate for themselves. Therefore, horizons are also formed by our own subjective perceptions. In practice, these two sides of horizons for action are linked, because what is available affects what we perceive to be possible and what we perceive as desirable can alter the available options as when young people or their parents arrange placements with local employers they already know.

Perceptions are rooted in the identity of the young person. This, in turn, is strongly influenced by their life histories, the interactions they have with significant others, their experiences and the social and cultural background that is part of their identity. However, that cultural background does not determine the choices they make in a mechanistic sense. A strength of our model of decision making is that it renders unnecessary the tendency, partly derived from the structure of the English language, to categorise actions and decisions as either determined by some external force, or the result of unfettered free will. Neither view fits the experiences reported to us.

The second dimension of career decision making is the social interactions with others who have some influence on the process. Young people are not the only ones who choose. Often, what happened more closely resembled employers choosing their trainees. What the stories reveal is a complex system of negotiation, bargaining and sometimes struggle, within what, following Bourdieu, we call the youth training *field*. The young people, their employers, their parents, their careers officers and their training providers were all players in the field. They had resources of varying types and quality, which produced unequal power relations. The resulting placements were as much an outcome of the interactions between such players, as they were of choices made by the young people. The stories reveal that the interactions in the field and the pragmatic decisions of young people are completely interrelated. It is not possible to understand either outside the context of the other.

The third and final part of careership concerns progression over time. We argue that career decisions are often transitory in nature, and that much of the current literature and policy thinking is unrealistically wedded to a view that career trajectories, as they are often called, are largely predictable. That is, that they are determined by choices made and/or by the social and cultural structures within which people live and work. In contrast, we argue that the future of a career trajectory is partly unknown. It is for this reason that we replace the mathematical metaphor of trajectory with the looser term 'careership'. Career paths can either change or be confirmed in a complex variety of ways. We suggest that this can be best understood through the concepts of *turning points* linked by periods of *routine*. Turning points are times when a person changes direction or at least considers such a change, and we suggest there are three types:

1. Those forced by unexpected external events (e.g. redundancy)

2. Those built in to the structure of British life (e.g. when a young person has to choose whether to leave school or continue in full-time education at 16+)

3. Those initiated by the young people themselves, for a variety of reasons.

Routines also contribute to change (or confirmation) and are related to the turning points. Once more, there are three types:

1. Some routines confirm original choices, so that a pathway chosen becomes deeply ingrained.

2. Others can be contradictory, as when subsequent experience causes a person to regret the choice made and/or to consider a different career.

3. Finally, routine can sometimes socialise a person into accepting as appropriate a career that was reluctantly entered into, perhaps because nothing better was available at the time.

We claim that the experiences recounted in the stories which follow, and this model of careership that derives from them, fundamentally challenge some of the premises upon which the current vocational education and training policies in Britain are based. We claim that these policies are naively individualistic, ignoring the complexities of decision making, of interrelationships in the field and of the uncertainty of careership. Further, we suggest that they are inherently and mistakenly *technically rational*. By this we mean that they take an industrial metaphor for people and society, which sees people acting with a consistency, predictability and controllability more sensibly associated with inanimate machines. There is an emphasis on efficiency, planning and controlling structures and procedures. These include a belief in 'free markets', which we argue depend on unrealistic assumptions about decision making and largely ignore the complex reality of culturally embedded social life.

Finally, we argue, in Chapter 9, that our model of careership can make a small contribution to long-standing theoretical questions in sociology and related social sciences, about the balance between individual freedom of choice and structural and cultural constraints on that choice.

THE STRUCTURE OF THE BOOK

Chapter 1 sets the context for the study. In it, we begin by discussing what is known about the nature of the transition to work, predominantly in Britain. This is followed by a brief discussion of the changing nature of employment and the implications of these changes for VET policy. We then describe recent changes to VET policy in Britain, which form the more immediate backdrop to the study. Next we focus down to examine the nature of the Training Credits initiative itself, as exemplified in the particular pilot scheme that was the focus of our investigation. There follows a brief description of the research that was actually carried out.

The stories in subsequent chapters are a synthesis of what participants told us and the ways in which we made sense of what we were told. Much of the middle part of the book is in the form of stories, told largely in the participants' own words.

We have presented these stories in a variety of ways. Chapter 2 shows the place within the scheme of those stakeholders other than the young people. This is done through extensive use of quotations, selected to represent both commonalities and differences within and between stakeholder groups. Those quotations are presented according to current writing conventions. They are indented, gaps in what is transcribed are indicated by ellipses (...), and words not actually spoken are in square brackets. That chapter, with Chapter 1, provides the context through which the stories that follow can be understood.

Chapters 3 and 4 each tell the story of one young person. Helen and Laura were picked because the progression through Training Credits was not smooth for them. Both faced at least one major transformation of their career during the period of our research. Their stories raise important issues about the transition to work and the nature of career development. Both these stories, and those that follow, are told through the voices of several individuals who contributed to the action. In these stories we have broken some of the customary conventions of research writing. Thus, in places, we have changed a word or two in the transcript, if by so doing we can express more clearly, in an extract, what we were told in a longer interview. We have minimised the use of square brackets and ellipses, and eschewed indented quotations, so that the constant shift of margin width and print size does not break the flow of the text or encourage the reader to skip the quotations.

In Chapters 5 and 6, four more stories are told, though now we concentrate on key parts of the stories, grouped to raise particular issues. In Chapter 5 we meet two young women, Elaine and Alison, who each used the Training Credit to take some control over their own training. We focus on why and how they did that, and the extent of the control that resulted from their actions and those of other stakeholders. In Chapter 6, the focus is on the problematic relationship between on and off the job training. For Becky, a traditional, examination-based, off-the-job course was causing problems. For Clive, it was the National Vocational Qualifications (NVQ) approach, tied to the necessity of collecting on the job evidence that proved impossibly difficult.

In Chapter 7, we break from the format of stories. We use the experiences of the four remaining young people to explore two things. Firstly, all four experienced fairly unproblematic career progression, in conventional, gender stereotypical occupations. Their experiences form a necessary balance to the problems in the other stories. Secondly, within each of their experiences there are critical incidents and issues which add to the our understanding of the overall complexity of the transition from school to work, in the context of the Training Credits scheme. In this chapter and the final two, we revert to the conventional style for reporting quotations that was used in Chapters 1 and 2.

In Chapters 8 and 9, we synthesise our findings and move beyond description into interpretation. In Chapter 8, we return to the idea of pragmatically rational career decision making, in relation to current policies for careers education and guidance. This is more broadly located in a critique of the technical rationality and excessive individualism of current British policy towards VET. In the final chapter, we develop the model of careership further, in order to engage with the theoretical questions about agency, social structure and culture in the transition to work. Throughout the book we have tried to keep jargon to a minimum, but some use of specialist language was unavoidable, especially in Chapter 9.

No author can control the way a book is read. Those interested in the lived experiences of young people could skip Chapter 1, and stop before Chapters 8 and 9. We have deliberately confined most of our theoretical analysis to the final chapter, so that the rest of the book can stand without it. Those readers especially interested in theory or policy could skip the middle chapters, and move straight from Chapter 1 to the two final chapters. We hope that you will resist the second temptation. Our analysis is nothing without the stories upon which it is built. It is the accounts of the experiences of our interviewees that form the heart of this book and make the complexity of the transition from school to work real and accessible.

1

Training Credits and the Transition to Work in Post-Thatcherite Britain

STRUCTURAL INEQUALITIES IN THE TRANSITION TO WORK

There are consistent differences between the career paths of young people from different backgrounds in many societies. In Britain, possibly to a greater extent than elsewhere in the world, these differences are partly class related. 20 years ago, Ashton and Field (1976) identified three broadly different types of work. These they called 'long-term career jobs', which were dominated by the middle classes; 'working-class career jobs' which included technical, clerical and skilled manual occupations; and 'low-skill' jobs including unskilled manual and shop work.

Since they wrote, there have been major changes to the British educational system, to the labour market and to the entry to work. Yet despite these changes, recent research – for example the ESRC 16–19 Initiative, the Employment Department Youth Cohort Study and the Scottish Young People's Surveys – still confirms the general validity of the Ashton and Field classification (Furlong, 1992; Roberts, 1993). In Britain in the late 1980s, there was a stratified youth labour market, so that Ashton and Field's three categories could be further sub-divided. For example, Roberts and Parsell (1992) identify three different types of Youth Training Scheme (YTS) experience, based predominantly on the chances of acquiring a job at the end of training. Contributors in Bates and Riseborough (1993) describe considerable differences between experiences, attitudes and background of young people across a range of post-16 education and training provision. These studies confirm deep-seated inequalities in the British labour market and that entry into the different career trajectories was largely dependent on levels of qualification gained at 16+. This, in turn, was strongly influenced by social class, which was itself a major independent factor in explaining career route. Gender still marked out strongly the type of occupational area likely to be entered (Griffin, 1985) and ethnic origin further restricted opportunities for some groups (Blackman, 1987; Cross and Wrench, 1991). Finally, Banks *et al.* (1992) show that geographical location was a significant factor, owing to variations in unemployment and job opportunities.

Such analyses often imply a determinist viewpoint that we claim underestimates the contested nature of social reproduction and the degree of choice that faces many individuals. For example, Furlong (1992) explores such career patterns but although he acknowledges the importance of what he calls the 'subjective realities' of young people in making career decisions, the nature of his work makes it difficult for these to be examined. Consequently, his and other similar large-scale survey studies, though they provide rich and valuable descriptive data, do relatively little to help us understand how and why such patterns persist. Contributors in Bates and Riseborough (1993) provide snapshot insights into the widely differing experiences of different groups of young people, and show how, *once on a chosen route*, they are socialised into a narrow, focused set of goals and ambitions, for some groups significantly different from those with which courses were begun (Bates, 1990, 1993). They do not, however, explore the processes by which the original choices were made.

Some studies in other national contexts lay more emphasis on the processes through which such different pathways are stratified. Gaskell (1992) explores the ways in which gender influences career progression in Canada. Okano (1993) shows how, in Japan, young people's location in a hierarchical career structure is influenced by their cultural resources, influenced by a stratified pattern of schooling. Frykholm and Nitzler (1993) describe a situation in Sweden that is reminiscent of what Bates and Riseborough (1993) describe in Britain, but focus on the process whereby educational pathways are reinforced. Drawing from such overseas studies and a process-oriented analysis in Britain by Brown (1987), we present an analysis of the social processes by which such patterns of inequality, and the degree of individual variation within such patterns, are produced out of the life courses and decision making of young people and others. Whereas the prime focal point in these studies is schooling, our analysis focuses directly on career decision making, the transition into work and experiences beyond full-time education.

There is a sharp contrast between the implicit determinism of much contemporary research on the transition to work in Britain and the bold assertions that British policy should be based on assumptions of individual free choice and markets derived, in turn, from an increasingly dominant belief in a new 'post-Fordist' world. It is the tensions and space between these perspectives that this book explores.

POST-FORDISM AND THE LOW-SKILLS EQUILIBRIUM

There is a widespread belief that the nature of employment and industrial organisation are in the process of rapid and radical transformation. Piore and Sabel (1984) distinguished between traditional manufacturing, based on Fordist mass production techniques supporting a hierarchical bureaucracy, and the 'new way' of flexible specialisation. For other writers, such as Murray (1991), 'post-Fordism' is the term used, to describe changes which included flexible specialisation. Brown and Lauder (1992) present one of many accounts of the differences between Fordism and post-Fordism. The latter is seen as located in global markets rather than protected national markets, to be based on flexible production systems, with flatter and flexible organisational structures. The workforce has to be multi-skilled and flexible, with high trust and shared responsibility in teams. There are many accounts of such practices spreading into large 'leading edge' employers, often based on Japanese styles of management.

What drives all this is the need for continual change in order to remain competitive in widely fluctuating markets. Such endemic change can be either supply or demand led, either based on new technologies or responding to new markets. The present is future-directed, as firms continually rethink their place in the market and constantly search for higher quality, through approaches such as Total Quality Management.

Post-Fordism brings an accentuated division between core and periphery workers (Atkinson and Meager, 1991). Those in the core have relatively secure jobs but must constantly re-skill. They are likely to be (relatively) well paid. Peripheral workers lack job security. They are employed on temporary or part-time contracts or are sub-contractors to the main firm.

It is widely believed that future employment will be increasingly restricted to well-educated and trained workers. Both core and periphery workers need high levels of education to adapt continually to new and more demanding work opportunities. Those lacking such qualities will be increasingly unable to get employment, whilst firms will survive only if there is a pool of highly educated 'knowledge workers' (Reich, 1991) for them to draw on.

Whilst this post-Fordist model is global in its vision, it has had a particular impact in the British context. For example, in one influential article, Finegold and Soskice (1991) argue that Britain faces an industrial crisis. British industry is trapped in a low skills equilibrium of low pay, low levels of education and training, short term financial costings and poor quality output. They argue that this low skills equilibrium is potentially disastrous, and Finegold (1991) goes on to claim that major policy shifts are necessary to break into the alternative high skills equilibrium. Some, but only some, of those shifts must be to VET policy.

Such post-Fordist beliefs are widely accepted as the contextual imperative for new VET policy in Britain, by policy makers and pressure groups as different as the Conservative Government, the Labour opposition, the Confederation of British Industry (CBI) and the Trades Union Congress (TUC). This view is sometimes over-simplified into the two virtuous circles that many believe should be the focus of VET policy.

Firstly, high skills leads to high productivity which leads to high wages. Secondly, high investment in training leads to high standards which leads to high aspirations (Ball, 1991). This is a far cry from the complexity of the original Finegold and Soskice analysis. Similarly, many enthusiasts for the post-Fordist future oversimplify the nature and extent of the changes, overlooking Harvey's (1989:338) warning that neither Fordism nor post-Fordism are homogeneous, and that 'the oppositions [between them] ... are never so clear cut, and the "structure of feeling" in any society is always a synthetic movement between the two'. There are ongoing debates about the nature and extent of post-Fordism and its implications for education and training (for example, contrast Brown and Lauder, 1992 and Young, 1993 with Jones and Hatcher, 1994 and Avis et al., 1996). Maguire (1995) argues that a significant and continuing proportion of youth employment will be into relatively low skill jobs, and that many firms will carry on operating in ways far removed from post-Fordism. The stories told in this book support his position, and challenge the extent to which post-Fordist approaches have influenced many small employers and at least some medium-sized firms in Britain. Marsh (1988), Roberts (1991) and Petersen and Mortimer (1994) remind us of the now all-pervading mass unemployment, which could be seen as creating a further category of non-worker, beyond the periphery. Our main concern is not with the reality or otherwise of such employment changes, but with the effect of a belief in post-Fordism on evolving VET policy and practice.

RECENT CHANGES IN VET POLICY IN BRITAIN

Ever since the mid-1970s, VET has had a high political profile in Britain. There has been almost universal agreement that not only was British VET largely inadequate, but also that its dramatic improvement was a necessary condition for the country's future economic prosperity. The first major policy of the Conservative government on this issue was the New Training Initiative (NTI) in 1981 (ED/DES, 1981). This set the ambitious agenda of improving the competitiveness of British industry through improvements to VET. The NTI was integral to the rapid rise of the Manpower Services Commission (MSC). The history of the policy period, and the ways in which the broad objectives of the NTI were gradually undermined by the more pressing political need to reduce rapidly rising youth unemployment, has been well documented elsewhere (Ainley and Corney, 1990; Evans, 1992; Skilbeck et al., 1994). In essence, the activity and budget of the MSC became dominated by the provision of the YTS, a training programme for 16+ school leavers.

Evans (1992) suggests that the decade of MSC and YTS was an anomalous centralist, interventionist period in British VET policy. Lee et *al.* (1990) disagree, suggesting that YTS always retained strong voluntarist principles. Both agree that the post-MSC and YTS period marked a dramatic increase in voluntarism as, towards the end of the 1980s, the Thatcher government introduced major changes to British VET policy that were more consistent with their individualist market principles. These included the end of the MSC, transmogrified and emasculated, eventually, into the Training, Enterprise and Employment Directorate (TEED) of the Employment Department [2]. Day-to-day provision of VET was devolved to 82 TECs in England and Wales and to 22 Local Enterprise Companies in Scotland. Evans (1992) discusses the policy imperatives behind their creation and Bennett *et al.* (1994) analyse their successes and failures in action. The latter demonstrate tensions between the principle of devolved responsibility and decision-making, upon which the TECs were supposedly founded, and the pressures from the Civil Service culture and the needs of Treasury accountability which led to increasingly stultifying economic control by TEED.

One unsolved problem of the 1980s had been the means of ensuring that training provided on YTS was of high quality. For Lee *et al.* (1992) strong central regulation was required, which would curtail the freedom of employers to train as they liked. Such approaches were opposed by the employers themselves and were anathema to a government bent on reducing red tape and public expenditure. Within this post-MSC policy climate, one of the leading British employers' organisations, the CBI, came up with a seductively simple solution. Training quality was to be ensured through a customer driven training market (CBI, 1989, 1993). This thinking proved highly influential on government policy.

THE NEW VET POLICY PARADIGM: INDIVIDUALISM AND THE TRAINING MARKET

The recent changes in VET policy and the ideological climate within which they have been introduced have resulted in a new paradigm for VET in Britain, based on individualism, choice and market forces (Hodkinson and Sparkes, 1995b). By paradigm, we mean a belief system about VET that is widely subscribed to and which, in the way Kuhn (1970) described for science, limits the understanding of those who accept it, so that questionable and problematic issues become self-evident truths, whilst other possible viewpoints are obscured. For the CBI, the central, organising idea of this paradigm was 'careership', but they do not use the term in the same way we do.

Careership gives pride of place to the individual and his or her responsibility for self-development in a market environment. It bridges the long-standing academic–vocational divide through four key elements:

– Relevant qualifications and the transferable core skills needed by employers and employees alike ....
– An individual focus through personal profiles incorporating records of achievement and individual action plans, in education and training.
– High class professional and independent careers advice and guidance.
– Incentives for all young people through financial credits, to empower and motivate them and arm them with real influence and buying power in a new education and training market. (CBI, 1993: 13)

The assumption was that if each young person took responsibility for their own education and training and were given a voucher, or Training Credit, to buy education or training of their own choice, their individual purchases would drive a market in training provision. This would ensure the most efficient use of training resources and force training providers to raise the quality of their courses to attract customers for their services. Because young people who are making choices about education or training are surrounded by others with vested interests, such as teachers who may want them to stay on to make sixth form courses viable, neutral careers guidance was seen as essential. To help young people take responsibility and choose, individual action planning procedures were to be used. These would form a lifelong record, showing past achievements and identifying future goals.

These CBI proposals were not adopted in totality. Early effects were mainly upon Youth Training (YT), the successor to YTS. A pilot scheme for Training Credits [3] was introduced in 11 areas from 1991, with a further 9 areas in a second pilot phase from 1993. In 1991 the decision was made that Training Credits should cover the whole of England, Scotland and Wales by 1996, eventually brought forward to 1995. In expanding the original pilot into national training policy, the Employment Department made explicit the the intention to change the locus of control of training from providers to individuals and employers:

In particular, public funding is routed through the individual young person rather than through a training provider. This aims:
– to increase young people's motivation to train, by giving them choice and control, and making obvious to them the scale of investment available to support their training;
– to enhance the market in training provision. Providers will be paid according to their ability to attract trainees holding credits;
– to enhance employer involvement. Where a young person with a credit is in a job, the employer can agree to organise the training. (ED/DES, 1991:35)

A recent White Paper (1994) on VET and industrial performance took this individualist agenda further: 'A fulfilled workforce meeting individual targets, driven by the will to perform to their individual best, will be a world class workforce' (p. 30). It went on to commit the Government to 'better careers education and guidance to help young people choose the best paths to their future' and 'greater responsiveness by providers to the needs of their customers – learners and employers – including closer examination of the learning credits approach to education and training' (p. 49). Learning credits were described as an extension of the Training Credit idea, to cover all education and training provision post-16. These policy imperatives are sustained a year later (White Paper, 1995), although the government still held back from a firm commitment to a voucher based approach for the whole of post-16 education and training.

Changes to VET funding also emphasise the individualist, market-forces approach. Funding for post-16 education or training in Britain is increasingly based on two principles. The first is that funding follows recruitment, so that the amount of funding earned by a provider depends on the number of students or trainees recruited. In response to the distortions which could follow such an approach, a proportion of the funding is only awarded once the course has been successfully completed and the qualification awarded. This is supposed to ensure that providers only recruit those suited to the courses and that training has to be of high quality.

The final pieces of the jigsaw are the continued growth of NVQs and the introduction of National Targets for Education and Training (NTETS). NVQs were proposed by the Del Ville Report (MSC/DES, 1986) and have been gradually developed since. Like the other parts of this new paradigm, they are controversial. The Government has consistently supported them as a corner-stone of VET policy, though they are now seen as only relevant to those not in full-time education. Their novel approach to training qualifications is described and advocated by Jessup (1991). This includes a focus on qualification rather than training provision. Consequently, in the absence of a conventional syllabus, the type of training provided is entirely dependent on achieving the elements of competence which make up units of the NVQ sought. Because competence is measured in the work place, NVQs apparently offered a mechanism to control the quality of on-the-job work experience, something sadly lacking under the YTS (Lee et al., 1990). An identical qualification structure is envisaged for all occupational areas and the qualifications are organised in five levels, so that Level 2 equates to craft skills, and Level 3 to technicians or supervisors. The system has been attacked by academics from all parts of the political spectrum (Smithers, 1993; Hyland, 1994) yet continues its development largely unchecked, though a recent report (Beaumont, 1996) has recommended some major modifications. Its focus on the individualist acquisition of competence and the measurement of outcomes dovetails with the rest of the markets paradigm.

The NTETS also originated from the CBI. They are a commitment by the government and others to raise the level of qualifications held by the British population, as part of the drive to upskill the workforce. For example, the latest White Paper (1995) sets the target of 60% of the age group with NVQ level 3 or its equivalent by the age of 21. TEC funding is increasingly geared to meeting these targets, so that outcome-related funding for training is reinforced.

Training Credits was the first and purest form of the new VET policies to be introduced and operated. It made an ideal focus for an investigation of the wider assumptions that underpin this new policy paradigm. We argue, in Chapter 7, that this paradigm is based on fundamental misunderstandings of the culture, beliefs, actions and interactions of those involved, which are an inappropriate basis for policy decisions. Before that, we need to explain briefly how the Training Credits pilot scheme was intended to operate.

TRAINING CREDITS AND THE PILOT SCHEME

33,000 young people were in training using Training Credits in July 1993 (ED, 1993), which was towards the end of our fieldwork. However, it is difficult to draw any conclusions from this figure, because the pilot schemes were deliberately targeted and operated in very different ways in different areas. As the prospectus for the initiative stated:

> The schemes to be selected are likely to include:
> – a significant number of pilots which provide credits to all young people entering the labour market within two years of minimum school leaving age, with a significant minimum value for the credit;
> – pilots which are more selective, for example by offering credits for apprentice or technician level training only, credits limited to small companies or shortage sectors, or to support Compacts and other business–education partnerships. (ED, 1990: 8)

We studied one of the first pilot schemes, which broadly fitted into the former category.

The details of the origin of the Training Credits initiative were examined by MacDonald and Coffield (1993) and Unwin (1993). Readers wishing to gain a broader understanding of the initiative as a whole are referred to them and to the official evaluation reports. The first year of the pilot was evaluated in all 11 areas, and a composite report was produced by Coopers & Lybrand Deloitte (1992). A summary was later published by the Employment Department (ED, 1992). The National Foundation for Educational Research carried out an evaluation of the second year, focusing on three sample schemes (Sims and Stoney, 1993).

The pilot scheme we studied had five key components:

1. Training providers were to be treated as suppliers in a market-place, rather than as partners in training provision.

2. Young people would be given enhanced careers guidance in school, associated with a Careers Guidance Action Plan (CGAP).

3. The young people were intended to select a training programme in negotiation with their employer.

4. Training providers had to be approved by the TEC, and were given the status of Approved Trainers. Approved Trainers could be employers, Further Education (FE) Colleges or private training organisations. The TEC carried out no training directly.

5. All training programmes had to lead to either an NVQ or an officially recognised NVQ-equivalent qualification.

As described in the original submission to TEED, the CGAP for this scheme was divided into four sequential parts:

Part 1 explored the young person's existing achievements, with a particular focus on 'the skills I have gained'.

Part 2 specified career aims, the skills required for these aims, and 'how I can work towards my aims'.

Part 3 described the planned learning programme.

Part 4 to be undertaken after training was completed, was a review of the learning programme.

Though the detailed nature of the action planning forms had changed several times between this submission and our fieldwork, the basic structure of the process had been retained. At the time when we interviewed, which was the second year of the pilot scheme, Part 1 was left to the schools. The Careers Service worked with pupils to complete Parts 2 and 3. Part 4 was to be done by the Careers Service after training had been finished.

The intended decision making process is shown in Figure 1.1. Once part 3 of the CGAP had been completed the young person was issued with the Training Credit. This was a voucher with duplicate pages, like a sales voucher from a credit card. This specified the agreed training programme in the chosen occupational area. Armed with the Credit, a young person selected an employer/work placement. Some found jobs. There was an organisation set up to help others find work placements. Originally, several private training providers acted as what were called Licensed Providers. After accusations that Licensed Providers favoured their own supposedly independent training branches, they were replaced by a

Placement Service funded separately by the TEC. Small-scale changes to the CGAP, within the same occupational area, could be easily negotiated. However, if a change of occupational area was required, the young person had to return to the Careers Service, for a further counselling session, prior to the issuing of a new credit. There was no limit to the number of new credits a young person could have in this way.

Once a placement was gained, the intention was that the young person and the employer would together select an appropriate training programme. At this point the voucher was used, and employer, training provider and young person were each supposed to keep one of the duplicate slips, whilst one went to the TEC. The Approved Trainer received profile payments, from the TEC, at regular intervals during the first year of training; 20% was held back until the training was completed, and a further 10% until the qualification was awarded. There was no time limit on these final payments, and training could take as short or as long a time as it required to complete. However, with the exception of those with special training needs, Training Credits had to be issued before the 18th birthday, training had to commence before the 19th birthday and had to be complete by the 23rd birthday. During the period of our fieldwork, the TEC raised the age limit for issuing a credit to the 19th birthday.

The young people participating in the scheme had all left full-time education. There were two main types of trainee. Those with 'employed status' had been issued with a contract of employment by an employer. That employer paid whatever wages he or she thought fit. As the young person was employed, costs of travelling to work were to be borne by them. The Training Credit paid for any training provided by an Approved Trainer that fitted the CGAP and lead to an appropriate qualification. It also paid for travel to any off-the-job training that was provided. Other young people had 'trainee status'. They were placed with an employer who undertook to work with the Approved Trainer to train them up to the agreed qualification. The employer had to pay a training allowance that must at least equal the minimums laid down nationally. These were £29.50 at 16+ and £35 at 17+, amounts that had not changed for 10 years. Travel expenses to work were paid to the young person by the TEC. In neither case was the employer paid to provide the training, unless he or she was also the Approved Trainer.

The procedures in this scheme were constantly changing during the 3-year pilot period. The above account summarises the system that applied to our interviewees at the time of our fieldwork, as accurately as we are able. The constant change was because the TEC took a proactive view to piloting and deliberately intervened to sharpen up and refine the scheme as they went along. It lies beyond the scope of this book to explore such changes. Our case study is located in a quite specific time period, as well as in a particular scheme.

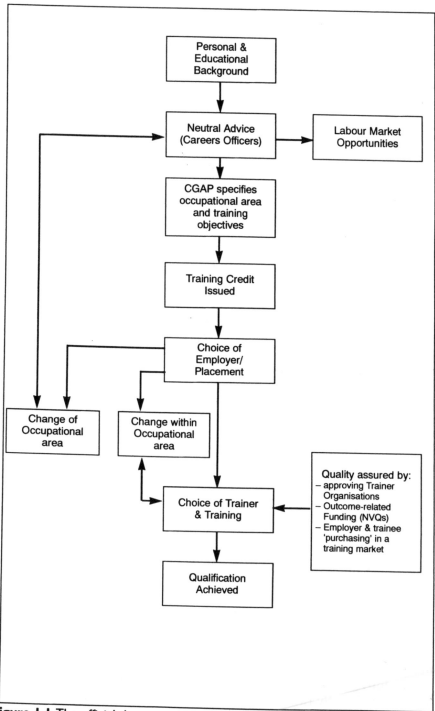

Figure 1.1 The official decision making process

THE TRAINING CREDITS IN ACTION PROJECT

In studying this Training Credits scheme, we approached the enquiry from within an interpretative framework (Smith, 1989). We adopted an 18-month longitudinal perspective to data collection, with four interview sweeps. After each sweep, data was analysed and used to focus questioning in subsequent sweeps. We focused on the second cohort of Training Credits trainees, following 10 young people from their final term in school until they were 15 months or more into their training. Sampling was in two stages. We began by interviewing 115 school pupils, mainly in small single-gender groups. Of these, 91 were in Year 11 and 26 in the sixth form; 59 were boys and 56 girls. They were attending six secondary schools, selected to give geographical spread. Pupils were selected, by their careers teachers, as being likely to at least consider using Training Credits. We also interviewed ten careers officers and eight careers teachers from those schools.

From the 115 pupils, we selected 14 to follow through, though this was rapidly reduced to 11 and eventually 10 (Table 1.1). They were selected as interesting cases who would be using Training Credits – with a gender mix, from different geographical locations and working in different occupational areas. We attempted to balance cases where unusual features were apparent with those that appeared to be more straightforward. For each trainee we also interviewed parents, employer(s), training providers and those finding placements. All such network members were interviewed in sweeps 2 and 4 and some in sweep 3. We also interviewed four TEC officials, in sweeps 2 and 4.

Interviews were semi-structured and tape-recorded. Each researcher took responsibility for whole networks, to maximise understanding of interrelationships. Regular team meetings ensured consistency of approach and we used standardised but open-ended interview schedules, separately drawn up for each stakeholder group and each sweep.

Analysis was at three levels which overlapped chronologically. We began by examining each stakeholder perspective separately. Secondly, we took each trainee as the centre of a network and built up his or her career story through a mixture of stakeholder perceptions. Analysis was done through repeated listening to tapes, to tease out harmonies and dissonances within and between perceptions. Thirdly we focused on specific issues raised by both types of story and by relevant literature, and synthesised these elements heuristically into a more comprehensive, theoretically rich picture of the Training Credits scheme and decision-making within it.

Our study focused on one of the original Training Credits pilot schemes, in a predominantly rural area with a labour market dominated by small firms, with geographical variations in unemployment and an almost

Table 1.1 The core sample

Pseudonym	Occupational area(s)	Termination of fieldwork
Henry*	Accountancy in local government	In sweep 2. Not using YCs
John	Car maintenance, small garage	In Sweep 2. Too similar to Peter
Martin	Motor mechanic, small garage. Redundant. Shop job with no training	In Sweep 2. No longer using YCs
Jenny	Hairdressing, small salon	End of Sweep 3. Employer refused interviews
Sam*	Engineering, medium-sized company	End of Sweep 4
Elaine*	Clerical work in Local Authority	End of Sweep 4
Peter	Motor mechanic, small garage	End of Sweep 4
Clive	Car valeting and sales, small garage	End of Sweep 4
Helen	Car body repair, small garage, then shop work	End of Sweep 4
Alison	Riding, two different stables and trainers	End of Sweep 4
David	Farm work, small farm then full-time college	End of Sweep 4
Becky	Dental surgery assistance, small practice	End of Sweep 4
Frances	Shop work, two training places, then part-time work	End of Sweep 4
Laura	Shop work, then nursery school, then secretarial training, the last without YCs	End of Sweep 4

*These young people left school from the sixth form.

exclusively white population. The pilot began in 1991 and was initially funded for 3 years, ending in March 1994. We began our study in April 1992 and fieldwork ended in December 1993. The first 2 years of the pilot scheme were particularly difficult, because an economic recession was at its height. This meant that an initiative designed for a predicted labour shortage was actually introduced at a time of glut. As Unwin (1993:221) says, 'the training credits initiative could not have been launched at a worse time, as employers of all sizes and in all sectors stopped recruiting young people'. Our early interviews with scheme participants were dominated by fears about jobs (Hodkinson and Sparkes, 1995a). At the same time, as Unwin also points out, staying on rates in full-time post 16 education were rising rapidly (Raffe, 1992). Since our study was completed, this rise in staying on rates has continued, though with some signs of levelling off in 1994. However, the recession officially ended in 1993, and national unemployment figures have continued to drop, albeit slowly. This means that, at the time of writing (November 1995), the context for the Training Credits scheme is somewhat different from that reported here. It should also be remembered that our fieldwork took place early in the history of the pilot scheme. As time passes, those people living and working with Training Credits will become more acclimatised, and TEC procedures were already being further adapted. The experiences of later cohorts may differ from the one studied here.

Before we move to the stories of the individual trainees, it is necessary to do a little more scene setting. In the next chapter, we examine the different stakeholder groups who were involved in the Training Credits process.

2

Stakeholders and Training Credits

We interviewed a range of stakeholders. These were:

- school pupils who were considering the use of credits;
- the trainees who did actually use them;
- the parents of those trainees;
- the careers teachers in school and the careers officers they worked with, who together were responsible for the guidance leading up to the issuing of a credit;
- the employers for whom the trainees worked;
- the trainers who provided off-the-job training to the trainees and were also involved in the placement of trainees;
- TEC officials who were responsible for the overall operation of the pilot scheme.

This chapter positions these different stakeholder groups in relation to the Training Credits initiative.

There were two types. School pupils, trainees, parents and small employers viewed Training Credits from a purely personal perspective. They were users or potential users of the Credit system. The careers officers, careers teachers, trainers and TEC officials were concerned with the Training Credits system through their own professional involvement within it, though their views of the system are coloured by their personal perceptions of rewards and costs. Larger employers sometimes fall into the second group as well as the first, especially when they are heavily involved in organising their own training.

Stakeholder groups engaged with Training Credits in two different stages. The first was the operation of CGAP in schools, when decisions were made to use Credits or not and which occupation to aim for. School pupils, careers teachers, careers officers, parents and training providers were involved at this stage. The second stage was the placement of trainees and undertaking the training. In this stage, trainees, employers, training providers and parents were involved. Careers Officers became involved, in some cases, when a new Credit has to be issued. TEC officials took an over-view role throughout but, as they were remote from the experiences of the young people whom this book is about, we have excluded them here.

It should be remembered that stakeholders of the same type are a diverse set of individuals, with varying personal histories and beliefs, working in different institutions and settings. The picture painted here simplifies these complexities to establish patterns.

USERS, CUSTOMERS OR CLIENTS

School Pupils

School pupils are potential Credit holders. The CGAP process was designed to help them plan their careers, using Credits if appropriate. We interviewed 44 boys and 45 girls in Year 11 [4]; 14 boys and 10 girls in Year 12, and 1 boy and 1 girl in Year 13. Interviews were conducted mainly in single-gender small groups, in March and April 1992. Perhaps because our sample was selected by the schools, we interviewed only a few pupils who belonged to the type of counter culture identified by Hargreaves (1967) and Willis (1977). Only one pupil, the Year 13 female, was classified as having Special Educational Needs.

Within the diverse sets of interests and opinions presented to us, a pattern can be discerned. Most pupils could be positioned along a continuum with regard to their opinions about Training Credits. This continuum is best explained by describing four typical positions.

(i) Knowledgeable and Committed

Those who knew most about Training Credits had clear career objectives involving their use. Furthermore, they had shown some initiative and had directly approached either a Licensed Provider or an Approved Trainer for information. This group were the most positive about the value of Credits, though this may sometimes have been based on inflated hopes, partly fuelled by Licensed Providers who had an interest in presenting Training Credits in the best light:

> Well I mean if you didn't get a job [on YTS] they chucked you out and that was it, but the woman at [named Licensed Provider] said most of our people that joined us have got a job now – they like employ you if you're halfway through your training and they think you're good enough they'll employ you anyway, and your training just stops and becomes a job (m) [5].

Pupils of this type had made a commitment to leaving rather than staying on at school, and many had a clear idea what job they wished to go into.

> I just can't see the point in staying in school and then getting all your all different grades. You might get higher grades, but there's no guarantee you're going to get a job at the end of it, so what's the point of waiting another year if you're not going to get a job? Just no point (f).

Some pupils were determined to leave, despite pressures to stay on:

> There's a lot of people in our year that want to go to College, and they treat you as a bit of a dropout if you want to go out and get a job, sort of thing. There's only about three or four of us going out and getting jobs. A lot of them [are] going on to university studying law. They're all saying "oh we'll be earning more money than you" (m).

These pupils were already committed to entering the labour market.

Knowledge about Training Credits followed that decision rather than preceding it. The trainees, whose stories we tell later, came mainly from this group.

(ii) Generally Interested

The next group was those pupils intending to leave school but who did not see Training Credits as relevant to their job aspirations, or lacked clear objectives as to the chosen career, or lacked the initiative to make contact with training organisations themselves. This group relied on the careers officer and school to inform them and many were concerned by their lack of understanding:

> It's [Training Credits] good but they should simplify it a bit because when we're having our careers interview, they're confusing a lot of people. Just the way they're saying how it should be used, like. One person saying one thing, another person saying another thing. It's like a bit complicated (m).

(iii) No Knowledge of Interest

Those Year 11 pupils who had decided to stay in school formed the third group: 'I don't know what I'm going to do, so that's why I'm staying on at school. I don't know what I'm interested in yet. Its got to be creative' (f). They knew little about Training Credits and could see no point in finding out. They felt that Credits were irrelevant to their career aspirations and, in some cases, low status:

> I think they [careers officer?] might have mentioned it [Training Credits]. I said I weren't going to do nothing with that, so they went off the subject. ... I knew I was going to stay on into the 6th form, so I didn't think there was much point (m).

(iv) Antipathy and Ignorance

The fourth group knew least and were vehemently opposed to the whole notion of Training Credits. There were two types of pupil in this group, but they shared similar perceptions of Credits. Many were Year 12 pupils who had finished a one year course. We also identified a small number of Year 11 pupils, mainly male, who seemed extremely anti any official body – school, the careers service or training organisations. Their rejection of Credits was part of a more general attack on the situation in which they found themselves:

> Nah, I don't like it [school]. I don't get on with teachers so much. In the school they seem to boss me about. I can behave sometimes. I behaved better on work experience ... cos they just treat you better outside. They just treat you as an adult (m).

Both groups of pupils in this category associated Training Credits with

YTS and regarded both as inappropriate and beneath them:

> I think they're [Training Credits] a waste of time. Because if you give them the Training Credit which is worth £30 or something, then your employer's only got to pay you £30 and the people who I know who are on them at the moment – they are a complete waste of time (m6).

> Ain't it called YTS any more then? (g).

That many Year 12 pupils held such views was unsurprising. They had chosen to stay on rather than take up Training Credits and were then faced with having to choose that which they previously rejected, even though they were a year older. They had received little careers guidance about Credits while in the sixth form [6]. Finally, Training Credits were still new and the sixth formers were working on 'old' understanding.

For this group, Training Credits were a potential threat. As they moved from school to the labour market, they might be forced to consider an initiative they regarded as inappropriate:

> I had one of them phoning up my house. One of them phoned up my house! 'Can she come up to the careers office to speak about it'. And I went up there and she was there going on about YTS and Training Credits. I didn't want to. I just, I think it's a waste of time to be honest. My mum wouldn't let me go on it anyway. ... Because she's seen people do YTS and don't get a job at the end of it. You know, now they're unemployed. If you get a job at the end of it, like firm, then you've got everything going for you. But they say they can't guarantee you a job at the end of it. (f6)

Parents

Research has consistently shown that parents have a significant informal influence on career decisions made by young people (Taylor, 1992) and that working-class parents often play a significant role in finding jobs for their offspring (Moore, 1988; Wallace et al., 1993). Yet they were largely ignored in the official Training Credits procedures.

We interviewed 20 parents of the 11 trainees who formed our core sample for this study. Most were confused by the Training Credits processes.

> I didn't know anything about Training Credits, not until very long ago. I still don't know what it really is to be honest. ... Only because Jenny mentioned it, about what she was going to earn, and how much Jim was going to give her. She thought he would only pay her the £30 a week. We thought, well, you can't really live on that. But he pays her the Training Credits, and I think he pays her the wage as well. I'm not sure.

Several pointed out that they had received little information on Training Credits. They relied on conversations with their child which at times was problematic as the following comment illustrates, in which a parent talks about how she attempted to assess the quality of training and the type of day her daughter has had at work:

Well she doesn't really talk much about it. But then it was the same with school. I don't like to keep on about it. I've noticed that, because I'd like to think she was doing something interesting, and she is happy at work, I'd say "how did work go today?" She's go "um". After a while she said, "You always mention work when I come in" ... I'm sort of hoping she'll say, "You never guess what I had to do today" ... A lot of the time I just don't ask.

Many parents drew upon their earlier experiences of YTS, when another of their children had been involved:

Nothing, absolutely nothing [received about Training Credits] ...The only thing, was that booklet down there, was what he came home with the day he got his credits. That's all that we've had, and that we knew about it. ... When our daughter left school, which was 4 years ago, it was the YTS scheme then. Of course, then, the government used to pay so much, and the firm used to pay so much ... I didn't know whether it was the same thing. I just didn't know.

Parental understanding about Training Credits frequently came about by having to deal with a crisis situation. One mother had a problem in setting her daughter up with a placement:

I find now [after sorting out the problem] I do understand the Training Credits because I've had it explained to me thoroughly. Hopefully, by someone who knows what they are talking about. ... they change the system quite a bit. It's hard for people who aren't in touch with it to keep on top of it. Even just phoning up and saying, "Oh, my daughters doing a YTS", or using certain abbreviations that are out of date, can confuse people. Then I had to rethink. So that's something that's hard.

Parents judged the costs and rewards of involvement in Training Credits according to their hopes for their children. A recurring theme was fear of exploitation. This sometimes focused on low rates of training allowance, and sometimes on prospects for permanent employment.

Small Employers

Small employers dominated the labour market in the area of our study, and 14 of the 16 employers we interviewed were of this type. Employers are key decision-makers in the school to work transition. They determine whether a young person is taken on, their status, the duration of the job or placement, the nature of the job and of the on-the-job training.

The 14 small employers we interviewed were largely marginalised and some were alienated from the Credits system. Although all had at least one trainee or employee using a credit, they knew little about how the system worked and some were uninterested in finding out more:

E [I know] nothing about Training Credits, no. ... A lady 'phoned me about 3 months ago, and I was talking to her about all this, and I said that I really would like to have something, just to read about it. We don't have anything at all. And she said 'oh yes, we'll get that sorted out' ... she was going to get things sorted out to send out to the likes of myself, and she never got back to me.

I Do you know anything about the funding arrangements for Training Credits? [Pause]

About how the training's paid for and everything like that?
E   I take it it's just through the government isn't it?

Like parents, they were often unable to distinguish between Training Credits and YTS.

From my point of view it's [Training Credits] an irrelevance, really. I mean there's no difference between that and YTS, as far as I am concerned. ...
... what a trainee wants, is a job and some training. End of story. And they don't give a damn, I don't think, how its provided. What we should all be interested in is the most cost effective way of providing sensible training for the employee.

Some took no interest in the current off-the-job training or in the detailed paperwork for the scheme, leaving all this for the trainer:

If somebody says "oh they've got to go to College one day a week" – they've got to go to College one day a week. How its arranged, and what they do, if they have to go I mean they could be studying modern art or whatever ... it doesn't worry me. If somebody says they've got to go there, they've got to go there. I'd rather them not study modern art, but you know (laughs).

Employers saw taking on a trainee as worthwhile, either because it was a cheap source of labour and/or because they saw it as providing a service to the young person and the community. However, the costs, in time and effort, of understanding and operating the system fully, were seen as too high. Some regarded giving non-situation-specific training as too high a cost, compared with the benefits of a trainee learning to do things the way the employers did them in their own firms. Large employers might see this equation differently, but the small employers found it difficult to devote time to general training and administration rather than doing the work that protects the 'bottom line'.

Problems arose within the Training Credits scheme, because it assumed a central role for employers and pupils as users, yet neither group had much involvement in operation of the scheme. They merely got on with work and training, largely as they saw fit. Users focused on Training Credits in terms of what the system could do for them, given their own idiosyncratic situation and intentions. Many found the system baffling and could see little point in even finding out about it, unless they perceived that Credits were either necessary or appropriate for their own needs. For some pupils, there was a 'Catch 22' that rendered the system dysfunctional: you don't know that Training Credits can help until you find out about them, but you don't find out about them until you know they might help. Some of the pupils most antagonised by Training Credits were quite likely to need to use them. One employer wanted a system that did some of the things Training Credits were supposed to do, but had no interest in finding out that this was already partly possible.

We have reported elsewhere (Hodkinson and Sparkes, 1994) that the market for training provision, much emphasised in the official literature for Training Credits, proved to be largely mythical. This was partly because employers chose to work with trainers they knew rather than shop around. As will be seen in subsequent chapters, trainees did not act as customers for training either. We return to this problem in Chapter 8.

PROFESSIONAL INVOLVEMENT IN THE SYSTEM

Careers Teachers

Though careers guidance was highlighted in the plans for this scheme, the role of careers teachers in providing this guidance was played down. There are three possible reasons for this. Harris (1992) suggests that careers teachers are 'marginal' actors, that are seen as peripheral to the main functioning of the school. This marginality may have allowed them to be overlooked or taken for granted in the rush to design the new system. Alternatively, much stress was placed in official documents on the importance of 'neutral guidance' – neutral in the sense that the provider of guidance has no vested interest in the outcome of that guidance. Careers teachers may have been associated with the partisan interests of the school. Finally, the view of career decision making in the Training Credits prospectus emphasised individual action planning and careers guidance rather than careers education. But in practice, the careers teachers played a pivotal role in the operation of the credits scheme (Sparkes and Hodkinson, 1996). This was because they were the point of contact between the school, which gave lots of careers advice to pupils, and the new scheme. We interviewed eight careers teachers. Four were male and four were female.

The marginal positioning of careers teachers in schools was mirrored and reinforced by their marginality in the Training Credits scheme and especially its introduction:

> It was all left so very late. ... The first we knew was when we came back to school in September and it was a *fait accomplis*. Then everyone was scrabbling around, 'God, it's here. We've got it. We've got to get to organised'. The Careers Service were running around like headless chickens. Then the actual licences [for training] and so on weren't actually settled until late February, ... I was actually in the situation where I said, 'Look I am not going to stand up in front of our kids and in effect tell them 'Look we have got this thing called Training Credits, but what the hell it is I don't know' (laughs) ... Very often people don't understand the time scale of guidance in schools.

Several teachers felt alienated from the Training Credits process due to the apparent lack of consultation with them by the TEC.

> Total lack of consultation, as far as I can see, with the people who seem delivering the goods. ... I've been involved in no consultation whatsoever ... There is very little information for them [the pupils]. ... I've had nothing sent through of any use that I can hand out to kids. I've had to either originate it myself, or write off to the training people and get them sent to me, and then I've handed them out to the kids. Now, I mean, is that

a good way of selling things? ... A total lack of consultation.

Though alienated, some had sympathy with the principles of the scheme.

[The best thing about Training Credits is] the fact that pupils are free to use a training pathway as suits them best. That they are going out with a positive view, 'this is mine and I can use it'. So they are taking responsibility for themselves, which I think the pupils going out to work, that's what they feel they want to be doing.

For others, alienation and lack of ownership resulted in a hankering after the earlier YTS system, into which they had invested much time and effort.

From our point of view the old YTS system was just beginning to come good, I think. There was a general understanding of it, a lot of work had actually gone into talking to parents, talking to kids about that system. I think it's unfortunate that it couldn't have been married up more closely really. The message seemed to be, 'YTS is dead and buried, now we've got this system'. Then trying to explain how the new system worked in comparison to YTS caused a lot of confusion for everyone, professionals included to begin with.

For many of these careers teachers, the personal costs of introducing Training Credits far outweighed the rewards and it is unsurprising that some looked back with regret on the loss of the YTS scheme they had expended so much effort to develop.

Careers Officers

Careers officers were much more central in the scheme and 30 new careers officers were appointed using pilot funding. Of the ten officers we interviewed five were new appointments under the Training Credits initiative. Only one was male. Lawrence (1992) shows that careers officers are also a marginalised profession, lying between schools and employers and now the TECs. Many of Lawrence's sample complained of marginalisation in schools and knew very little about the careers education programmes in the schools where they worked. Yet we found a marked contrast between the feelings of careers teachers and careers officers towards Training Credits. Several officers felt that the introduction of Credits had raised the profile of careers education and guidance in schools.

They get a lot more guidance now because it's [the Training Credits pilot] helped us, it's helped our staff, we've got more resources ... I feel now we're beginning to give the young people the service a lot of us want to give them, that certainly in [named county] we haven't been able to do before.

There was a feeling of overwork and not enough time despite increased resources, but the pressures were positively received rather than seen as burdensome.

We're very stretched. ... It's very strange, but because we've contracted to give more work, it's spiralling. The schools are actually asking for more. I was talking to one colleague this morning, and he says to me 'God! I did a bit of work in Year 9 [14 year olds] last year, only a bit, and I had to find the time to do it. I've just been asked to go in Year 8! [13 year olds]'... it's done a lot for the careers service, this extra funding and everything, extra staff, but it generates more [demand].

There was a marked absence of the sorts of negative comment reported by Lawrence (1992). Sims and Stoney (1993) confirm that in other pilot areas the Training Credits initiative had also raised the profile and morale of the careers service. This centrality of careers officers to the scheme is not surprising. In addition to the points made in relation to careers teachers above, in the scheme under investigation, one of the inner group who planned the pilot bid and wrote the submission was then a Chief Careers Officer in the area. For most officers, the rewards of the introduction of Training Credits far outweighed the costs.

Most were in favour of action planning, but there was one dissenting point of view:

> The CGAP thingies ... I think it's useful for them to have some sort of written record [of the interview] but I don't think it has to be done when they're there. I don't think it should be such – it's their statement – I think this is a load of twaddle in a way.

For this officer, costs appeared to outweigh rewards. She was engaged in some difficult battles in the school, which she felt had criticised her unfairly for advice she had given.

> I mean I'm not, I don't push Training Credits, they're an alternative way, but sometimes it doesn't go down well [with the school] that you're giving them alternatives, really. I have to say that.

Added to these tensions at work, the principles of action planning, aimed at an end goal, clashed with this officer's view of her professional role. She saw career guidance as being supportive, non-directional counselling. However, this officer was an exception and others were largely positive about their enhanced roles and about Training Credits and CGAP in principle.

Training Providers

The position of training providers in the Training Credits scheme was ambiguous. On the one hand they were central in the sense that the rationale was to produce high quality training. New categories of Licensed Provider and Approved Trainer had been created. The former were those organisations successful in a round of competitive tendering and who combined a training role with a placement function. The latter status, which did not officially involve placing young people, was available to any organisation who met the TEC criteria. On the other hand, the deliberate use of market mechanisms meant that training organisations were not seen as part of a collaborative professional community to provide high quality training. Rather, they were supposed to compete to deliver that quality more efficiently that their rivals.

Furthermore, the use of NVQs to accredit training shifted the focus firmly to employers, whether they were Approved Trainers themselves or not. Most training assessment had to be done in the workplace, and any off-the-job training was simply to supplement that which was learned in the workplace. This further marginalised professional trainers.

We interviewed 40 trainers working for 15 organisations. Three of these were run by Local Education Authorities (LEAs), seven were private commercial organisations and five were FE Colleges. Interviewees included managers, those providing the training and those responsible for placing trainees with employers. Sometimes these roles overlapped. When our first interviews were conducted, four of these organisations were Licensed Providers. Before the research was completed Licensed Providers had been abolished (see Chapter 1) and these organisations became Approved Trainers. In practice, all Approved Trainers claimed that they retained a placement role.

Of all the people we interviewed, only the TEC officials had a clearer grasp of the details of the Training Credits scheme than the trainers. For trainers the scheme was of central importance. They talked in detail about the complexities and intricacies of the scheme. The following, for example, is one trainer talking about problems with performance-related funding under Training Credits. Note that, as well as the predictable concern about loss of money to her organisation, she was also concerned to bend the official system, so that a trainee who had lost a placement could continue training until he or she found another one:

> It's an enormous problem because it's something you have no control over. You can control it to a certain extent, the performance of the young people that stay with you, but you can't control those that are going to drop off the end long before you get there, for a variety of reasons – they were away, they go back to school, they become pregnant, any amount of reasons – you can do nothing to control it. The ones that lose their jobs usually I can do something about. I say to them "don't worry about it, I'll take you off my TEC return we'll keep you here and keep training you, so you're still going down the road to NVQ and hopefully within a month I'll find another job for you." And that's only a small percentage of the ones you lose.

Despite detailed knowledge and practical experience, trainers felt they were not consulted about the scheme or the changes to it: 'nobody has consulted with the Approved Trainers [about the new placement service that was to replace Licensed Providers] nobody has discussed with the Approved Trainers. If they have I don't know about it. Where is consultation?' Many felt that things were getting worse for them. 'The funding's been cut this year by about 10% – there's no increase. The amount of work that has to be done is getting greater. I'm not sure if they want to push Approved Trainers out.'

There was widespread dissatisfaction with the Training Credits system. Things were seen to be getting progressively worse, for employers and trainees as well as the trainers themselves:

They reduced the funding by about 60% and on top of that they withheld another 30%. ... So you have to target when you think you're going to get that. With hairdressers that's going to be round about 2 years. We get the last 20% on certification. In Band B there's 5 payments, every 12 weeks ... [then] you have to go 12 months before you can collect your last 30%. Which causes an enormous cash flow problem. So what tends to happen is you tend to train down to the [minimum] because that's all you can afford to do. There is no add on anywhere, whereas 12 months ago we used to do for care and catering, the basic hygiene certificate, first aid certificate – all extras, all things the employers want.

We feel that the old YTS programme had quality and was becoming accepted by parents and by young people. The flexibility that came in on YT, in fact, in some ways reduced the quality. We felt, therefore, there weren't the mandatory requirements for things like developing social skills and computer inputs .... We feel that Training Credits have put in tremendous blocks on the move towards acceptance of work based training that was occurring with the old YT programme.

The position of trainers within the Training Credits scheme was paradoxical. These were people who lived and breathed training but many felt threatened by the initiative, that they were neither consulted nor valued by the TEC and that quality of training was declining for young people and employers.

We could probably cram someone through [to NVQ level 2] in about 9 months ... Basically we've put a ceiling on it 'cos we feel (a) we're not doing ourselves justice and (b) we're definitely not doing the trainee justice, so we're sticking out ... and saying well it's 2 years. ... And doing it that way you can lose out to other people, competitors.

While it is possible that there is some special pleading in these responses, the weight of negative feeling from the interviews was overwhelming. Trainers felt alienated by the scheme and saw costs far outweighing any possible rewards.

There were problems because of the marginality of these training providers. The supposed focus of the Training Credits initiative was the provision of quality training. Whatever type of training provision is introduced, the role played by training providers in a scheme must be crucial to achieving that quality. Training Credits were supposed to raise training quality through a mixture of market pressures and performance indicators. As far as could be ascertained in our data, the market pressures failed to work as intended because neither the trainee nor the small employer shopped around as customers. Developing strong links with employers over time was the key strategy for trainer survival, which is why those Approved Trainers who were not also Licensed Providers continued to place young people. The competition was to find placements and trainees, not improve training quality.

We have seen the ways in which trainers felt some the performance indicators, and especially the funding system, were pressuring them to reduce quality rather than raise it. The way to maximise profit seemed to be to get trainees through to an NVQ qualification in the shortest time possible. Many trainers felt penalised if they tried to do any more than that, though most claimed they were still providing more, as they felt both employers and trainees deserved it. We return to this issue in Chapter 8.

THE TECHNICAL APPROACH TO THE INTRODUCTION OF TRAINING CREDITS

Given the nature of its inception and the speed with which Training Credits were introduced, it is not surprising that their introduction was framed within what is often called a 'technological' perspective (House, 1979). The features of this perspective are outlined in more detail elsewhere (Hord, 1987; Nicholls, 1983). Here, it is worth mentioning that it assumes a *passive* practitioner who is willing to accept the innovation within a process which involves a division of labour with a clear separation of roles and functions.

Talking of such a technological perspective that infused the major centrally funded curriculum projects that were spawned in the 1970s, Rudduck (1986:9) notes that they were, 'arrogantly simplistic and somewhat neglectful of the school's sense of its own identity ... The ownership of meaning remained with its originators. Many teachers felt as though they were puppets dangling from the threads of someone else's invention'. Such an image rings true for the careers teachers and training providers we interviewed.

Rudduck (1991:31) argues that we are beginning to see change not simply as a technical problem but a shared cultural problem that requires attention to context and to the creation of shared meaning within working groups. It is informative to insert 'training provider' for 'teacher' in what follows:

> Teachers must come to feel that they recognise as significant the problem or situation that is defining the agenda for change, and that they are partners in the planning of change ... If an initiative for change comes from outside the school, then the staff will need to give local meaning to the abstractions of national or regional policy. There must be opportunities for collaborative analysis of the need for change, of the strategies by which change is to be achieved, and of the criteria for judging what progress towards change teachers and pupils are making. Teachers must feel as individuals and as members of a working group that they own and are in control of the problem of change. Dialogue within working groups is crucial, "not as a matter of empty courtesy or ritualistic adherence to some vague democratic ethos" (Sarason, 1982:217), but to bring people in on the logic of planned change.

Others have commented that change is not a neutral process and that there are winners and losers, defined by the perceptions of the individual

(Sparkes, 1989). As Fullan (1991:127) notes:

> Change is a highly personal experience – each and every one of the teachers who will be affected by change must have the opportunity to work through this experience in a way in which the rewards at least equal the cost. The fact that those who advocate and develop changes get more rewards than costs, and those who are expected to implement them experience more costs than rewards, goes a long way to explaining why the more things change, the more they remain the same.

For careers teachers and trainers the costs of introducing Training Credits were often high, while the rewards appeared to be much less significant. An additional problem was the radical nature of the initiative, as perceived by these groups. In different ways, both had invested much time and effort into YTS. Yet before they had really absorbed the change from YTS to YT, the Training Credits pilot scheme was upon them. Rudduck (1991:30–31), once more, highlights the risks of such an innovation strategy:

> Many teachers question, in the face of planned change, why there appears to be so little regard for what they have already accomplished. Change involves the adaption or abandonment of practices that are familiar and therefore comfortable. If change is seen as a denial of a person's professional past, then his or her investment in a change programme will at most be slender ... Change can threaten the basis of one's occupational identity. It is important, therefore, that those who are to be involved in change are helped to see that there is a continuity of experience and in the professional knowledge that experience creates.

This help does not appear to have been given to either careers teachers or trainers and the alienation of the latter jeopardised the ultimate success of the Training Credits initiative.

We now move on to tell the stories of our ten sample trainees, largely through their own words and those of the other stakeholders they engaged with. These longitudinal studies, focusing on the idiosyncratic experiences of these young people over an 18-month period, give a different perspective of the transition to work from that presented here. While reading these stories, the general Training Credits framework and the stakeholder positions need to be borne constantly in mind. In Chapters 8 and 9, we draw together policy and theoretical issues from a synthesis of both perspectives. Some of the issues discussed here will be returned to and fleshed out more fully there.

3

Anticipations and Forced Change: Helen's Story

One of the central ideas in this book is that career progression can be seen as periods of routine interspersed with turning points. Helen's story illustrates this idea. We follow her training through two different turning points and the periods of routine that followed each of them. We begin with Helen's successful attempt to secure a place as a trainee in car body repairing. This is followed by a period when she worked on that training programme. She was placed in a local garage for four days per week, with a regular day a week in a local FE college. However, long before her training was complete, Helen was made redundant. We explore her second turning point as she changed careers and took up a training place in a local record shop. Finally we see how, once in the shop, her view of her own career identity changed and car body repairing became a hobby rather than a career.

BECOMING A CAR SPRAYER

Helen came from a working-class family. Her father attended a local secondary modern school before leaving to take up an apprenticeship and he has been a fitter with several large companies. Unfortunately, about two and a half years before our fieldwork commenced, he sustained a back injury at work that would not heal. He was diagnosed as having cancer of the spine and had undergone several major operations and a series of treatments. Helen's mother had also attended a local secondary modern school and left without any formal qualifications. Helen seemed to get on well with both of her parents who were very supportive of her in the transition from school to work.

In our first interview Helen commented: 'I work at a garage called Langley's in the city. I got the information from my dad for work experience. Then I asked them if I could work for them in the summer holidays. At the end of the summer holidays he asked me if I wanted a job. It's interesting, you get to meet a lot of people. At the moment I'll be rubbing down cars, a bit of spraying when I can, and that's about it.'

When asked what got her interested in cars, she replied: 'my dad. He's a mechanic. He used to work for a large national company. He doesn't work at the moment. He's ill at the moment. My mum, she wasn't surprised because she knew I was going to end up with a man's job. It's mostly men that do it, but there is another girl working there where I'm working. My friends aren't that surprised really. I discussed it with the careers officer. She just wrote things down, what I've got to do in college and everything.'

Helen's parents influenced her decision. Her father commented, 'Basically, she wanted to do a bit of art work. She wanted to go painting. What we said was, "Why not get trained with something as a background", so that she had something to fall back on. Between us we talked about it. The spraying, she didn't want to go into sign writing. We said, "Oh, what about car spraying?" She said, "I wouldn't mind having a go at that". So that was a way in to give her something she could get interested in. I think I suggested that one. She's always been good with her hands. She gets that off me. She's a tomboy at heart. The choice was left up to her really.'

Helen's mother said 'Yes we did guide her career choice. We sat down and talked to her. Well, she talked to her dad mostly on that side of it. He sat her down and said, "what do you really want to do?" First of all, she would perhaps go into window dressing and then as soon as she was old enough take an HGV [Heavy Goods Vehicle] licence to be a lorry driver. But then she decided that perhaps she didn't want to get stuck in a shop all the time and looked at other things. He [dad] went through all the sort of jobs that might be available. It came down to car spraying. She liked that idea because she loves drawing. In the end, once she's finished her training she wants to start training to do all these diagrams on cars, customised cars. She loves stencil work and all that sort of stuff. So her dad said to her, "What about car spraying?" And she jumped right in there for that.'

Her mother was not surprised that Helen had ended up in a car-related trade. 'Well, I knew she wouldn't take a woman's job [laughs]. My husband used to go out on a lot of breakdowns, get called out, and Helen always used to go with him and help him. She fed the brake pipes right the way through in a coach once, and she was only 4. So she's been getting grease under her fingernails since she was tiny. So I knew she wouldn't take a woman's job. Other people are all a bit shocked at first, when she tells them what she does. Then they sort of look at her and see that she's really into it.'

Her father's contacts were important in guiding Helen into her chosen career. He was instrumental in arranging her school work experience at a small body repair garage, Langley's. 'She spent a couple weeks down there in the summer holidays and she enjoyed it. So I said "let's get the ball rolling, and get the two weeks work experience down there in the November". We went down and he said, "you can come in in the summer and work". So she went in and enjoyed it'. His prior business relationship with the owner of the garage played a strong part in Helen being offered her first job there. 'I've known him through the trade for quite some time.

I said, "Well, we'll see if we can have a word with him, and see if I can get you in with him. If not go around a couple of other places and see what we can do". I've known him about 10 years. Basically, from the company before, we used to get all our vans repaired there. So just business contacts really. It's a nice tight-knit small company which I think is ideal for what Helen wants. She is going to learn everything from start to finish. She's been issued with all the equipment now which gives you heart in them, that they are doing the job properly. We touch wood, that she has got a job. She's being occupied.'

The owner of Langley's confirmed the importance of his contact with Helen's father. 'I know Helen's father. They had a bit of bad luck in the family with his illness. But prior to that she had come down here, sort of two weeks from the school basically, just to see what it's all about. With a view of us maybe employing her at a later date. He was in the motor trade. He was working for a company on the industrial estate. They were on the mechanical side, and we used to do their bodywork. So we got to know him, and he used to come over here, we used to go over there, and that sort of thing. And he said, "Oh, I've got a daughter leaving school and can she come down for this two weeks?". I think she came down during the summer, 12 months back, part-time, cash in her pocket.'

Helen made a good impression on the garage owner whilst on her school experience, and he was prepared to offer her a job when she left school. 'Well, when she came down she was such a success we said, "yes, no problem". As time went on, and the recession bit a little bit more, we found ourselves in a position where just taking on anything or anybody wouldn't have been a good move. Unfortunately, at the time I said to Helen, "look, yes, you're still in the running. But not at the moment". This was July time, when she left school I believe. So, anyway, as time went on, things sort of bucked up, so we gave her the option to come and she was more than willing. I think this was back in September. But I did tell her that things could go either way at any time, and she came here under that understanding. It's ongoing. Unless something drastic goes wrong, she's here for keeps, no problem at all.'

As with many small companies in the late 1980s and early 1990s, Langley's had felt the impact of the economic recession. Therefore, despite having been promised a job when she left school, Helen suddenly found herself without the job she wanted. Her father recalled the problems of keeping her motivated and the worry it caused them. 'When she heard that she hadn't got a job she went down hill. She couldn't be bothered. It's frustrating. That made me bad. It was just unfortunate that the recession came in just as she was about to start work. She had a letter from him saying she couldn't start down there. That was a worry for her, and as I say, it upset me a bit. I said, "We'll just have to look around and see if anybody else can take you in". Everybody was laying people off. It's unfortunate, but that's the way it went. They weren't prepared to take on a trainee at that time. They were laying off their own staff.'

Helen's mother also remembered. 'Every interview she went to, she got a reply in the post saying no. It just made her even more down. She got very very depressed. There wasn't a lot I could do for her. Obviously, I tried to keep her occupied as much as I could. You do don't you, but she was very down and she wouldn't get out of bed some days until dinnertime. Then she'd sit in there watching the box. When she was home it was really worrying. Even when it was good to have her home, because she was here to help with her dad, I just wished she could have found something. To watch her go out, two or three times, to interviews and come home with her face down here because she hadn't got anything. She really was depressed. It pulls me down as well. I don't like to see either of my kids unhappy.'

Family contacts were approached to see if any other jobs were available in a range of areas including large stores. As Helen said, 'anywhere really'. Applications were made without any real desire for the jobs on offer. When Helen was asked questions on forms about her ideal employment she wrote car spraying. 'I couldn't help that. It's just what I wanted to do'. Yet had Helen been offered a job she would have accepted it. Luckily, due to an uplift in trade, the owner of Langley's garage was able to re-offer Helen her job, in the September of 1992, beginning with a two month trial period. He said, 'I can't say we are over the recession, but we are over the worst. From Easter till probably mid-August it was quite bleak, although we were paying our way. We were making our figures every month. You just couldn't look forward at all, there was nothing to look forward to. It looked we would be like this for ever more. There were people going down owing us money. Everything looked so negative. But in the last two or three months its gone to back where it was before, within reason, relatively speaking. People are paying their bills better now, less bad debts, the percentage of people going bankrupt is less, as it affects us anyway. I can't see us reversing any more now. I think we are going uphill, but we are going uphill quicker than we were before [laughs].'

Local contacts were important in determining who gained access to limited job opportunities. This is evident in the following statement by the employer about how he appointed Helen. 'We rarely have to advertise positions because, especially youngsters like that, I'd rather them come to us with a pedigree rather than taking them off the street. It's like buying a puppy isn't it? It's better if they come recommended [laughs]. I treat all of them, our YTS, very much like puppies. They need close supervision, they need training. Because if they don't get the training now, it's like a dog sort of three years old without training – they are wild aren't they?' He was fond of the 'puppy' metaphor when describing his young employees.

Talking of the kind of person he would look for to join his work force he commented, 'From my point of view someone that would get on with other members of staff. We are not in inverted commas, "I'm the boss", but it's not that sort of boss–worker relationship. It's very much they call me Joe, or whatever, unless in front of customers. I know the families, they know my family. It's a very close-knit company really. You can't really afford to have anybody alien on the company at all. They have to fit in. Helen is quiet. I suppose most of our staff are quiet people. They come from nice families. I'm not prejudiced or a snob or anything, but they come from good working-class families. They got good breeding, or the sort of the breeding that we want. None of us are terribly educated people. None of us are scholars. They are practical. Seventy five per cent of their work is practical anyway.'

In the eyes of her employer, Helen had the potential to be a good 'puppy' and had the right kind of 'breeding' to fit in with the 'family' atmosphere at the garage. It was within this family atmosphere that Helen would get her training. 'Helen has fitted in with Martin, who is our top-flight guy, and he's sort of bringing her up the same way that he brought up Sally. He'll show her what to do and how to do it. She's always within shouting distance of him. I just let them get on with it. I know what Martin is like. If he does a job he'll do it properly, and also with his training, the girls – he's trained them exceptionally well. I think he likes it. He's just like a mother hen really [laughs]. He likes to take them under his wing, he likes to be responsible for them. Some people are like that and he's probably the best one out there for it. We've got a foreman, Peter, who takes on the panel beating side of it under his wing, and he's like a family man. He's got children, or had younger children. Like I was saying, it's a family kind of thing. Most people treat them like their own children. At the moment Helen's doing preparation, masking, rubbing down, on the paint side of it. We are not expecting them to do a re-spray in a week type of thing. They have a section they have to learn and they learn it. Once they've done that they go onto something else and work their way up.'

This system had worked well with a previous female trainee who was still employed by the garage. Her success, coupled with the garage owner's knowledge of Helen's background, helped to shape his views. 'We have a woman painter already, you see. She's, what, 22 now. We've seen her through probably 3 years of her training and coming out of her training. I was a little bit apprehensive when she came along. She came to us, clinging to the side of another painter, to be honest. Their company had gone bust, I don't quite know the circumstances, but the company had closed. Martin is a top-flight painter. He's incredible and she was his prodigy, really, she came along with him. On the understanding if Martin came, could she come. Well, yes, to get one I'll put up with the other as it were. But we didn't have to put up with her. She's fitted in well. I thought we would get a lot of leg pulling or whatever, but she holds her own. She's a good painter anyway, the guys respect that, and that's really what it's all about. The same with Helen, she doesn't get any leg pulling here at all. They respect her for what she is, as long as she can do the job. If they want to go around filing their nails in the workshop and painting their nails, well they would get their leg pulled. But they fit in well. Neither of them are tomboys, but they don't mind getting dirty, and they don't mind mucking in and pushing a car, or whatever it may be. So, she's doing well. It's early days for Helen, but if she goes along the lines that I think she will, there will be no problems at all with her.'

During the first few months of her job Helen was getting on well. In October 1992 she was happy and found the work interesting and challenging. She enjoyed being around cars and got on well with Martin. 'He tells me to do stuff and he checks before he sprays it. So if it's wrong you have to do it again.' The part of the job Helen did not like was the repetition. 'Doing the same things over and over again. Because all I'm doing is rubbing down things, like bonnets and bumpers. It's boring sometimes, especially when I have to do bonnets one after the other.' Helen felt that she would get more interesting tasks as her skills improved and she gained knowledge. She got on well with the garage owner. 'He's a good laugh. We get on well with him. Just talk about anything.' Likewise, the owner was happy with Helen's progress. He commented, 'Helen will be a top-flight painter and sprayer. Yes, I'm sure she will. I don't want to train people, or make use of them for 4 or 5 years and then say, "Thank you very much we don't want you any more". Because they are no good to me if they don't progress. They have got to be able to feel confident enough to do a job that is suitable to go out of our doors.'

Her employer saw Helen as a good investment and she passed her trial period. To him, she was someone who would stay with the company and do a good job for them. 'It's OK taking people on from, like, the outside world. But they are not trained your way. Each garage, although we are doing the same job, will have a different method, albeit one or two quirks. But it is a different method of achieving the same thing. If they come here, and they are still a puppy we can teach them the way to do it, our way to do it. They are the people that we want. If we have to employ outside, it takes a long time for them to change into our sort of system. I relate very much to bringing up, or training animals of any description.'

DISILLUSIONMENT AND FORCED CHANGE

In the first week of May 1993, Helen lost her job at the garage. When asked why, she replied 'there isn't enough work. Well, that was before this week. It's packed in there this week. Last Thursday they told me I was leaving, and another girl, a secretary was going. They said, "as you know we're not getting much business in the trade and the recession's just hit us". I don't blame them really because he hasn't had much in really. It was noticeable, it was hard to find things to do. You'd get about three people working on the same car. It was getting quite bad.'

In Helen's eyes, the recession was the cause of her redundancy. However, her employer gave a different view, that was never expressed to Helen. 'Work had got tight but that wasn't, I wouldn't say, of great importance. It didn't reflect the fact that we got rid of her. It was merely on the pretence of that. Unfortunately, Helen was a lovely girl. Very enthusiastic to start with and then it just went. I tried all sorts of encouragements, bribes, everything, to get things moving again. Through the grapevine I heard she'd picked up with a boyfriend, or a man friend, or something. I think that was her downfall to be honest. To get Helen to walk from here to the door, it probably would have taken, exaggerated, 10 minutes. She was so slow, I thought she was going to stop [laughs]. Very unfortunate, because what she did she did thoroughly, but she put an awful lot of time into creating that. In this business, time is against us. She couldn't grasp the fact that we get a price for a job and that price is based on selling labour, and we have a labour rate which covers everything in the workshop. She couldn't grasp that if we were getting 5 hours to do that, granted she was on a lower pay rate, but she couldn't grasp that she had to keep within the parameter. But personally, she was a great kid.'

He talked of a gradual change in Helen's attitude and how this impacted upon working relationships in the garage. 'She was with Martin in the workshop, and he is our top-flight painter, as I mentioned before, he had a lot of time for her, in the beginning, and she was responding to that. And Martin, he wouldn't change, he doesn't fluctuate, Martin is Martin. But come the end he literally pushed her to one side because he didn't want to know her, because she wasn't responding to him. He's the guy, he's not going to be prepared to put in his time teaching someone who is not really interested. It isn't that she was doing things wrong as such, not practically wrong. But, whereas before she may have been intent and concentrating on what he was saying, it was now with a cigarette in the air [gives a distracted look]. She had a good opportunity, especially with Martin. I know maybe I'm a little bit biased because he works for me, but he is a tremendous guy. His skill is second to none and he has got so much patience. For somebody to blow an opportunity like that to work with Martin, I think it's criminal really. Certainly, a lack of appreciation.'

He continued 'besides the odd sort of jolly up comments, she had two verbal warnings from myself. Telling her about her lack of speed, lack of interest or whatever. Then, just maybe 3 or 4 weeks or so after that, we just went very quiet. Instead of helping herself, because in her eyes she had nothing to do, she sort of abused the situation. If she had stood up, got a brush or helped somebody else. But she abused it. Unfortunately while she was here she took up smoking as well, and smoking has to be regulated quite tightly out in a workshop like that. Obviously there are designated areas where smoking shouldn't take place. I mean, she knows all the rules and regulations, and I'm sure that college will tell the same. But at one stage there, she had a 5 litre can of thinners in one hand with a rag in the other hand and a cigarette in the same hand as the rag. She was sort of wiping off. How I didn't go mad I don't know. I could have kicked her literally, because that could have put us all out of business if that had gone up. Plus, it could have maimed her for life. She was preoccupied, I think, I mean I know her father is quite desperately ill, but I thought she was preoccupied besides that. She had her friends, as I say she took up smoking. I don't know.'

Eventually he decided that Helen would have to be dismissed. He did not like having to sack anybody. He spoke of feeling 'let down' which coloured his views about taking on another young trainee in the future. 'At the moment we've closed it down. I feel a little bit hurt about it because, I may have said last time, they are very much a family out there. I sound as if I'm old now, but somebody of Helen's age, they could be my daughter, and when somebody blows a good opportunity like that, which I feel she had, I feel a little bit resentful. I think it would probably be better to do without somebody for a while, than take somebody else on and have that resentment in me, maybe being taken out on them.'

Helen, not surprisingly, saw things differently. After a 'honeymoon' in the early months, she was concerned around the lack of progress in her on-site training and the mundane jobs she was continually given. Just after she left the garage, she recalled, 'I wasn't doing much spraying down at Langley's, only at Christmas when they were in a good mood. I wasn't happy with the training, not really, because they didn't tell me if I was doing anything wrong. Most of the time I was clearing up. I know it's where you're supposed to start off, but I was doing it nearly every day. Sweeping up. Tidying up the paint shop and cleaning the booths, the outside, cleaning the paint off windows. I was doing that nearly everyday all day. The only time I did anything was when Martin, who was training me, was getting a bit too busy and couldn't cope with it, and he asked me to do some of it. That was the only time I'd get anything done. I would have liked to know, and get them to tell me if I was doing something wrong. Which way do you do it right. The little bits I get wrong, and how to mask up properly, and a bit of painting. Even a little tiny bit once a week, that would do. But I didn't get much done.'

Helen felt let down by the lack of progress in her training. This was reinforced when she compared her progress with that of her peers attending her college course. 'The lads at college, two of them are the same age as me, they get paid more, they do more, they are actually left on their own to do something. Some of them aren't even capable of it but they are made to do it.' For Helen, the worlds of garage and college were totally different. 'At college I've been painting and spraying, and bodywork and panel beating. I've never done that down Langley's, nothing to do with panel beating at Langley's. I'm getting better at that, but I only do it at college. The lads are giving me help now. I'm doing more at college than I would have been doing at Langley's. I learn the most at college. I'm happy with the college course. It's brilliant that is. I'm learning a lot, a lot more than I would be at work. Little bits like how to weld, how the paint gun works – which I've never been shown at work, what paints do to metal and how to mix them. It's really interesting.'

Helen's view of the quality of her training at college is in direct contrast to her employer's view of what went on outside of his garage. For him, Helen's day at college was defined as a 'day off'. He described it as, 'A pain in the backside to be honest. Because we don't overstaff anything here, we can't afford to, so when anybody is out, even if it's just a youngster like that it's a problem. They all play a part and we miss them. Helen isn't quite to that position where she is missed a great deal, but you think, "Ah, where is she", sort of thing. The other lad, he goes Thursdays, and we've got to really alter the whole workshop around because, he's only a lad, but he's out, he's not here with us.'

The garage owner did not value the training given by the college. When asked if he could provide all the training that he felt Helen required without the need of a day at college he replied, 'Oh yes, without a doubt. I don't know what her views would be on that. Yes, I'm sure we could, no problem at all there'. College was seen as a necessary evil and the employer saw this 'time out' as interfering with his main priority. As he described matters, 'My priority is to have the staff here. I mean, obviously the priority is to get the work out the door. But if people say they've got to do a day at college, they have to. We realise we've got them 4 days a week and then we make the most of them then. You get varying opinions on college, their training. Some say its good, some say it's boring. In some cases they are not even on the course they are supposed to be on. One is a panel beater and he's on a paint course. We had that 2 years back. There was one of our lads, a panel beater, and he was on a paint course because they didn't have a panel beating course for him.'

The employer also held a negative view of what was actually taught on the college course. 'The college are far behind. They are teaching these lads to spray cellulose. Cellulose just isn't used in the motor trade anymore. Even for people like us we get left behind. Especially with paint technology these days. It' so far advanced. Its a mystery to us so God knows what the college thinks to it.' He recalled a conversation with one of his trainees: 'He comes back and says "Oh we did so and so today". And I'm thinking, "Why on earth are you doing that? I used to do that when I was a boy". I'm sure that they are totally out of date. They need to join a few associations. They need to get fed the same information that a garage would do. They have to retrain their tutors, or upgrade them, to help us deal with these young lads. I think it's people who are out of touch with the trade, which are trying to teach these kids what they are doing.'

Another comment emphasised the gap that he saw between small employers like himself and the college staff. 'There seems to be a void between them and us. They are sort of teachers, and we are the, sort of, scum. We are the manual workers, we don't even read the same books as they read, so they can't communicate with people like us. That's how I think they feel about us. It may be true in most cases. Some people you just cannot relate to. It's no wonder the trainees resent what they are being taught, and the people they are being taught by as well.'

He felt he did not have the time to spend finding out what the college course was about. When asked what he knew about off-site training he responded, 'Not much really, to be honest'. Equally, his awareness of Training Credits was limited. He commented, 'I think it was bandied about at the time, but no one discussed it with me personally. Well, they may have mentioned something. They may have mentioned the fact of Training Credits assuming I would know. I'm not an intelligent guy so unless people tell me I'm not going to find out. But as you say, it didn't worry me too much. I wanted Helen on the workshop, train her up, and if or when she goes to college, I accepted the fact she would have to go one day, and how it's paid for was really incidental to me.' Similarly, NVQs were a meaningless term to him. When asked what they meant he replied, 'I was just going to ask you what it stood for, but you just explained it [laughs]. That's the first time I've heard of that.'

The employer found it difficult to find time to talk to the liaison officer from the college. 'If the liaison officer comes down from the college, to be honest I haven't always got time to sit with her. I chat with her about, not so much about what they are doing, we get a report every so often. It's like a school report at the end of term, "Helen is doing well". It's about six words. Funnily enough, she was down yesterday checking up on Helen. They are supposed to send in something to the college. But neither of the kids seem to know what they should have been sending in.'

However, the liaison officer assumed that the employer would understand the system. She said, 'they knew about Training Credits anyhow because we have got another lad in there. So they knew what it involved, that for their contribution they were there for 4 days a week. They knew before what they had to do, their contribution was the on-job training and then they would be expected to come into college on day a week for their off-job training. So they knew exactly what the training was that Helen was going to go through. They knew which course she was going to come in on. My role after that was, once she was in her placement I then had to go and activate her credits. That's just going through all the paper-work and making sure that he knows about the pay, holidays and sickness. We had the employer and Helen in there and signed up all the credits.'

With regard to the quality of training provided by Langley's, the liaison officer commented, 'She was going through what she had to do. I mean Langley's' is a good placement. We have got some really grotty ones around so she could have been in somewhere far worse. So yes, she was getting training down there, and she was obviously getting her training in college.' Even after two monitoring visits, the liaison officer was not told by the employer of his concerns about Helen. 'She was obviously going to have to start off with the grotty things and then gradually work her way up as she got more proficient at that. The reports we had from down there, her work was quite satisfactory. So whether she was expecting more out of it I don't really know. But you know what it's like, sometimes there is not a lot of work around so you have to do the grotty jobs. I know she was having a bit of a problem with the boss down there and she wasn't very happy. I think she felt that he was picking on her and he was giving her all the grotty things and he was finding fault in what she was doing and everything. It couldn't have been because she is a girl because they have another girl down there. So whether she wasn't up to scratch and he was trying to bring her up to scratch I don't really know, because shortly after that my job changed here and a little while after that she decided she was going to do something else. I'm not quite sure what she is doing, but I know that she has gone into something completely different.'

WINNING THE BATTLE BUT LOSING THE WAR?

Despite the brevity of Helen's stay at Langley's Garage, the fact that she got in at all is worthy of note. The liaison officer commented, 'we had a period when we couldn't really find her anything. Plus, because she is a girl, a lot of employers obviously wouldn't take her on. Whereas when the market is very buoyant they will say, "yes, we'll give her a try". But when it's not they are not willing to take that chance.'

We have seen how Helen got Langley's to 'take a chance' on her. This was a no small victory. Likewise, Helen encountered gender discrimination at college, but felt she had won the battle to be accepted by the young men on her course. 'I'm the only girl in that group. It's a bit odd at times. I get on well with them sometimes. There's one lad in there who is a bit of an idiot because he jokes about anything. He's just getting at me sometimes and I just get fed up with it. Some of them didn't talk to me because I don't think they liked the idea of a girl going on that sort of course. Just sort of leaving me out really – going to lunch with all the other lads. All the lads went to lunch all together, in the pub or whatever, and I was just left there. So I started going around town. But it's all right now. Some of them are all right, a good laugh.'

Helen felt that she had to prove herself to the others. 'Sometimes, yes, at the beginning. Panel beating is not really what I wanted to do, and I wasn't getting on too well with that. But on the paint side I was getting on quite well and the others weren't. They are pretty useless at car spraying but they are better than me at panel beating. So they were taking the Mick out of me while I was doing the body work but I could say "well you're good at this but crap at the other where I'm good". So it worked out really.'

By May 1993 she commented 'The lads at college accept me now, but its taken a long time. You just have to get used to it I suppose. I'm happier now that I've got to know them and how they felt about things, like me in college working with them. All the sexist remarks I've got to put up with, that's all right now, "women shouldn't be working in this job, they should be at home tied to the kitchen sink". I just laugh. I say, "oh shut up, you should be making the tea". They just shut up then. It didn't put me off, not really, I just kept thinking to myself, "I'm going to get through, no matter what they say". I didn't get along with everyone first of all but now I've got to know everyone on the course, we get on really well.'

Despite having won her battle for acceptance at college, Helen lacked the confidence to discuss training with her employer. When asked if she ever discussed this with him she responded, 'not with him. He can be a bit scary. You have got to be able to catch him in a good mood really, and that's not very often. Not with the rest of them because he knows them really well because they have been there for years. But with me and Daniel [the other trainee], he's in his second year at college. He didn't want to ask about a pay rise because he didn't know what Joe would say. I wouldn't either if I was Daniel. He's 18 now and he should have got more money, but he hasn't got it all, he's only got about £8 more. He wouldn't ask. Most of the time Joe is out, so it's hard to get time to talk to him. When you do talk to him he might be in a bad mood.'

This raises questions about the idealism of the Training Credit scheme whereby, in theory, if the trainee was not happy with their training they could negotiate an improvement. Such a strategy seemed dangerous to Helen. In discussing the idea of complaining to the employer about the quality of training, she commented 'I don't think many people would do that. It depends what their employer is like really. It's a big decision. Just to keep the job is the thing. You see, you never know what he is going to say. He might say "If you don't like it go". I didn't discuss it with him, no, not really. When I left yesterday, I gave him all my equipment back, my mask and everything. He said, "Would you go into the trade again if you got another job?" I said, "I don't know". And he said, "Oh, all right then". He didn't actually talk. He didn't want to find out what was going to be happening or whatever.'

BACK IN THE MARKET-PLACE

When asked what she would like do now her garage placement had been lost, Helen replied 'work in a clothes shop. I think it's partly that I'm fed up with what's happened to me'. Her mother said 'she will get really depressed. She's very down at the moment. No job, no money. I mean, she didn't have much money before but she got through on her £30 a week. But now she is home all day.' On receiving a telephone call from the careers office, Helen told them that she had some ideas about what she wanted to do, and they encouraged her to contact them if she changed her mind about going back into car bodywork. Helen said, 'I've been looking for other jobs in clothes shops, or anywhere. But an application form came from Sainsbury's, so I'll send that off, see about that one. I'm going to Tesco's to see if there are any jobs in there. If nothing comes up from those two, I'll start trying clothes shops. I asked a friend, who worked in C&A, if any jobs were going. She said, "Not at the moment, but if there is I'll let you know, I'll ask around". My brother's friend, she works in there. If I don't get any answers from there I'll look around. I did try Superdrug before I got the job at Langley's. They asked me for an interview, so if I don't get anything I'll try them again.'

Despite not being sure which kind of job she would go into, Helen still wanted to complete the college course. She felt that if she could get a job in retailing she might be able to finance the course herself. 'Once I finish my 3 year course and I'm qualified, I'll probably look for a garage job then.' It is interesting to note how Helen rated her chances of finding another garage job at that time. 'Not much of a good chance because there are not many jobs like that around. Quite a lot of people are getting laid off in that area. You see all these blokes without work who usually do car spraying or whatever, and they are qualified. I'm not qualified and they're be going for the same jobs as me. They stand a better chance than me. You always see these adverts in the paper for qualified people with experience. That's why I want to do my course. Once I've finished my course I'll probably be able to get a job because I'm qualified.'

Meanwhile Helen had got an interview in a shoe shop. 'It all happened in one day. I went to the careers centre and they put me in touch with the bloke at the Licensed Provider's. He got me the interview in the shoe shop. I went for that one. I was at college that day. So I had to go for the interview and then go to college in a skirt and top which was a bit embarrassing. When I was at college they 'phoned up my mum and said they really liked me and do I want the job? But I didn't. It was really quiet in there. They weren't getting much business.'

Helen's decision to turn down the job in the shoe shop was influenced by a range of factors which included the advice she was getting from her friends and family. As her mother explained, 'she was so upset at losing her job, and getting advice from so many different people. She was very influenced by the girl that works down at Langley's Garage. She told her that the same thing had happened to her and that instead of finding another job in the same line, she paid for her college course and got a part-time job in pubs and waitressing. Helen was thinking about doing the same thing. I didn't want her to do that. She would probably would have lost interest in it altogether in the end if she did that. I let it go, and let her think about it for over a week, to think about it and make her own decisions and then I took her into the careers office. Her brother had a chat with her, late one night, kept her up to two o'clock. He told her to go for a trade rather than a shoe shop, or any shop. I was glad that he spoke to her because she wouldn't listen to me. Her dad didn't have a lot to say but he agreed with me.'

Following this Helen got an interview at a large garage. 'I went for an interview last week at Big Garage. It went really well. I got a job application. Filled that in. The health and safety form I had to fill in. I sent it all back and I haven't heard from them yet. I asked him about college, that I would need time off for college. He said "Yes, you get that automatically."'

When asked what she would do if she didn't get the job in Big Garage, Helen replied, 'keep on looking for jobs in garages. I've got a bridging allowance that lasts for eight weeks, so it's eight weeks. If I don't find a job by then I'll have to think about giving my course up. I'm just waiting to hear from Big Garage. If I don't get that one I'm going to start writing off to everyone. I'm definitely going to carry on with my course at college, whatever. I've got to find a way to keep on it. I've got to find out how much it costs to stay on it. I rang my tutors and they don't know who to get in touch with to find out.'

Helen did not get the job in Big Garage. She was disappointed. 'It was a nice place. A dream garage. It was massive. Got your own space to work in. It was brilliant.' So it was back to the careers centre where, now, she was not looking for anything specific. 'I was just looking for anything I could get really – anything'. A job advertisement for a training placement at a large record shop caught her eye. 'I've always liked that shop. I wondered what it would be like to work in there. I don't know, I like music.'

Following an interview, Helen was offered the placement in the record shop. However, she still wanted to complete her training in paint spraying. The ideal situation would have been, 'I'd like to finish my course on body repair. Get my qualifications. Once that's over get an actual job and start out on my own'. When she originally got the job in the record shop, Helen saw it as a stopover to provide an income, 'to see what else comes up in the meantime'. She negotiated a day off a week from her job in the record shop to go to college. The manager of the shop was sympathetic and was prepared to give the day off as long as Helen worked

Saturdays to make it up. But, because Helen was not now employed by a garage and was using Training Credits for her NVQ in retailing, she was no longer eligible for the body repair course. 'They found out. I went twice, once a week. I had to fill in this form the first day I was there. They got that back and found out that I wasn't working at Langley's Garage and that I was working at the record shop, and they kicked me out in the second week.'

Helen enjoyed working at the record shop. 'It's a good laugh'. She got on well with her boss and with the other members of staff who invited her out to their Christmas dinner. Helen was also happy with the training she was getting in the shop. 'They go though everything with you. You learn a lot more there. Even though I didn't know what to do at all in the beginning. They take you through it all. If you forget anything they just go through it again. It takes you at least two weeks to get used to it because it swaps around a lot. Plus I started when we had the sale stock in. It was a bit hectic.'

The manager of the record shop was happy with Helen and the progress she was making, 8 weeks into her job. 'I hope that I will take her on, when the training is finished. It's sometimes dictated by head counts from head office. If I can't take her on she'll be able to go for another job and in interview be confident and be able to say "Well I've done this, and I've had this responsibility". And people saying "yes, she's a bright girl". If at the end of her time if I had a vacancy I'd definitely take her on.'

Having settled into work at the record shop, Helen remained unsure about her future as there were no guarantees of a job at the end. 'I don't know what I really want to do. It all depends how far I get in this company.' When asked what she thought she would be doing in a year's time she replied, 'I'll probably still be working in the record shop', and expressed a desire to progress to NVQ level 2 in retailing after she had completed the level 1 that she was currently working on. In contrast to her thoughts 6 months earlier, Helen did not not see the record shop as a stopover, and signalled some ambitions to progress within the company. 'I wouldn't mind getting a bit higher in it. It's quite interesting'. She talked of the possibilities of making it to assistant manager. Helen was aware that this might prove difficult but her conversations with a security guard at the shop indicated it could happen. The security guard's wife had started as a YTS trainee with the record company and worked her way up to assistant manager, 'So it can happen'. Helen also indicated that if the money was right, she might be prepared to leave the area and move to another part of the country.

Helen remained unsure about the future. 'I don't know. It depends if I get a job at the end of the year. I think I've got a good chance.' When asked what she might be doing in 5 years time Helen replied, 'I don't usually look that far ahead. I don't look into the future, I take it a day at a time. I did when I was at Langley's Garage, so I don't think it's a good idea.' Her thoughts about becoming a car sprayer, and in particular a customised car sprayer, were still there but not so central. She said, 'It's part-time now, cash on the side. I still fancy doing it for some extra cash. A bit of a hobby isn't it – my hobby.' To this end, in June 1993, Helen bought an old car that she was working on with her father. She was spraying it and learning about the mechanics of the car from her father as part of her hobby.

Looking back over the previous year and a half, Helen commented, 'I don't think I would have gone for a job in Langley's Garage for a start. I was a bit slow. When I first started there we weren't having many cars in. That was before the recession, I should have realised that when we hit the recession I would have been out of a job. I might have looked for another job, I'm not sure what kinds really. I was a bit in two minds about to go into car spraying or a clothes shop. Now I'm in a record store. It might have been that it was the first job that came up that I was interested in. I think I jumped in a bit too quick. I should have stayed at school and done my GCSEs, even though I got seven passes, but they are not very good grades, I should have got them higher. Another year at college perhaps, then looked for another job that I would have been more able to get. I'm not sure what kind of job.'

When asked what advice she would give to someone like herself thinking about leaving school, Helen gave an interesting response. 'Nowadays there aren't many jobs. All my jobs I got by chance. Everybody is staying on at school or college. I'd advise them to stay on at the moment. I think it goes both ways. Everybody is saying that if you stay on at college to get your grades and pass all your exams, then you get out and you've still got to get a job. But then you come straight out of school to get a job, sometimes it's easy, sometimes it's hard.'

Helen's experience supports her view that sometimes it's hard and sometimes it's easy. For her, the biggest hurt remains losing her job at Langley's Garage. 'I'm still disappointed. I would have liked to finish my 3 years and then actually got a full-time job and decent money. If I pass level 1 NVQ in retailing and a job crops up in car spraying, I don't know what I'm going to do.' These uncertainties remain for Helen and it is possible that what has now become her hobby might, in the future, become her job again.

COMMENTARY

One feature that stands out from Helen's story is that she cannot be portrayed as either a dupe moved by larger forces or as a decision maker controlling her own future. She demonstrated considerable strength of character, backed up by personal and family resources, in taking a stereotypically male job and in holding her own as the only young woman on the college training programme. An optimistic interpretation of these events suggests that she had taken advantage of a slightly more liberal attitude to gender equality in the early 1990s and had proactively counteracted the remaining prejudices and pressures against her as a female. Up to this point her story hints at the successes of the Training Credits policy, built as it was on the assumption that such proactive choosing should and could be the norm.

But things went wrong. We do not know whether her gender had anything to do with her eventual dismissal, but her employer's remarks about her having a boyfriend suggest that it might have. What we do know is that she was suddenly forced to reconsider her future, at a turning point that was sprung upon her unexpectedly. At this point, Helen was driven by forces beyond her control. She tried but failed to get another garage placement. She tried but failed to keep her car spraying training going whilst working in the record shop. She turned down one shop placement but eventually took another. As a result, Helen had reverted to type, in a stereotypically female working-class job.

This transformation into a shop worker was partly unpredictable and might at some point be reversed. In Chapter 9, we will argue that such unpredictability is a central feature of career progression and careership. Perhaps more predictable was the fact that, once in a record shop, Helen was gradually socialised into accepting that this might be her career and the car spraying, which is what she still really wanted to do, was relegated to the status of a hobby.

In the next chapter we meet Laura. Like Helen, her story involves a complex pattern of routines and turning points. Even more than for Helen, her early progress into the world of work was characterised by uncertainty, change and struggle.

4

Victim, Fool or Rebel?: Laura's Story

Laura's experiences also demonstrate the significance of a combination of routines and turning points in her career progression. However, to a much greater extent than for Helen, the routines in Laura's life prepared the way for some dramatic changes in direction. Once more, much of what happened to her was unpredictable at the start. Her story emphasises another feature we have already met but not yet commented on. The business of finding or losing a placement was not simply a matter of choice. Rather, it was a complex interaction between stakeholders, using widely different and unequally distributed resources. These interactions – between parents, young people, employers, training providers and careers officers – consist of negotiations, alliances, struggle and conflict.

BECOMING A BEAUTICIAN

Laura found the immediate transition from school difficult when she left in the summer of 1992. 'It was all like rushed. We just done careers lessons on a Friday, and then after that Friday it was all over all forgotten about. They should make it more, because it's a big leap into work. And when I got out here I was frightened because I didn't know what I wanted to do. I mean I honestly don't think they give you enough, not so much education, advice. You know, that's all you ask for is like, "well, what do I do when?" Another thing I find difficult is in school they don't treat you like a young adult – they want you to act like one but they don't treat you like one – then all of a sudden, just like that, you're out in an adult's world and it's really confusing. I felt really lost when I first left school.'

Laura had a careers interview at the start of her final year and a follow-up group session near Easter. In the earlier interview she was given information about hairdressing, which was what she thought she might want to do. Laura then completed a period of work experience at the hairdresser's salon where her older sister was employed. 'I was going to do hairdressing until I done my work experience. I hated it because I worked with my sister. They compared me to my sister all the time and we're totally different. The worst thing was they treated me like her little sister.' By Easter, Laura decided she might like to be a beautician. 'It was ages ago I thought about being a beautician, but I gave up hope on it because what I really wanted to do was just be a make-up artist. And then like, the beginning of this year, my mum said something to me about it and I thought about it again, thought I'd go for it.'

She found the group careers session unhelpful because she was told she could not use Training Credits to become a beautician, because the normal route to this career is a full-time college course. 'She just gave me all this information on college. But I don't want to go to college. I was told in the group session that I didn't need Training Credits because I couldn't do training for beautician. "There isn't any training for it" she said, the careers officer. She went, " you don't need Training Credits for that."'

Laura hoped to get a job with training or, failing that, a placement using Training Credits. At this time Laura thought she had found a way to become a beautician without doing a full-time course. 'Me and my mum found it out. It was in the local paper. So we went in and spoke to the Licensed Provider on Tuesday, and that's how we found out all the information. I can definitely do beautician training. It's retail training, like working somewhere like Debenham's, and then training on retail and beautician at the same time.'

She knew from the trainer that she would need Training Credits but was unsure how to get them. She lacked confidence in the careers officer but saw the her again, completed her CGAP and got her Credits, right at the end of the school year. 'That was in school I got issued with them. That was for retail beautician, so I could use them in retail. She just asked me what I was aiming for, what I thought I'd achieve by training as a beautician. That was all.'

However, the hoped for training place did not materialise. 'The trainer couldn't get me anything. The person I actually went to, she was in retail and I sort of got backed into a corner to doing retail. So I was put into a fashion chain shop and I hated it. I thought from the first week it would get better and it never did. I left after about 2 months. It wasn't even retail beautician they got me in, it was a fashion shop. It was nothing to do with what I wanted. I don't think they really considered what I wanted to do, I think she thought, I can't even see her trying very hard, I think she thought, "I can't get her anything in beautician, so I'll just put her in retail." 'Cos she said to me, "I remember you saying your second choice would be fashion." Well I never said that. My mum was with me and she can't remember me saying it either.'

Whereas Helen was gradually socialised into seeing herself as a shop worker, Laura's experiences reinforced her dislike of retail work and she decided to leave. 'Half of it was the manageress and the deputy manageress, I just didn't get on with them. But I just took the final step one day when I'd had enough. I went sick and then I just couldn't pluck up the courage to go back. I wasn't really enjoying the work either, 'cos it wasn't what I wanted to do.'

A further problem was that Laura couldn't see any progress in her training. 'The only thing I got trained in was on the till. I was supposed to be doing a training scheme that the shop do themselves, called "Aiming for Excellence", but I never started on that. I had people from the trainers coming round and assessing me and when I left I got a little booklet saying what I could do so far. I know I wasn't going to get day release, I wasn't going to go to college, because they said it wasn't worth it, because what they were teaching at college most people had already learned in the shop anyway, so there wasn't a day release any more. That's what I thought Training Credits were for, to pay for your training. Well I wasn't really getting any so called training. They didn't really help me when I got into difficulty.' Relationships with other staff, perceptions of lack of training and of an inadequate level of support from the trainer will recur as factors throughout Laura's story.

It was not possible to fully explain why Laura was placed in a fashion shop, because the trainer who had dealt with her had left the area by the time we interviewed, in the autumn of 1992. Her successor had met Laura, and recalled that Laura had come in response to an advertisement for a beauty consultant's post in a store, but that it was already filled. She was fairly certain that Laura had been happy about going into a fashion shop instead, but thought that she became disillusioned by the usual retail problems, like standing up all day.

The manageress of the shop where Laura had her placement recalled 'every time a placement comes up I ring the trainer, and he just sorts somebody out. They always come in here to interview with me, and its, "oh, it's what I want to do". Laura complained a lot of being tired, complained a lot of finding it was hard work, she was sick quite a lot, I don't know, I mean you've got to give them the benefit of the doubt, but I did think at the time that it was it was always after like, a heavy few days, she'd go sick, and I think it was because she was worn out, basically. I just don't think she could stand the pace.'

By August 1992, Laura had given up on the beautician idea. As her careers officer said: 'she'd a lot of qualities there, but she was being a bit unrealistic right from the beginning and sort of learned the hard way.'

TRANSITION TRAINING

This left Laura unsure what to do. 'I went to the careers centre and I spoke to the careers adviser and she gave me a lot of choices. She asked me what I wanted to do. I said I wasn't sure so she mentioned a thing called Transition Training, and I'm starting that on the 5th October. I've seen her once or twice since I left school. She's been really helpful and she's been really understanding about me wanting to give up the shop. She hasn't said "Well you've had your chance".'

The careers officer confirmed what happened. 'Laura came in to see me and she was thinking of working with animals. She was also interested in mechanics and catering. So basically, had a job been there and had she been very focused, I could have done a new CGAP 3 with her, she could have had a new Training Credit issued and could have started on a completely new course. As it is, because she had those different ideas and was feeling very down about it and wasn't sure, I was a bit wary of her jumping into something else very quickly. So I suggested that we could talk about Transition Training, and when I told her a little bit more about it she sounded very encouraged and thought it was for her.' Transition Training lasted up to 6 months for those who were judged to be not ready for work. It included placement sampling, and the employer did not have to pay the training allowance.

The careers officer said 'in a second interview with Laura we did her action plan for Transition Training. It varied a little bit from what she'd told me the first time. We left it with animals, painting and decorating and office work. The catering and the mechanics fell off a bit.' Her Licensed Provider said, about what Laura wanted to do when beginning Transition Training, 'Laura said she wanted to become a Redcoat. And very early on it was very difficult to get anything else out of her except that she wanted to be a Redcoat.' No one else mentioned an interest in Redcoat work at all.

Laura was enthusiastic about starting Transition Training. 'I think it's quite good, this Transition Training, 'cos it will help me find out what job I want and if I'm suitable to the jobs I want to do. So I do think it's a good thing. I mean I hadn't heard about it before I left school. I only found out about it after this job at the shop didn't work out. If I'd known about it when I left school I probably would have gone straight in to it, 'cos it would have helped me a lot'. She continued 'Transition Training can show you the bad side of jobs as well. Something you might have your heart set on might be something that was totally wrong for you. So its a good idea. I think I'm quite looking forward to doing it as well. If you find a job part way through you can just give Transition Training up. And then, if it's not right for you, if you do work there and you're not very happy, you can go back to it. If you've only used up like three of your months, then you can go back to it. I think through this Transition Training I'll be able to find out what I want to do. But they can't guarantee, it's not 100%, that you'll get a job at the end. The only thing I am worried about is if I don't get anything at the end and after that 6 months I'm back to square one again. I've got nothing, no money, no job. As far as I know you can only go on it once and only for 6 months.'

At all times Laura had her family's support. Her mother made sure she understood what was going on, by asking for information and sometimes speaking to people like the careers officer and trainers herself. What the family was not able to do was provide local contacts, in career areas that Laura was interested in, which might have helped her find a job. They were happy with Laura's decision to take Transition Training. 'My parents are quite pleased actually. When I gave up the job they didn't mind, because they knew I wasn't happy in it. Then when I said about the Transition Training, my mum thought at first it was a bit of a waste of time, because you'd just be there for 6 months dossing around. But then, when I explained it to her properly, she's quite looking forward to me doing it, so that I can find what I want to do, because she thinks my confidence has been knocked a bit through this job, because I was so unhappy there. She even asked if she could do it herself!'

All concerned with Laura saw the Transition Training as a success. She enjoyed the activities and the company of the twelve other young people with her on the induction week. The Licensed Provider described Laura's subsequent progress through Transition Training, where her first placement was in a nursery school. 'We looked at child care with a view to that being useful for when she does start maybe doing a Redcoat's job, come the summer. And then, you know, the Redcoat disappeared. Basically, she found what she wanted. She did a week's induction to start with. Apart from that, most of her work has been done at the workplace, because she's responded so well to the workplace and it's met her needs, all down the line, with confidence, communication – the normal things that young people seem to have blocks on, they all disappeared with Laura straight away. She just found her little niche, as it were. There was no question of Laura coming out of her first placement on Transition Training after 4 weeks, because she was so well settled there and the employer had suggested that there could be a job here, because she is so suited both to the workplace and the job itself.'

THE NURSERY SCHOOL

Laura and her mother were pleased that she had found something she liked so much so quickly. At the same time, both recognised that child care was not an area for which she had shown any previous interest. But Laura was really enjoying working with children and didn't mind the low pay (£29.50 plus travel), because she was so happy in the job. Both she and her mother saw this as a long-term prospect for employment and, provided she got some qualifications, there seemed to be promotion possibilities as well.

The nursery school placement had become available because the headmistress of the school contacted the Licensed Provider. 'I actually rang up one of the trainers that I knew, I've had dealings with her over a number of years. I rang her up, told her how we were expanding up here, told her that I was looking for young people to train out and to take on to staff, and could she get back to me if she could come up with somebody.'

The headmistress was pleased with Laura and liked the Transition Training system, which allowed her a month's free trial with a potential trainee. 'When we started taking girls on these training schemes they came and the paperwork was done and started and after a week or two we found that they were absolutely unsuitable, everything had been done and yet it was just a waste of time. I spoke to the Licensed Provider about a month, because it takes a month to be able to tell whether someone is suitable, and also for them to tell whether they're going to fit in to that situation, and whether working with children is really what they want to do. But, then again, Laura – a couple of days she was here, and I knew and she knew, and she has literally lit up from inside. The children love her, she loves the children. The parents have accepted her well and certainly the other members of staff have accepted her well. So she has just fitted in.'

When this interview took place Laura had done about a month at the school. The head was planning to employ her. 'When ever I take a student like this, I always say that there is every possibility of a job and I do not take them unless there was a possibility. I feel it's immoral to take them unless you can offer them something. We're opening an under-three section, so she could actually choose whether she stays in the group that she's in or whether she would like to work with babies and toddlers. I would like to take her on an employed basis.'

At this stage, the only person with concerns about Laura's situation was the careers officer. 'Unfortunately, we do get the kids who come in who've been matched up with something that we haven't ever talked to them about. The way Laura's gone isn't ideal. It's turned out good for her but, I mean, they don't pay much attention to what goes into the action plan, do they?'

One problem was Laura's training. The employer was concerned about giving Laura time off work for off-the-job training in spite of having used trainees under YTS, when day release had been compulsory. 'It's going to be very difficult for me, because I have to find somebody to take her place on the one day when she is training off-the-job and that is not ideal. It's not ideal for the group of children and I have to be able to rely on my staff, really.'

She was aware that an NVQ in child care was being introduced which might allow all of the training to be given on-the-job. But this might also be problematic. 'It's not just placements you're asked for but it's the training, and the assessments are going to put quite a burden on the internal assessors. We have one girl in our Kindergarten department, and there's a teacher in charge of that department. She's got quite a bit of experience and she's been used to making judgements, and she feels that she is totally competent at assessing that girl without having to do an assessors course. I sent her to an information day, and she found out about all the evidence she's going to have to collect, and quite frankly she is not enamoured at all. It will be a lot of work for her. I foresee not actually taking students, because staff balk against the requirements that are being asked. They see them as unreasonable, and that the responsibility is being decentralised and passed out to the employer.'

The headteacher wasn't happy with either day release to college or a system where the bulk of the training and assessment was done at work. There is a sense in which she did not want any training programme that had a cost to her as an employer. She would have preferred a system where the trainees spent a year full time gaining practical experience and then, if they were bright enough, went on to a full-time college course (thus not disrupting the school or costing a day's work) to gain an NNEB (Nursery Nursing Examination Board) qualification, which she considered to be the best for the job.

The Training Credits system was supposed to encourage employer and trainee together to select a trainer and training programme that fulfils their requirements. When we mentioned this to Laura's Licensed Provider, he said 'our trainer, I know, is going to see the headteacher. She's also got the address of two others that do child care and I've encouraged employers to get in touch with all of them, to see what training is offered, so they can make the right decision. It's up to the Approved Trainer to negotiate to suit the bill.'

Laura stopped Transition Training, following a meeting involving herself, the Licensed Provider and the careers officer, and went on to work at the Nursery School after Christmas 1992. She did a new CGAP and had a new Training Credit issued. However, the process of choosing an appropriate training course does not seem to have taken place. The headteacher said 'it just happened. Laura would prefer to stay with somebody she knows. So Laura probably chose.' But Laura said, 'I remember the Licensed Provider said "you and the headteacher can decide who your trainer can be, you know, who you can go with". But one day a trainer from his company just walked into the room I was working in and they said "well this is your new training officer". So it was really decided for me. I think the head could have had a lot to do with it, she's a very strong willed woman.'

The 'chosen' Approved Trainer said, 'when Laura finished Transition Training, she was coming near the end, and I was asked to pick it up and do the link. So I had to go out and see the placement provider , make sure that everything was OK. I first met the headteacher a number of years ago, with a young girl they took on, and it appears she does like our firm. It would have been her and Laura's choice in who they had as an Approved Trainer. It would have been explained to them and it's likely that the headteacher asked for us.' There were reasons why that trainer might have been chosen, but nobody remembered making the decision.

THE LOSS OF THE PLACEMENT

From the time when she was taken on Laura's apparently ideal situation deteriorated to the point where she resigned, at the end of May. 'It all went downhill after I left Transition Training and was taken on as a YTS.' Laura became unhappy as a result of poor relations with some staff and the headteacher, a dramatic change from a few months earlier. 'There was like quite a bit of problems with my boss and me. Apparently, the girl who I worked with in the room, told my boss that we were leaving her out. The headmistress knew the girl I was working with, they all went to church together, so they knew each other socially as well. This girl from the kitchen used to come down some days to help out, because I was her friend. When she came in my work didn't change, I can guarantee that. We used to have a laugh in there. Anyway, the girl in charge used to muck around a lot, and I think she gets jealous because my friend in the kitchen was coming down. She went up and told the headteacher that my work was slipping. Since I've left, she's caused trouble for other people as well. She made my life a misery while I was there.'

The employer's version of affairs was different. 'The whole time she was on Transition Training she really couldn't do enough to please. The moment that we took her on her attitude changed. She got on with everybody and everybody thought she was a super girl. Suddenly, there were waves in her room between the staff. Laura didn't mention it to me, she should have done, but she didn't. She mentioned it to the trainer, so the trainer came to me. We addressed the situation. We talked to Laura about her way forward. I also spoke to the staff in the room. For a time, 2 or 3 weeks, it was better. But then it drifted back. But I noticed it wasn't only that. When Laura started with us she was very smart. Now she put a lot of weight on when she was with us. And she started – I would think there were changes going on outside of her working environment – and she started trying wearing very short things, which is very unsuitable when you're working with children and you're bending around. It's not nice. I might be old fashioned, but I like some grace. I don't like things like that. Her make-up got very pronounced whereas before it was discrete, very, very nice.'

'I had to talk to Laura about her attitude on a couple of occasions. I changed the staff, put another girl in there. She got very friendly with the new girl. They were not good to work together and, although Laura had never refused to do what the room leader requested, this other girl did and Laura was quite thrilled about it. I wouldn't be surprised if Laura might have egged her on.' When interviewing Laura at about this time, we also noticed a dramatic change in her appearance. She seemed to have put on weight and her clothes seemed brash and garish.

The trainer's perception was closer to that of the employer than of Laura. 'The placement provider I know very well. And yes, I know that mother actually said I was too friendly with her and Laura didn't feel she was able to talk to me on her own. Now Laura's rung me up on a number of occasions asking me things and I've actually acted straight away. There have been occasions where Laura could quite rightly have asked to see me separately. The headteacher had some very clear points about Laura and I think she had valid points. She's a nice lady and she certainly wouldn't be conjuring them up. Laura's quite forceful and it's easy for her to get into the gossiping syndrome. And I've actually seen her actively doing that in here, when she's been on courses. Laura is insecure, but I am concerned she does appear to have let herself go, her appearance, whether there's an underlying reason there outside? I think the difference is when she's on Transition Training she's got a training officer who's giving her an awful lot of support. But now she's a basic trainee and she only sees the training officer every 8 weeks. Whether she enjoyed the extra support that she was getting from her training officer and suddenly found herself, ooh! and also being confronted with real work situations, about the way people should actually behave.'

Laura also stressed the value of the Licensed Provider's support on Transition Training. 'The Licensed Provider was fantastic for me, he came to see me really often and he always said to me, "is everything all right, are you sure everything's all right?" But I don't know, the trainer seemed really, she seemed on the edge of everything, like she cared more about my work than how I was feeling in the workplace. I felt more like a number to her, not a person.'

For whatever reason, in 6 months Laura seems to have changed from someone who made an effort to fit into the possibly rather staid middle-class school environment, to someone who apparently didn't fit in and resented criticism for not doing so. The trainer thought that mother might have reinforced Laura's negative feelings. 'I feel that the mum is a strong influence, definitely. She's underlying there because things that mum said to me quite strongly, I would talk to Laura about and she was quite reasonable about it. So she's obviously going back to mum. I mean it's not mum's fault, she's trying to protect her daughter. But she's going back to mum with very strong views, it appears, but when confronted or when in the placement, they're not as clear, they're not as strong.'

Laura's mother did not say a lot to us about this, but we didn't interview her until several months after Laura had resigned from the nursery school. 'She was very unhappy at the nursery school. It sort of deteriorated after Christmas. Up until Christmas she was fine and then after Christmas there was a problem with another member of staff and her employer, and she felt it would be in her best interests, as she was so desperately unhappy, to leave and try something else. There again, you see, she didn't start any form of training. But I think she would have stuck at it if she didn't have problems with the person at work.'

The NVQ training was a problem, and Laura had not been registered for it by the time she left. There were two difficulties resulting from the time at which Laura started working at the school. Firstly, as Laura said, 'I was told that I'd missed the start of the term for college, so I couldn't go there until the following September, and I wasn't getting anything, no training, nothing. The only thing I'd done in the 7 months I'd been there, including the Transition Training time, was a basic Food Hygiene course which wasn't really relevant to me, because it was more for people that work in kitchens. Apart from that, I had to do a couple of projects which I had no help on, all on my own, I didn't know what I was supposed to do.'

Secondly, she started just as the actual NVQ child care was being introduced nationally. The trainers said 'unfortunately we had problems with the NVQ at the time. The child care NVQ has been a very difficult publication to actually try and get on to, let alone carry out. So I explained to Laura and the workplace supervisor that it would be unlikely that we would be able to get it started immediately, but we would get her projects to start on and, as soon as I had any news and it was all clear, that I would get her registered.' Because NVQs are workplace based, Laura might have been able to start gaining her qualification at work. She knew she was learning things at work, but did not see this as proper training. 'Oh yes, I picked up a lot at work. Because obviously you will 'cos you're just there, aren't you? And you've got to pick it up haven't you but just nothing to say that I actually had a qualification.'

The employer's views about training have already been given. The delay in starting training probably suited her, as she had Laura 5 days a week and wasn't having to do any formal assessment. 'Let me just say that she couldn't join the proper course. She was actually working doing some things, so she wasn't wasting time, that would cover modules. I felt that unless she could do parts 1 and 2 previous to this September, she might just as well have gone on an NNEB course this September. I think she would have got funding.' There was no way to fund this option through Training Credits and Laura had had enough of full-time education.

Laura claimed that occasional visits to the Approved Trainer's premises had been frowned upon. 'My training officer reckoned that, because I was doing this project I should go to their centre. In there they've got a library. I should go there twice a month, and the head said "well that's not really any good, because we need you."'

Laura's expectations of training were based on what her sister had done, getting regular day release under YTS, and on the experiences of trainees already at the school, who had also gone to college one day a week. We asked, 'you felt you needed the off-the-job training did you?' 'Definitely, yes, because I didn't have any First Aid or anything. If a child had fallen over I wouldn't have known what to do properly. When you're working with children it is such a responsibility, because anything can happen.'

Because of the timing, Laura neither followed a traditional college course nor was the new NVQ-based course yet available. She was given a couple of projects to do which would be likely to count, eventually, towards her qualification. Here Laura's insecurity shows, for she felt she had no help or support in doing these, whereas both trainer and employer insist that she had as much support as she asked for and that she made a very good job of them. The trainer said 'whenever she asked me I gave her suggestions. And then when I talked it through with her, she came into the learning resources unit and I sat down and spent quite a lot of time with her going through it and giving her suggestions and ideas. And she wanted to cut me off and say, "yes, that's fine, I understand it." So, at the worst, she could always contact me. I used to leave her numerous messages to ring me, and she never did.' Her employer said 'she did see a similar project done by one of the other students. And I told her that she ought to do it slightly differently. She must get her own ideas and do something on her own. She did a wonderful job. She gave it to me and about 2 days after that she gave her notice in. But when I gave it to her back I said, "Laura this is wonderful work." The standard of her English, the neatness, the content, the presentation – brilliant.'

By the time Laura left, the trainer had obtained an open learning package which she thought was ideal for the child-care NVQ for reasonably bright trainees, and Laura would have started work on it straight away. Although it was not a taught course, she would have been required to have regular time off work to do it, which might have caused problems with the employer. But to suit the employer, it did look as if a peripatetic assessor could have been used for the on-the-job assessment. So the training problems could probably have been sorted out, but the relationships problems might have remained. And because of the poor relationship with the employer, Laura felt there was a lack of prospects. 'It would have been another – I don't know whether it's a year or two year course. And then what after that? I mean the head wasn't even sure if she could take me on after. After that I might not have anything, and I wouldn't know what it's like to get into a child care place with an NVQ. I don't know whether it's easy or what. But most people look for NNEBs, don't they?'

The employer and trainer both felt there might be factors outside work which had affected Laura's attitude to the job. In a later interview, Laura did talk in vague terms about a break-up with a boyfriend whom she had apparently been living with, but the time-scale she hinted at did not appear to coincide with the problems at the nursery school.

REJECTING THE SYSTEM

After leaving the nursery school, Laura stayed within the Training Credits system. She said 'I actually think the Training Credits are a good idea. It's just the training officers that are the problem. It's just picking the right training really, and who can do the best for you. I mean like I know I can start another job or another training job, and I know I'll have it all paid for by my Training Credits and that and there's no problem there. You feel secure with it really. There are a lot of people out there willing to help you as well, like the careers officer. She's really good. She said, "We'll always be here to help you." I think that's the sort of thing you need to hear. It makes you feel more like there's somebody there you can fall back on, you know. That's why I think the system's good really.'

The trainer felt that Laura's mother was less convinced. 'Mum's very opinionated on how wrong the employer was, and also me. But also she said that the scheme, Training Credits, were basically rubbish, and that she would find training for her daughter, well employment for her daughter. And then, about a fortnight later, I actually hear that she's coming through back on Training Credits doing clerical work.'

There had been a change in the system by then, in that all training places were now supposed to be advertised through the Careers Office. That's where Laura went. This time she had a clearer idea what she wanted to do, but it was another change of direction. 'I'd like to do this admin., because like there's so many different places you can work with it. My Mum she does this sort of thing, at the moment she's temping, she's working in the new newspaper offices. If I did get married and have children, you can always go back to it after 'cos it's that sort of thing. My mum, she's been teaching me how to type and where to put your fingers, you know, touch typing. She's been teaching me that and I find it quite interesting. And I mean it's not just typing is it? I'll have a try anyway.'

This conversation was in June 1993, when Laura was just starting to apply for clerical placements. By October she still didn't have one and had given up on the Training Credits system. Preliminary interviews for most of the jobs and training placements were arranged through the Approved Training organisations, including the same company who had acted as trainer for her nursery school placement. She was interviewed by the same trainer, with whom she did not get on particularly well. At this stage, we spoke to two different trainers, working for the same firm. For clarity, we will call the trainer we have already met number one, and the other number two. Trainer one said 'it just turned out that I was interviewing on the day that Laura came in. So I think she was a bit shocked to see me. I'm not quite sure. She's got like a little fear, as if she's going to get told off.'

We interviewed trainer number two the following October. 'Laura came in for an interview after she was actually referred to us from careers. So I interviewed her for a clerical placement, and then I saw her about 3 or 4 weeks later, when she came in with her mum, to actually talk about her future and basically find out what she really wanted to do.'

Both trainers doubted her suitability for clerical jobs. Number one said,

'I hope that she makes a go of clerical, but I was really trying to get her to give me genuine reasons of why does she want to do clerical, and she couldn't. We had the CV sent to us, very badly written. We needed the CV to send to an employer we had in mind. But trainer number two said, "I can't send it". Because there were spelling mistakes on it. But Laura's let herself down, because normally I would have expected her to provide a good CV, with a lot of thought into it, and it hadn't, it wasn't very good. This is peculiar, if she was seriously trying to get a job, and she certainly sounded as if she was.'

Trainer two said, 'the impression she gave me was that she wanted to do something, but she was getting disheartened with it so she was going to go against the system, and bleach her hair and things like that. I was honest with her, and I said "you're not going to get a reception position, looking the way you do." She agreed with it all, but she didn't do anything about it.'

This was a girl who had been attractive enough to be accepted by a fashion shop a year ago, and whose project was praised for its neatness and English, only a few months earlier. A further problem was seen to be her difficulties in getting along with working colleagues. 'You saw about the problem with her child care when she had a few problems getting on with people down there. I mean, if she's going to have that, then she's not suited to clerical, because you're in an office with, it could be you and one other person, or it could be you and three other people, day after day' (trainer two).

Trainer two said that when Laura was offered interviews for clerical jobs, she had twice failed to turn up. Laura said she had only been offered one. Consistently, in Laura's story, it is when things are not going well that there are diverse perceptions of events. From the trainers we heard of a lack of interest and commitment on Laura's part, and from Laura and her mother we heard of a lack of interest from the trainers. Her mother said, 'You see, the last time we went to the careers office, she saw a few jobs she liked. She saw the careers officer, who gave her details, phoned up the training organisation and someone there was going to get in touch with Laura. Well, nothing had happened, she'd lost her bridging loan. I phoned the careers officer myself, who I felt has been quite supportive, and explained that the Approved Trainers had done nothing. She got on to them and got back to me and said that the chappie that was going to do the interviews was on holiday, she'd get in touch with Laura the following week. And I've heard nothing since.'

Laura said, 'I went to the Approved Trainer's and I told them. I didn't hear anything from them for 3 weeks. I told them I wanted to be a clerical assistant. I phoned up and I said "look! What's going on, I haven't heard anything, you said you'd try and get me a place." She said "well I've sent your CV off to a company, I'm waiting to see if they can do anything." So my mum phoned up, because she said to me, "well what did she say?" and I told her, and she said "well I don't really understand that, why is she just sending it to one? Surely she should be sending it out in bulk and hoping that she gets one back." So my mum phoned up, and about 2 minutes after I phoned,the trainer was out, surprise, surprise! So they said "we'll give her a message and she'll get back to you". A week later she came up with this job and I thought, "I'm not doing that, it's a waste of time". And I haven't heard anything from them since.

'I tried another training organisation. They said because I haven't got any qualifications, they can't do anything for me. I went for a job at [named company], and she says to me, "can you use a word-processor?" and I said, "no," and she said , "well you can't have the job then." She said, "sorry, this is no good for you, they need somebody that works a word-processor." So I said, "well, how am I supposed to get the training?" How am I supposed to have the training if I can't get the training? It's just a vicious circle.'

Laura only had one interview with an employer over a period of several months of trying for jobs through the careers service and Approved Trainers. According to Laura, this interview was rearranged several times, but in spite of that she was very hopeful about it. But at the interview she got the impression that all they wanted was someone to make the tea and take files up to an attic store. 'I'd gone there and I thought "yeah, I'm going to get a job now, I know I am." I'd gone there and I made a really big effort and well I came out feeling really miserable. She 'phoned me back a couple of weeks later. I think she said she wanted me for a second interview, and I said "no, it's allright thank you." The Approved Trainers had another 'very good' girl working there by the time we interviewed them. They thought this girl was very happy and was certainly not just making tea.

It seems surprising that Laura didn't obtain a training placement, for many Approved Trainers were then complaining of a shortage of trainees, as more pupils stayed on at school than in the previous year. But the trainers were unconvinced of Laura's suitability and commitment and Laura was no longer prepared to accept just any job. 'I said to them I wanted to be a clerical assistant. I mean the position they wanted me at the solicitor's they called it office junior, that's not the same thing as a clerical assistant is it? I mean there's no point in me getting a YTS now, because I'm 18 in January. I don't really want the YTS wage. It's too hard a struggle really.'

She was no longer interested in going on 'job searches' and 'inductions'. 'I went to the careers office and they said "come in for this week, this job week." I don't want to do that, I just want to get a job. I don't want to go to other job clubs and all that lot. I mean its a waste of time. All right, she said, "ooh, you'll be getting £35 a week." But that's not what I want. I don't want to be like, try this place, try that place. I want a steady job.' Trainer number two suggested that she was being unrealistic. 'At that age they have to expect that they've got to start at the bottom. She wants to go in and just do a job straight away.'

So Laura and the Approved Trainers gave up on one another, and Laura became disillusioned. 'If a school leaver came to me now and said to me, "I've just left school, what do you think I should do?" I'd say to them "don't bother doing a YTS", I'd say, "because you're not treated very well." And I'd advise them to do something like I'm doing now, get trained themselves. Because I don't know if it's just me or what, but it doesn't seem to be working out very well, and a lot of people I've spoken to have said that. I think what's wrong with Training Credits is that the trainees are being abused. I know I was, in both places really. I mean, you're a trainee when it suits them and when it doesn't matter to them, you're anything. When they want work, you've got all the responsibilities of all the other people. I've got Training Credits here at home now but they're not doing me any good. I can't use them because I haven't got a job. They're not paying for my training.'

Laura claimed to spend a lot of time replying to newspaper advertisements for jobs, going to the job centre and cold calling, with no results. 'I was getting letters back saying I was too young. That's why I'm going to wait and write properly – I mean I am writing now, a couple a week – but I'll start writing properly, more seriously, in January, when I'm 18. I think employers'll take you more seriously then. I mean they think of you as an adult then. Employers are looking for typing. Some places are looking for 70 words a minute, which is an awful lot I think, very, very fast. They're looking for word-processing, computer skills. Some people are looking for shorthand.'

Not having a job, Laura, with her mother's encouragement, had set out to get some of those qualifications. She rejected the careers officer's advice in favour of mum's, as the informal network asserted itself over the formal, official system. 'I told the careers officer that I wanted to do this thing at the private training organisation and all she could say was, "oh, go to the college of further education, go to the college of further education!" Whereas I didn't want to go to the college of further education, 'cos my mum goes to this other place, and my mum said it's really, really good.'

The trainer she was now working with provided open learning training in office skills, resulting in their own and nationally recognised diplomas. Laura had done a telephone techniques day, nearly completed Royal Society of Arts (RSA) stage one typing, was about to start word processing and intended to continue to higher levels until such time as she got a job. She was as enthusiastic about this training as she had been about the nursery school a year earlier. 'I think starting at this trainer's was the best thing I've ever done. It's excellent. The people there are really nice. She's given me a lot more confidence. She's very, very good at her job. I go in nearly every day. You do it on your own, you do it at your own speed. I know I'm getting a lot more attention there than I would anywhere else. She gives you one on one attention. If you need her you just say "can I have a bit of help". She'll sit with you for the whole lesson if you want. When I first went there, she sat with me every time I went in, the whole 2 hours.'

This trainer was not approved for Training Credits, which pleased Laura. 'If they'd opened for Training Credits you get a different standard of people with them. When you go in there now everybody's really nice, and nobody's too loud or anything like that. If you go to one of these Training Credits places, there were a lot of people there that are really rough looking. And some of them are so vulgar and loud' – an interesting comment from somebody who was criticised for appearance and gossiping a little earlier.

As she had turned her back on Training Credits, Laura's family, which was not well off, had to pay for her training. 'I don't get too miserable about it. It's just, it's my mum really, she's got to support me. She's not getting anything for me. I mean, the family allowance has stopped. She's got to buy everything for me, she's got to buy my clothes, she's got to buy everything, because I haven't got a penny.' Her mother said 'I haven't resented paying for the training. I've resented having no help at all. The fact that if she was sort of eighteen and a half, and hadn't worked since the day she left school, she could get "unemployment", but because she's younger, she can't get any help. Because I work, I can't get any help.'

Laura was too bruised by the system to give it another go. Rightly or wrongly, pride and dignity were more important to her and her mother than a little money. Once she was 18, she would be able to claim income support, but she had high hopes that age and certificates would bring a job. In spite of the lack of money, Laura and her mother were happy with this position. Her mother said 'I mean, obviously, it's no good her just taking any job that's offered her if she's not going to be happy, because we'd be back in the same situation. My only worry is, what will she do if she doesn't find a job when she's got her qualifications? But when she's 18, obviously other avenues open up. I mean, she can always do part time up in a pub or something, just to get some money. There's a lot you can do when you're 18 that you can't before. I've spoken to a girl I know at a temp. agency, and they'll take you at 18. She said, "Certainly, send her along, we'll find her a job."'

COMMENTARY

There was a cyclical pattern to Laura's training career. She began each cycle with naive over-enthusiasm, following a 'choice' based on a combination of whim and opportunity. In the early stages there were sometimes glowing reports of her attitude and ability. There followed a period of tension at work. During this stage there were usually personal relationship problems and worries about lack of 'proper training'. This led to a stage of disillusion, when things got worse and were seen in a negative light by all concerned. This was ended by Laura leaving. Laura then dismissed any thoughts of working in that occupational area, and began the cycle again, choosing something completely different.

In telling Laura's story, it would be easy to paint either of two opposite pictures. One is of Laura as victim, never getting the opportunities she wants, being manipulated by trainers and employers to fit their agendas and being exploited rather than trained. From this perspective, her actions were a form of resistance – preserving her dignity and self-respect. The other story is of Laura as inadequate and irresponsible, unable to relate to work colleagues, with unrealistic ambitions, lacking perseverance when things got difficult and progressively making life harder than it needed to be for herself. There are elements of truth in both these stories, but it is in the overlapping of them that we can best make sense of what happened.

Laura was relatively able compared with many 16-year-old trainees, gaining a grade C in General Certificate of Secondary Education (GCSE) science. She could be personable, enthusiastic and hard working. But she was deeply insecure and didn't know how to cope when left on her own or when things went wrong. She was at her best when given close support, on Transition Training and with the clerical tutor. Because things were going so well when she was supported, the nursery school head and the Licensed Provider over-estimated her ability to cope with the stresses of regular work on her own. She was given something of a raw deal, in that her conception of proper, off-the-job training was never given to her, either in the shop or in the school, and there were indications that her employers saw such training as a luxury to be avoided. When things began to go wrong, Laura lacked the confidence or personal skills to deal with the situation, eventually ending the pain by making a clean break.

Relationships with her mum were both a strength and a problem. Mum was always there for her daughter, always prepared to take her side. Like many parents, she did not fully understand the official Training Credits system, despite working hard to find out what was happening at each stage. Our impression was that she left well alone when things were going well but, once things went wrong, fought her daughter's corner with force and verbal aggression. This unintentionally reinforced Laura's own sense of unfairness and the trainers' and employers' feelings that Laura and her mother were difficult and unreasonable. As mum and Laura lost faith with the Approved Trainers, they reverted to the traditional pattern of local networking.

It would be a mistake to interpret Laura's cycle of hope and despair too rigidly, for there were important differences between each cycle. As she gains maturity, we must hope that success can be sustained in some future situation. Some employers may set greater store by the traditional clerical qualifications, that she was finally working for, than the new NVQs, which Training Credits training had to use. What is certain is that Laura represents a failure for the Training Credits system. She had ability but had not been trained. At the time of our final interview she did not officially exist, being neither in receipt of training nor officially unemployed. But she was not work shy, nor looking for an easy life. She and her parents were accepting considerable costs to support her clerical training. Despite repeated failures she had not given up and was apparently working hard towards her latest chosen future.

The contrast between Laura's story and the vision of empowered individualism in the official Training Credits rhetoric is stark. In the next chapter, we turn to two young people who had more success in controlling their own training careers and got much closer to the ideals that the Training Credits scheme espoused.

5

Choice, Empowerment and Unsatisfactory Training: Elaine and Alison

A central principle of Training Credits was the empowerment of young people through 'spending' the credit. For most of our sample there was little sense of such customer power. In this chapter we focus on the two trainees who got closest to using the credit in the way in which it was intended. Elaine was proactive in ensuring that her employer provided access to training and she chose the training programme she would follow. Alison, having completed her NVQ level 2 at one college and with one employer, took the initiative to change both, as she progressed to level 3.

Elaine and Alison had something else in common. Both followed an NVQ or NVQ-type competence-based training programme and both found the training experience partly unsatisfactory. In this chapter we are concerned with the juxtaposition of empowered choice and unsatisfactory training. Elaine chose her training at the outset, but it did not entirely live up to her hopes and expectations. Possibly because of this disillusionment, she refused the opportunity to take up level 3 training the year after. Alison exercised her choice after a partly unsatisfactory experience, in the hope that a new placement and a new trainer would improve her prospects. We begin with Elaine.

ELAINE'S STORY: EMPOWERMENT AND DISILLUSION

Elaine was academically the most able of our sample. 'I got six GCSE passes. I was going to stay on for 'A' levels originally, but I decided against it. I wanted to work. But by the time I'd changed my mind most of the training places had gone, so I decided I'd make the most of it the next year. So in the sixth form at school I've done a business and administration course at NVQ 1, sociology GCSE, accounting GCSE, and I've done RSA 1 typing. I got distinction in that and I'm doing RSA 2 at the end of this month [June 1992].'

For several years she had intended to go into office work, having tried it and enjoyed it on various periods of work experience. During her year in the sixth form she had to do one day a week work experience. Her parents helped her to find a place. They targeted large companies, where they felt she would have more chance of eventually getting a job. Elaine obtained a work experience place with the local Council, where her sister had done YTS training and had subsequently gained employment.

Elaine's sixth form timetable left one day a week without lessons and she chose to use this for additional work experience. She impressed her employers, so that when a junior post became available she was appointed. This was in April 1992, just before her examinations. Whilst at school, she had completed her GCSEs (passing Sociology) and part 1 of the RSA 2, but did not finish the NVQ 1. Her employer said 'She certainly created a favourable impression as far as the managers were concerned, in the offices that she spent time in. And luckily for Elaine, and for us really, about the time that her work experience and her school year came to an end a vacancy occurred in our legal section and Elaine got the job.'

Much of the initiative to take her training further came from Elaine herself. 'When I was at work I talked to the city solicitor and he said "would you like to carry on learning?" and I said "yes". I knew I was entitled to training so I asked my administrative officer about it.' There was some doubt about whether her training could be financed. 'I talked to him and he said, "Well it's not quite as easy as that. There might not be enough money in the budget". And I said, "well I think I'm still entitled to Training Credits even though I've spent an extra year at school". When I went to the Approved Trainers, they told me that everybody under 18 is entitled to training, even people in full-time jobs. So I explained that to him and he 'phoned personnel and they confirmed what I'd said.'

Elaine organised an interview with the careers officer, completed a CGAP and collected a Training Credit for clerical training. 'I've done an aim, worked out a plan of action sort of thing, and the careers officer's written out what I'm going to do and everything, what help I think I need, support etc., and that'll be typed up and I'll pick up my Training Credits. I'll take them into personnel and then they sort out the courses.'

The Council had a training officer. They had been a managing agent under YTS, organising training for trainees employed by the Council and for some placed with other employers. Reduced funding meant that they now no longer took trainees themselves, but they still acted as an Approved Trainer for trainees placed with other employers. The training officer organised this.

Elaine made her own decision about what training course to follow, in consultation with the training officer. She said 'about the beginning of August they started to arrange things for me. It was all up to me totally, I could do whatever. I was going to do ILEX [Institute of Legal Executives] but decided I didn't really want to go into something specifically like legal work before I found out much about it, so I've done something more general now. I could choose the private training provider or I could do a

BTEC [Business and Technician Education Council] course at FE college or I could do a personal assistant course, anything really.'

Elaine did not follow the preference of her employer, who said 'to be honest, we tended to lead her towards either the BTEC or ILEX, because they tend to have a higher regard by employers at this stage'. When asked why she chose the NVQ, Elaine said 'I don't know, I think it was because I'd started the NVQ 1 and not quite finished it, so I thought I can carry on with it and when I finish it, it will be an NVQ 2 which is higher again. It was something I was already comfortable with and I quite enjoyed doing. If I ever got promotion to legal assistant, then you automatically start on ILEX anyway.' Her employer commented 'Her reasons were quite valid I think. We discussed it in detail, and the pros and cons of it all. It was her decision.'

With the agreement of the training officer, she chose to have her off-the-job training from the Approved Trainer she had previously visited from school. They are subsequently referred to as the training provider, as they were not acting as a full Approved Trainer for Elaine's programme. Elaine's employers acted as her official Approved Trainer. They cashed the credit, carried out the administration and 'on-the-job' monitoring, but bought in the 'off-the-job' training and NVQ validation from the training provider. The training manager commented 'we've had a lot to do with the training provider. They've done a lot of work for us and also provide training. We find them a very sympathetic and flexible training provider.'

Elaine had one day a week off-the-job with the training provider. The Council training officer said, 'The only thing that she will do at the training provider's is to support what she can't do at work. So there is a reception simulated unit at the training provider's, but she wouldn't do that. I've an arrangement with them that if she does it in work then there's no need to do it at the trainers. It's assessed here.'

However, the training provider claimed to do everything connected with Elaine's NVQ, except monitoring her progress at work. 'The Council are Approved Trainers still, but they simply don't deliver any in-house clerical programme any longer. The Council pays us to provide her with off-the-job training, end of story. I don't monitor her or anything. Assessment, in order to satisfy NVQ, is done by our assessors in house. But in addition to that, the candidate log book that they all fill out can be filled in at work when they achieve an element within a unit. It can be signed off by their supervisor and dated, and there could be dozens of those within a unit. But in order for us to be absolutely convinced they have achieved full competency we cover everything with them in here as well.'

Elaine took some responsibility for her own work-based training, making sure that she did the necessary work for the NVQ in her own department and arranging to work for other departments. Her employer

said 'I look after the sort of admin. of the department and things like faxes
are sent from our office, and she did actually come in to me and say, when
we are sending faxes could she sort of come along and see what was going
on, because it was one of the things needed for her course.' Elaine said 'I
did have a little go on reception at the training provider's, but nobody
comes in really. So on Tuesdays and Thursdays from 9 till 11 for about 6
weeks I did experience on the reception in the Council building. It was
really good.'

Elaine had the full co-operation of her employers. She collected
evidence of the tasks she had performed at work, as this was needed for
assessment. At times she found the evidence she had to provide
somewhat trivial in relation to the work she was doing. 'I had to log all
telephone calls. Say somebody 'phoned up and they just wanted to know
what time the Council building opened, I mean I wouldn't ask them their
name and log down the time. Most calls that you get are general
enquiries.' Such logging was sometimes the only way of providing
evidence of work done which would satisfy the assessment criteria. This
was the first indication that all was not going well with Elaine's chosen
training. 'You don't get actually assessed at work. You do things at work,
like the telephone calls and the reception, and then you use the logging
things from that to be assessed by the training provider.'

The training provider initially saw Elaine as a bright and committed
trainee who was likely to complete the NVQ early. But, after a very good
start, Elaine's achievement rate and attitude deteriorated. 'That is what is
so frustrating, somebody as bright as that. We were hoping to have her
verified at the end of this month. There's no way will she will reach that
now.'

In contrast, Elaine was doing extremely well at work. 'I'm taking on
new responsibilities at work. I'm the clerk and then there's four legal
trainees and a legal executive, who all do conveyancing work like council
house sales. I've been doing some of the things that the legal trainees do,
like mortgage redemptions. The city solicitor's in charge of our
department and his secretary left at the end of March. So somebody went
in to do all her secretarial duties and I got to do the other half of her duties,
which were the legal library, and I got a pay rise.' Her employer confirmed
this. 'She's still in the same job, but her work is probably a bit more varied
now. Someone in an adjacent section is on maternity leave, so Elaine has
been helping them out. And she has taken on some other responsibilities,
so she's been accelerated an increment or two to recognise those
additional duties. She's getting on very well.'

Once she had been in the job for 6 months Elaine was finding the
training less interesting than work itself. 'Off-the-job training is the
shorter day by one hour, but work goes much faster because I'm interested
in the work. My time's used more effectively at work. Nobody's got any

enthusiasm for the training whatsoever. It's an insult to your intelligence. It's sort of "look up the address of something or other in the 'phone book". Things I knew how to do when I was five. It's all just "write everything down so it looks good on paper". I could have done it faster. But it doesn't stretch your brain power, you don't have to think about it. I told my tutor that today. I said "I spend four days of the week being treated like an adult and then I come here." Frankly you just get treated like a child really. About a month ago we were about five minutes late back from lunch, and it was sort of "if you do that again you'll stay in five minutes later after half past four". Not that we want to come and go as we please. Going to training is like going back to school again.'

Elaine couldn't be bothered to produce all the evidence necessary for the NVQ, because it was stuff she could do easily but which was not done at work exactly as the training provider required it in the log. So she was not completing units when she could have done. The training provider was aware of a problem. 'She's taking a very long time. I don't know why. She's a lovely girl. The work she produces is very good. She talks a lot. I don't know why and if you ask her she doesn't know why. I don't think she's even half way through yet. We have a mock training office. We try and make it as realistic as possible. We don't like classroom situations. Each unit is a work station. They do it at their own time, at their own pace. We don't try and let it take them too long because they tend to get bored. But on saying that there are some girls that you just cannot push. You know, most of them you say "right, verification is going to be the end of July". And most of them will put a spurt on at the last minute and get it done. Elaine, for some reason, is not one of those.' He felt that Elaine was mixing with the wrong people at training sessions.

At this time, the Council training officer was not aware of any problem. 'Her on-the-job training is tremendous. It's going along very, very nicely, and I think that reflects in her off-the-job training because we're hoping that she should be verified before Christmas.' The training officer and the training provider said they were often in touch with one another, yet their viewpoints on the training and on Elaine's progress were very different.

Elaine had hoped to finish her RSA 2 typing as well as the NVQ 2, but ended up doing the RSA in an evening class paid for by her parents. She said 'I want to do the second part of my RSA 2 typing and I was told that I could only do that if I finished my NVQ 2 before the end of the time available. They used to do RSA typing, but they don't do it any more because the Training Credits don't pay for those exams any more, they only pay for a certain amount of tuition which covers the NVQ.' The training provider confirmed this. 'The Training Credit provides for them to achieve an NVQ 2. But it is so unlikely that you could get a young person who could achieve it so quickly that you could afford to include other things. The NVQ 2 is their training. Keyboarding is covered but not to any specific single subject standard. It is an example of a traditional qualification valued by employers and trainees which cannot be paid for by Training Credits as they only pay for NVQ training.'

Elaine's training was less good than she had hoped. It did not provide the typing which she particularly wanted, proved to be unchallenging and boring. 'I wish I'd done something like Business and Finance instead of what I'm doing now. Or even though I didn't really want to specify and do something like ILEX, I wish I had done it now, because it would have been a start and if I hadn't carried it on then it still shows that you don't mind studying.'

The employer's advice to do ILEX may have been sound, but Elaine's desire not to commit herself to a specific field seems sensible. Maybe the BTEC course would have proved a more worthwhile compromise. It is also possible that a different approach to the teaching and assessment of the NVQ would have minimised her problems. If she could have been assessed at work on the units which she did at work, then she might have found the NVQ less tiresome. This was what the Council training officer had always envisaged. 'At the training provider's she'll be doing the things that she can't do in the office, to support requirements. We did have a conversation where I said to Elaine, "if you find you are repeating things, then speak and tell someone". The training provider can be flexible when they know the requirements.' However, the training provider did not see things like this. 'In order for us to be absolutely convinced they have achieved full competency we cover everything with them in here as well. We still simulate the unit even if they say, "well I do this at work".' In this case, the training provider's attempts to maintain standards acted as a deterrent to the trainee.

Elaine completed the NVQ 2 in just over a year, a period seen as quite satisfactory by her employers. They had eventually become aware that there was a problem at the training provider's. The training officer said 'she got sidetracked by work. With this restructuring that we've had, she was given extra duties. But we picked that up, well really it was a need to put her back on the straight and narrow and offer her support. And I said, "that's no problem, we can sort that out for the time that it takes you to achieve the bits and pieces for the NVQ". And we got her back on track. Possibly she used the excuse of over-work.' Elaine never blamed over-work when talking to us.

Once there was another verification event in sight, Elaine completed the remaining units rapidly. The training provider said 'she was a bit disgruntled I think, she said she did a lot of the work at work. I said to her, "why didn't you come and see me?" We never really got to grips with that. She's fine, we just had a little talk and she settled down. She's due to finish in December [1993]. She could have finished in July if she'd wanted to. With hindsight, there were several girls in there who weren't going to work who've since left. And it seems to me that since they left and since we've had the talk, she's really got her head down.' Elaine said 'I've done everything in the last like four months. It was better working rather than lazing around there, just because it goes faster. The actual work has always been easy there. Getting it done in the time was the difficulty.'

Once she had finished it, Elaine was content with her decision to do the NVQ. 'I might have done it faster if I'd done this one again, and maybe gone on to, is it a BTEC in Business and Finance, which I was quite interested in. A friend of mine is doing that. It's a bit more in depth. But then again if I went up to an employer and said, "I've got Business and Finance BTEC" or "I've got RSA NVQ 2 in Business and Administration", they might think mine was higher than hers anyway, even though hers is a lot more depth. Obviously it's going to have helped me, because any qualification you can get is good.'

Nevertheless, Elaine didn't intend to go on and do NVQ 3. She was in a better position than many young people who do use Training Credits to progress to this level, as she was good at her job and already had supervisory responsibility over a newcomer whom she had to train. The training officer said 'we've discussed what she was going to do if she'd achieved NVQ 2 and she was unsure then and I think she's still of the same mind. Where she is she could go either way. The level 3 in business admin. is sufficient for her to continue. But with her involvement in conveyancing and suchlike, if she settles to that area of the work she may well do the ILEX. I think I've been through this before and there is an NVQ equivalency for it. I think possibly in about nine months we might be deciding what to do next.'

Elaine said 'I've been offered NVQ 3. I spoke to a lady from the TEC and she said money is available. But it's not what I want at the moment.' As our fieldwork ended, Elaine preferred to do just the job which she found challenging, not training which she did not. She was in the fortunate position that the Council might pay for her to train at higher levels anyway, once her entitlement to Training Credits had expired.

FRUSTRATION AND CHOICE: ALISON'S STORY

Alison had known what job she wanted to do for some time. She had her own pony, had spent weekends and done a successful work experience at a local stables, and wanted to work with horses. Her mother, who had personal knowledge of the equestrian world, did not initially encourage her in this. 'I didn't really want her to go into this career, but as she's choosing it and she's happy at doing it and it's probably one of her best abilities, I will back her all the way through. I would rather she didn't go into the horse world because I have experienced it myself. I know how exploited you can be. It's hard work, it's dangerous.'

Alison considered other options, but was not deflected. 'I wasn't all that sure that I was going to work with horses when I left school. I was quite open to a lot of different things like working in the leisure industry and I could quite fancy going in the Navy, 'cos my brother's in the Navy and it's good. But I wasn't sure like the things I could do in the Navy.'

She decided her preferred route into the horse industry was using Training Credits. 'I just wanted to have practical experience first out. Like the trainers up there said, a lot of them did YTS first, and when they'd finished all their exams [following subsequent full-time courses] and went to an employer, the employer said, "Oh, she's been out and worked in the industry for a year or two so she's not just been in college, she knows what it is like working out and how hard work it is really". You've got to learn to cope with people of all sorts. I wanted to go out and work first to really make sure that's what I wanted to do.'

Her mother insisted that she should get good training. 'I didn't mind what she did so long as she went for some training, efficient training. Because we'd had such a bad experience with the oldest son doing YTS, I wanted to make sure the training she did was a good consistent one.' Choosing training was something the family thought about before Alison left school. Their connections with the horse world helped.

Alison: 'The careers officer said she'd put me in to see two trainers but I wasn't very keen on going to one of them because mum said that it was an agency'.

Mother: 'I wasn't too keen after our experience with Alison's brother of how that training organisation was run.'

Alison: 'Well County College had already been in touch with me and I'd already been up there and I liked it anyway. I was given some booklets from somewhere.'

Mother: 'From an agricultural show, they had a trade stand there.'

Alison: 'And there was a little pink leaflet saying "taster courses" that you could go on for 3 days. So I went up there and they told me about all the courses.'

Mother: 'Because we are like into agriculture anyway, we knew South College. You'd been to visit hadn't you? And then we went to visit County.'

Alison: 'I liked the South College as well but they said that because County was nearer, I might as well go there.'

County College was keen on providing opportunities for potential trainees to find out about the facilities they offered. The training manager said 'we go into schools and talk about careers in land based industry. We'll talk about the different courses that we offer, career opportunities and about the courses that can be bought with Training Credits. So the whole thing is presented. We then offer young people a chance to research in depth what we do. They can come in for a 3-day taster course. The parents join us for 2 hours on the last day and have a chance to see the facilities and meet the staff and talk about the various courses that we do. In addition, we run what we call mini open days. We like young people to come with their parents. We let them interview current full-time students, who will be ex-YT. Then those people show them round, so they got the story from them without any input from us. Then after that we will go over the various courses that we offer and look at the different training opportunities, full-time courses, and how the Training Credits work. I also explain how NVQs work. Some people we will never see again. That's fine, because they've researched us and they've gone. Those who are still interested will then need to make a choice depending on exam results. We keep in touch with them. They can come back again.'

So Alison chose training on the basis of considerable information about the college. She did not have as much information about the alternatives. Like many other young people, Alison went to a known training organisation first, County College, and used them to help her find a work placement. The college arranged a placement for her at the riding stables where she had done work experience from school. Although Alison knew that it was a good yard, she had reservations about going there having been 'bossed around' on work experience.

Alison: 'I wanted to go somewhere further away really and lodge there but the college liaison officer said she reckoned that there wasn't any other places.'

Mother: 'They put lots of obstacles in front of us. And it would be cheap. If she had gone further afield, where they'd had to pay her board and lodgings, it would have cost them more money.'

Alison fitted in well at the stables. Her employer said 'Alison's excellent. She's keen and she will do well in the horse job. I've had quite a lot of YTS's, most of which never stick the course and I've had a handful which were worth employing. I would definitely employ Alison.' She had worked with County College before and was happy with them. 'Alison approached me about a training place. I think she'd already spoken to County but I tend to send them in that direction because they do train them, which is more than I know of any others. We get very good support from them.'

Alison was working for a Pony Society Vocational Qualification, which was an NVQ level 2 equivalent. It had the same type of competence-based structure as a full NVQ and almost everyone talked as if it was an actual NVQ. Alison was expected to do much of her training at work. Progress at work would be checked by the college liaison officer, and the aim of the college course was to provide training in those areas not covered in sufficient depth at the particular stables. Alison said 'I'm going up to County for 6 weeks throughout the year. Just doing different things which I can't train up at the riding school or, if I can train, it'll be more advanced.'

Alison's college tutor described the structure of the training. 'I've taken the syllabus and divided it into approximately 10 weeks. I'll run all the modules twice over the year, because you get the hunting yards that are busy over the winter and quiet through the summer and vice-versa the riding stables. So the work provider then can choose. Whereas perhaps a student will be regularly clipping horses and therefore will have no need really to come in to college to clip horses, they might need to come in for perhaps for the loading of horses and the transportation of horses. They sit down with my liaison officer, the student and the work provider, and the work provider will say, "I can cover this, I can cover that, I don't think I can cover this subject in as much detail, I think she ought to attend the week here". And they also look at their own dates, knowing how busy they're going to be, and they decide. 'We also ran a 10 week foundation course through the summer. So those modules that I've just been talking about will be covered in those 10 weeks. The student will then go away with all the theory and some of the practice that they will need to reach to NVQ level 2. Alison came in for the first health and safety week and then she went back to the stable.'

So choices were made by Alison and her employer. Unfortunately it did not work out as smoothly as it should have done. Alison was only able to attend one week of the foundation course. 'I was going up there for the summer holidays for an 8-week course, but as I was working at a riding school it's really busy in the summer so I had to work.' This foundation programme was not compulsory but, because of the way the training worked out in that particular year, it would have been of considerable benefit to Alison. The college tutor said 'I made a boo-boo. I ran the 10 week foundation course. I then let a couple of weeks lapse and then I started my module weeks. What I didn't appreciate, it was obvious, was that they wouldn't come back in so soon. I thought the third that didn't do the foundation course would come in. But, of course, you only get one or two coming in for each module, then it's very hard to run a module week, using up a lot of lecturer time and facilities for only one or two people. We had to cancel a couple.'

Alison had problems with her chosen modules. 'On my yard I don't do any bandaging or anything like that. So I wanted to do things on that. And things that you mainly need for your exams, like that you're not sure on, say. My employer helped me pick them. Or I said what I'm not very good on or what I need practice on. But because there was other trainees we had to work it amongst us. We all had to go up at different weeks. But then they kept changing the weeks, a couple of times. So then you ended up with weeks that you didn't want, and the weeks you wanted had gone already. One week I was the only person there. They fitted me in with the full-time courses.'

These problems were confirmed by the college liaison officer. 'It was unfortunate that, because the foundation course started last year, we put on the module weeks from September to Christmas and of course we didn't have anything like the number of students, so we had to either cancel weeks or block people together for different subjects, and Alison got muddled around basically over that. So then the list went out for module weeks for the new year and that unfortunately had to be changed, so poor Alison felt that she'd tried twice, and then the third time she managed to get to college to do what she was supposed to. But again I understand there was the mix-up when she came in to do what she thought was one subject and somehow she was doing something different.'

Despite the existence of a local liaison officer, there were misunderstandings about arrangements. When the liaison officer first interviewed Alison and her mother, she was not aware that Alison had already done a taster course at the college. Then the first week that Alison was supposed to spend in college was not notified to the employer, who was expecting Alison at the stables. Her mother observed 'we put her on the train then I had a 'phone call from the employer at the riding school saying, "where's your daughter? She should be here working". I said, "oh but she's on her week health and safety course at County". I said, "well it was all booked and arranged, and I 'phoned the liaison officer the previous week for something and she knows". She said, "well I was at the liaison officer's on Friday, and she never told me". So then I'm 'phoning County saying, "is Alison really meant to be there?" Alison did stay there, she did need to go for the health and safety thing although her employer said she didn't really need to, but I was happier that she'd been on that.'

Alison had problems getting her assessments signed off. 'Every time I went up to County they said, "oh, we'll do your assessments at the end of the week", and then they'd forget or they didn't actually get them done. When I was up at County they said, "well who's been ticking them?" And I said, "well no one really, because I was told that you was meant to be doing them". And then it's been said, "oh well your employer should have done them as well".'

Alison went in for level 2 verification twice. On both occasions the college suddenly discovered that this capable trainee hadn't had all the elements signed off. The first time, 'they was like rushing trying to just finish them off really quickly, and then they said, "well no way we can put you in for it".' The liaison officer commented 'her employer did do some of the assessment in the end. I think there were one or two subjects which the college tutor thought that the employer could have signed but she didn't think she could. So I think that's how the muddle came that Alison hadn't got the assessments done prior to the original verification day.'

There were a few elements where Alison and her employer felt that she had been rushed through before she was ready. The employer said 'there were feeding and things that they'd ticked and signed. I wouldn't have signed them. They sent a whole pile back for me to sign, and I sent them back saying I wasn't signing them. One was preparing linseed and feeding a horse linseed. Now they ticked that and signed that as she knew how to do it. Now that is a dangerous thing because that could poison a horse, and she didn't know anything about it.'

Alison agreed. 'Most of the stuff I was OK on. It was mainly the stud work which I hadn't done a lot on. We've got a mare and foal where I worked – I didn't really have much to do with that though. I know a little bit through my own knowledge but not in depth at all which we were meant to know quite a bit about really. We went to a stud for a couple of days to watch a mare being teased and things like that. But that was my stud section ticked, really.'

But it wasn't all bad. 'I was going up to County for different weeks. I did a week on shoeing, a week on bandaging, a week on transporting horses and getting them ready for travelling. A lot of the time we went up to County we went over quite a lot of things over and over again so that we knew it quite well. And then when we went back to our work placement we were meant to practise them then and carry it on through.'

Alison was successfully verified for her level 2 just before 12 months were up and was satisfied with her progress. Her mother was dissatisfied with the inefficiency of the college. There was something else which bothered both of them. It was accepted by everyone we spoke to that although the NVQ approach was appropriate for assessing most trainees' capabilities, the traditional British Horse Society (BHS) qualifications had an international reputation and were the qualification that anyone 'in the know' wanted to get. Alison said 'they say the NVQ is the equivalent of the BHS but really it's not the equivalent, because they said themselves up at County, "oh, so and so's got her NVQ stage 2 but she wouldn't no way pass her BHS stage 1". I wanted to do both, just in case the NVQs aren't very good and a lot of employers didn't really seem to think much of that really. The NVQ's good really because a lot of people are nervous in exams and you don't have to do that, whereas you're not sure if they're very good as a qualification or not.'

The college training manager explained that 'if they are prepared to pay for the BHS exam themselves, we will provide them any extra tuition that is necessary because the industry at the moment perceives the BHS as quality because when they go overseas NVQ means nothing, whereas a BHS qualification will get a job in the US, Austria, New Zealand. We've had youngsters in Spain, in Belgium, ex-YT.' Alison did pass her BHS stage one as well as her NVQ 2, but her parents had to pay her entry fee, as they were told that the Training Credit would not fund it. The college tutor claimed that 'NVQ originally came out and we all moved over to NVQ and then it fell through. British Horse Society pulled out and of course they are our biggest awarding body. So the TEC were then saying we had to get our students through an NVQ level 2 equivalent. This year they stopped funding us for BHS NVQ equivalents. Then next year we're back to NVQ. It's changed every year I've been here.' Alison's mother later claimed that at least two other Approved Trainers were still putting trainees through the BHS stages as an NVQ equivalent.

By the end of the year Alison was satisfied with having achieved her NVQ 2 equivalent and her BHS Horse Management stage 1. She felt that she had had a good experience of working with horses at one of the best riding stables in the county. 'I think I've learnt a lot where I've been. Tuition, I didn't really get that much. I was showed once and then, "you know how to do it don't you, the way I like". But otherwise experience-wise I've done all sorts where I've been.' The owner was satisfied with Alison and hoped she would stay. 'I thought she would stay for another year, probably go to college for a year and then maybe come back as an instructor because there would have been a job here for her.'

However, Alison did not see her own best interest as to stay. 'I quite fancied doing another year somewhere else. I wasn't keen on going up to college yet for a full-time course, and I didn't particularly want to stay there because in a year I couldn't really learn that much more. So I thought I might as well get myself another year somewhere else. They were always saying, "oh we're so busy – well we'll do some so and so today, practise your plaiting or something". Then when we get round to it people would turn up for hacks and they'd say, "oh, you have to take a hack out now". It was always the customers first and then you fitted in when and if you could, and that was very rarely.'

The liaison officer had not helped Alison in her attempt to change stables. 'I was told when I 'phoned up the college that I wouldn't be able to be under them because the new stable was out of their area, by the liaison officer, and that I wouldn't be able to go anywhere else, only in this area. But I said to my tutor "I've got a new work placement and I won't be under this college any more", and she said, "ooh, why's that?" And I said, "well I was told I was out of the area". And she said, "oh no, that's not true".' When Alison asked the liaison officer about placements in different types of stables she had little to offer.

Alison :'It's just riding schools, which the one I was at is the top, round this area it's one of the best. I think that's all she's really got. 'Cos she said there's a hunting yard, the hunt masters yard and he's got two horses and a young one that needs breaking. But I was talking to a girl up at college and she was the one that was leaving there and she said, "well we do quite a lot in the hunting season". But the rest of the year she just does odd jobs round the farm. So I didn't really fancy that.'

Mother: 'The only conclusion that I come to was that the liaison officer didn't want to lose Alison's Training Credits. I think she thought we would give up on this work placement further away.'

Alison found a new placement for herself. 'I like doing breaking and schooling and I was looking in a horse magazine and I saw this livery yard with breaking and schooling and things and we just 'phoned up to see whether they wanted a YT. And she said she was actually looking for one at the time. We went up and I had an interview and I rode and everything, and she said I could start whenever I wanted to.' She was supported by her college tutor. 'She's gone to a very good yard. Alison found the job herself, and I am in total agreement that she did the right thing. Having worked in a riding school which is very, very good work experience, I think she was now due for a change. It's a dressage type of yard, competition yard livery, a lot of stud – she's got a stallion that they compete. I think it's a good career move.' But the liaison officer felt it was a mistake. 'I think Alison could be a little bit disillusioned after a little while, because I think it's essentially a livery yard, and they do a little bit of breaking and schooling. And I don't think being a student she will get much chance to be "hands on" to the job anyway.'

Her original employer felt that the decision was not entirely Alison's. 'There was someone at the college who was saying to her, every time she went up there, "don't waste your time at a riding school, why don't you go to an event yard" that was one of the instructors at the college.' But from what Alison said to us, she had always hoped for something different. There was considerable resentment from this employer. Fearing such a reaction, Alison did not tell her she was leaving until the last minute. The employer said 'we'd taken her to horse shows, we'd taken her to other places, we'd taken her on a show jumping course, we'd done an awful lot for her we really had. Everybody else knew she was going before I did. The college knew, everybody in the yard knew, which is very bad. She could have come to me and said.' She was concerned that Alison was not necessarily taking the right route for her talents, in moving away from riding schools. 'She's not going to be a high flying rider. She's not a bad little rider but when fences start going higher and things like that you know, it worries her. But I think she'll make a good instructor.'

After the choice of new stables, off-the-job training had to be considered. The new stable was a long way from County College, which, when added to the problems that had arisen in the previous year, resulted in Alison and her mother deciding to try somewhere else. This was supported by her new employer. ' I've always used South College. Alison spoke to County and seemed to think she could come here from them, but she actually wasn't very pleased with them. I suggested she try South because I thought they would be better because they seem to do quite a lot of theory and riding with them, whereas Alison said when she went to County very often she was the only one there. Going in on her own then she found they didn't really bother to teach her because she was the only one there.'

Alison herself wasn't concerned which college she attended, as she saw on-the-job training as more significant. 'I think really it doesn't make much difference because County haven't really given me that much training. I've only really been up for about six weeks. So it depends, if I'm getting more training where I am at work it won't really make much difference. I mean I'm not really bothered which college I go to. I think South will be a lot easier because I'll be nearer. The other YT girl that's there, she goes to South.' Having gained some information by 'phone and post, Alison said 'the good thing about South is when you go up there you're always the same group so you go through the same courses together.' Alison's mother did not want a repetition of the previous year's problems. She believed that South would put Alison in for the next BHS examination without charge.

Mother: 'South don't go along with NVQ, they are BHS examiners.'

Alison: 'Yes but the Training Credits is NVQ anyway, so I'll still be doing the NVQ.'

Mother: 'But their priority is to get you through your BHS stages. They pay for it.'

The only remaining problem was implementing the choice. This time, according to Alison's mother, the careers office was unhelpful. 'The only thing I was quite enlightened about was the fact that with the TEC you were allowed to take your Training Credits from one county to another. Whereas the liaison officer and the careers officers were adamant that you couldn't do that. If you're the type of person that won't dispute things I suppose you sit back and say, "oh this is what they've said". But I just felt that if Alison had Training Credits and they couldn't accommodate her to what she wanted to do in one county, then she had to find somewhere, and they were on offer in the other county as well. And if it was the same TEC for both counties, how could they say no? But I felt I was being conned and I felt the careers office should have that information available.'

Having sorted out that Alison could use her Training Credit for South College, the next problem was transferring it. County College had applied for credits for NVQ 3 for Alison as soon as she finished her NVQ 2, and they activated them straight away. The County training manager said that 'From her getting her level 2 verification, the level 3 discretionary Training Credit starts from the next day. So it has to be done because she's been at her work placement from the time she was verified until she actually left.'

The Training Credits system was designed to aid personal choices, yet it seems to have taken several months to complete the transfer and Alison did not get her travel and lodgings expenses until December, having moved in July. 'Apparently County had pocketed the discretionary credits for a second year. They knew in May I was leaving, and that was before my first year was even up. So I don't know how they managed to apply for a second year. But they didn't even know I wasn't still with them. I got a letter through about some new thing for your wages. And mum 'phoned up and said, "well she left there in July". It's all come through now anyway. I've got my money now.'

Three months in, the training at South College was not trouble free. Most of the problems related to the introduction of a new NVQ. But Alison was not unhappy. Her personal priority was the BHS stage 2 and 3 qualifications, rather than NVQ 3, and the training she was getting would help her towards them. However, her description of the training provided did not seem very different from her experiences with County College. 'South don't really do set weeks on things, you just come in and do a bit of everything really. Like this afternoon we're doing a practical, they usually do it on a set thing which you're working towards, say you would do bandaging. Or if you really needed practice on something else, say you were good at bandaging you could say, "oh, could I practise plaiting", something like that.'

The organisation at South College may have been, in reality, little better than County, but it didn't seem to be worrying Alison. 'The job itself's brilliant, really good. It's a totally different job really. I don't see a lot of people in the yard its actually with the horses I'm working all the time. We've got all sorts there. We've got two point-to-pointers, we've got two stallions, we've got lots that come for breaking and schooling and like we've got all the offspring from the stallion which the oldest of them are three now so they're breaking. Liveries, there's a bit of everything really there. My boss likes dressage so she encourages us to do it on some of the younger horses that she's got. I gained from what I did last year, but it's like different, on a higher standard now.'

Alison was undecided what to do after the current training was finished. 'If I want to, I'll be able to stay at the yard where I am for longer or, last time I was at South I thought "I would quite like to come here for a year full-time", but I think I'd probably find it boring. I'd quite like to go to another yard, I think. I do like working as a trainee at different yards. It was good when I moved because it was all new and there were lots of new horses to try. Eventually I'd like to go to America or somewhere to live. I don't really want to go back to my home county to find a job because there's not really much choice.'

COMMENTARY

In making choices, both Elaine and Alison utilised resources of various types. Both were determined and had a clear idea of what they wanted. Elaine demonstrated considerable self-confidence and was highly successful at work. This probably helped her employers to take her wishes seriously and, similarly, success and confidence allowed Alison the chance to get a place in a second stable when she wanted to move, despite resistance from other stakeholders.

Both utilised additional resources provided by their parents, as had Helen and Laura. Elaine's parents directed her towards a larger firm and found the work experience placement for her. Alison's mother's personal knowledge of the equestrian field proved invaluable, as did her determination to argue on her daughter's behalf, for example when originally told that the Training Credit could not be used for the new placement.

In Elaine's case, the willingness of her employers to allow her to choose was significant. Had they insisted on the ILEX course, it is unlikely Elaine would have refused or even argued. She chose because they encouraged her to do so. This may have partly because they were a larger organisation with a full-time training officer, who had been used to helping other trainees decide what they wanted to do.

As Sims and Stoney (1993) suggest about Training Credits in general, one of the main benefits of the new system may be that young people were more aware of their training entitlements. Elaine knew that she could use her Training Credit, and Alison knew that she could change both placement and training provider once she had completed her level 2. The possession of the Credit may have encouraged Elaine to consider several different types of training and encouraged her employers to recognise her right to choose. However, as we have already seen with Laura and Helen, such choices were far from universal. In Alison's case, the choices appear to have been made in the absence of a Training Credit. Alison and her mother both claim she was never issued with a Credit for her level 3. Instead, County College simply applied direct to the TEC for a new credit, even though Alison claims that she had already told them she wanted to leave. The choice was made because one period of training was completed and another one about to begin. It did not need a complex credit structure to enable this to happen, simply that the funding for the two courses be kept separate.

Alison faced some opposition on making her choice. Her employer and the college liaison officer tried to dissuade her, and the careers officer apparently advised her that she could not move outside her home county. It was not the possession of the Training Credit that enabled her to withstand these pressures, but her own determination and the support of her mother and the tutors in both colleges. Had any or all of these people also advised against the change, Alison would have found it harder to proceed.

Both Elaine's and Alison's stories are successes, if we concentrate on the broader details of choice, career progression, qualification achievement and success on the job. Yet when we look below the surface, both experienced partly unsatisfactory off-the-job training as, indeed, did

Helen and Laura. Elaine's choice of qualifications and training provider options did not result in a quality experience. It is difficult to see how, no matter how well informed, she could have predicted the rapid dislocation between responsibility, challenge and success at work, and boredom, triviality and repetition with the trainer. We can never know how things would have worked out had she made a different choice, but the greater demands of a BTEC course may have advanced her training further and faster, and might have encouraged her to continue to a higher level. Also, any off-the-job course may have seemed inferior to the buzz of doing a successful job.

Alison's choice seems to have been partly, though not mainly, a reaction to unsatisfactory elements in her first year of training. Yet there were early, if inconclusive, signs that the quality of training provided at the second college was little different from that which she found unsatisfactory at the first. These stories raise an important question for any voucher driven education or training scheme. How can we be sure that choices made by a purchaser, be it parent or young person, will increase the likelihood of a satisfactory learning experience? We continue the analysis of the issues around on- and off-the-job training in the next chapter, and return to questions of training quality in Chapter 8.

6

NVQs and On- and Off-the-Job Training: Clive and Becky

The difficulties experienced by Elaine and Alison are illustrative of a fundamental problem for most training schemes – the relationship between on- and off-the-job training. With Training Credits, the use of work-based NVQs was compulsory. However, at the time of our fieldwork the NVQ system had not been fully introduced, so for some occupational areas qualifications were used that were temporarily approved as NVQ equivalents. These older qualifications were often designed to be taught predominantly off-the-job, with a mixture of written and practical assessment. The NVQ approach revolutionised vocational qualifications and training in Britain, as briefly explained in Chapter 1. NVQs are described in terms of work-based competence. Assessment is a matter of proving, through evidence and observation, that the trainee can fulfil the performance criteria and thus demonstrate competence. The qualification is sub-divided into units and elements, which can be acquired in any order and learned in any manner. For NVQ-based training, on-the-job experience is vital. This the best way to learn many of the competence elements and work is the place where most of them have to be assessed.

Supposedly, NVQs have been drawn up by employers to meet employers' needs. However, Field (1995) argues that such employer influence is more rhetorical than real, and none of the predominantly small employers we spoke to showed any sense of ownership. Indeed, as with Helen's first employer, some knew nothing about NVQs at all. It was a combination of the Training Credits regulations and the NVQ focus on work-based practice which forced Helen to abandon her training, as a car body sprayer, when she lost her garage placement. In this chapter, we focus on the contrasting experiences of two other trainees, Clive and Becky.

Becky was training as a dental surgery assistant (DSA), and studying for an NVQ equivalent qualification. She was taught formally at the local hospital, on a course which was primarily theoretical and assessed by examination. She struggled with the level of academic work involved and by the end of our fieldwork the dentist providing this training feared that she might fail. Yet her work in the dental practice was fine. Becky might have done better on a competence-based NVQ course.

Clive was employed as a car sales trainee and appeared to spend most of his time valeting cars. His employer wanted him to get a business studies qualification as background to his job. He had to do a competence-based NVQ because there was one available. In the end he failed to achieve level 2, mainly because there was little opportunity to develop business and administration skills in the workplace. He might have been better served by a more traditional course, taught and assessed off-the-job. It is Clive's story we tell first.

CLIVE'S PROBLEMS WITH WORK-BASED COMPETENCE

Clive's job arose through work experience from school. 'It started when I did work experience. I went up there for a week, and they offered me a part-time job afterwards. On work experience week I was in the workshops and that – mending cars. And I started cleaning cars and doing bits and pieces. And now I'm gradually in the office more, doing filing and stuff like that. It's more sales than garage side, really. It's brilliant.'

The employer confirmed this. 'He initially came on a week's work experience and then, because he lives locally, he then wanted a part-time job, which we gave him, and he worked a full day on Saturdays, washing cars and things, and then he progressed on to working the petrol pumps, and he was a very very *very* exceptionally good lad. Very correct sense of responsibility etc. And it came up, what he was going to do when he left school, and having had a meeting with his parents, and because it was his wish, we agreed that he would start for me, working for me on the car sales side, and start at the bottom and work his way up.'

The car sales work was expanding fast, but the job was created for Clive because the employer liked him and knew the family. The employer said 'our business here is obviously very localised, it's very personalised. Consequently, the people who work for me are hand picked and we tend to take someone when someone suitable came along for what we want to do, rather than, if you like, being inundated with enquiries, or whatever. As Clive progressed along, he became obviously higher than the average ability and he seemed ideal to come and work with ourselves. I'm not interested in having someone employed here just to have a dead end job. He's a very very nice young man, exceptionally so. His whole family are. Which is another basis for when we employed him. Having met the whole family and done business with them, giving ourselves an insight into them, they are very very pleasant, and you can see just why he's the way he is.' Clive had employed status and his employer claimed his job was secure for the foreseeable future.

No one could remember exactly when the job was offered and accepted, but it was probably around January 1992. It happened before Clive had an interview with the careers officer to draw up his CGAP. Consequently,

Clive, his employer and his parents were operating outside the formal advice system, trying to get some training. The employer specified training in business studies, even though Clive was to be employed as a car sales trainee. He said 'the Training Credits side actually came in when I suggested that he should do some sort of formal qualification, and the one that sprang out, as far as I was concerned, was business studies, and with the aid of his Training Credit he was able to do that.'

Interviewer: 'He's working on the car sales side. You suggested business studies?'

Employer: 'Yes.'

Interviewer: 'Why did you think that was the best for you and for him?'

Employer: 'Not so much for me, but more for him, because I think it gives you an overall grounding and, more important, an overall insight into how business works. I just think for his future well being, if things didn't work out for ourselves, it would be a very good qualification for him to have.'

Interviewer: 'Were you involved in him choosing where to do the training?'

Employer: 'No. I left that entirely open. It was just more convenient to go the nearest town. The gentleman [training manager] who actually interviewed ourselves and him, I was very impressed with.'

Clive's father found the training for him, with a private training organisation. Clive said 'well, the employer just said I've got to find the training, and if I couldn't arrange anything, let him know, and he'd help. I rung the training centre up after dad had spoken to them, and asked them about it, and they said I'd have to get Training Credits. So then I saw the careers officer and she arranged to get them for me.'

Clive explained that the search for training had not been easy, a fact confirmed by his parents. Both he and they believed that the training organisation they had found was the only one which could offer day-release training of the type Clive needed. 'I tried all the colleges, and they wouldn't do a one day a week course, so dad rung up the training centre, and they said they'd do the same course as college for one day a week, but I had to use my Training Credits to do it.'

Early on, we were aware that the relationship between on- and off-the-job training might be problematic for Clive, because his actual job bore very little relation to the NVQ in Business and Administration that he was doing. In November 1992 we asked relevant stakeholders about this. Though specifying business studies, the employer knew nothing about NVQs. Our impression was that he saw training as a completely separate off-the-job process, giving broad background to the work Clive was doing. He wanted the trainers to get on with it and do it, and saw Clive's work in the garage as completely different.

The trainers were aware of a potential problem but felt that it was surmountable. Interestingly, the training tutor described Clive's job as clerical, not valeting cars. 'Clive's working in a garage. He's doing the clerical side in the garage. Clive's here mainly to do Business and Administration, but there are other aspects of the garage work that he's actually being offered the opportunity to sample, if you like. My main consideration is he actually gets his Business Administration qualification. If the employer wants to offer him experience of other areas, then if he's going to work in a garage I can see that could be very beneficial.'

'What I've found with Clive, he's very shy. I can see there's a lot of potential there, so I feel the first thing to do here is perhaps help to build his confidence, with groups, with me. Giving a little background knowledge underpinning skills, sort of gradually taking him through the NVQ. He's got three or four units he's working his way through, he's just completed a couple of them, then I think we'll probably sit down and talk about this. "Can you get experience at work doing this? If not, we need to look at you gaining experience here doing it, so I can actually assess you doing it." Or perhaps I could go in. Very probably what I will do is negotiate with the sponsor, you know, "is it possible for Clive to get experience doing XYZ here, with you?" It's much better in the work placement because it's a realistic situation. It is going to be difficult, yes. He hasn't been here long enough to sit down and work out a programme of how we're going to approach it. We're gradually working into at the moment "OK. Lets have a look at what you're doing. What you've done. Can you please remember when you do this to keep a daily log, or make a note, can you please collect some evidence to show that you are actually doing it." It does take a little while for the whole ethos of the NVQ, for them to actually understand what it's about.' Her use of the word 'sponsor' rather than 'employer' suggests she believed Clive was a trainee placed in the garage by her organisation, rather than an employee. This would also explain her assumption that his main work was clerical.

At this stage Clive hoped things would work out. 'Well, what I'm doing in the garage in't really what I'm doing at the training centre. But hopefully when I do bits and pieces and learn a lot, but I haven't really put it into practice yet.'

Interviewer: 'Do you think there's going to be any chance to put it into practice?'

Clive: 'Yeah. I hope so. Its quite important to get a decent qualification, because if I was to lose my job I'd need them to get another job. 'Cause if I was to come out unqualified 'cause I thought I had a job, and I lost my job, I'd have no qualifications, so no one would want me, really.'

In the summer of 1993 we only interviewed Clive and the training manager, having had repeated attempts to talk to the employer rebuffed. Our interviews took place soon after serious problems between the trainers, Clive and the employer had emerged. Clive said 'about a month ago the trainers said that I wasn't having enough experience at work and that they didn't think I should carry on with their course. They said that I should leave, basically. And I told my boss, and he rung them up and had words with them. And said that I'm not gonna leave. We're gonna stay there. And that they're gonna have to train me there. And he said that even if they don't train me, I'll still go in.'

Interviewer: 'Was this the problem that they're trying to train you for Business Studies and what you're doing is working with cars?'

Clive: 'Yeah. Because when I started the course I was told that I could do Business Studies at the training organisation and just go to work the rest of the time. But now they're saying that I've got to do things at work, and I've got to collect evidence or something, to say that I've been doing these things like faxing and photocopying and that. So it seems like all I've got to do at work is Business Studies, which is not what I'm there for.'

The training manager agreed about the basic problem. 'As time's gone by, they seem to be so busy, with cars coming in and out, Clive seems to be doing so much car valeting and the cleaning side, that he had very little input on the clerical side. We have had a meeting with the employer, and we always talk to Clive when he comes in about collecting evidence for the NVQ, and he says "yes yes yes" and the employer says "yes he does enough" or "he can do enough" to do the NVQ, but in the event, when we ask him to produce the evidence, it's very little. Now he's been in there nearly 12 months, and he's only managed to achieve two modules out of a possible nine. Two modules of NVQ 1.'

Clive confirmed that he sometimes lied to the trainers, to get out of a difficult situation. 'It was awkward, 'cause my boss was telling me one thing, and I went in to the training centre and they were telling me another. I had to lie a bit. I lied to the trainers, just to shut them up. They were getting on my nerves. They were really pressuring me.'

Both parties took different views of the causes of the problem. One aspect concerned Clive's status as an employee. Clive felt the training organisation misunderstood that, a view supported by our earlier interview with the training tutor. 'At the training centre, they seem to think that I got my job through them, which I didn't. I had my job way before, and they didn't seem to understand that. They keep sending someone round, saying I've got to fill in these forms to say I've been at work every day. They're saying I have to earn a basic wage of £29 or something, which I don't. I earn a lot more. And they were saying "right. When you go in to work tomorrow, you have a word with your boss and see if you can do this. And this." And I had a word with him, and he said "well, basically its nothing to do with them what you do here. They can't dictate how much you earn, they can't dictate what you do. You go to them separate. You know, you go there, get your qualification and leave", he said, "and what you do here is nothing to do with them." And they don't seem to work that way.'

By the time we spoke to the training manager he knew Clive was employed. 'As he's in employed status, it's difficult to you know actually say to the company "right. Let's have this done". We could do that if he was a trainee, but as he's an employee of the company, I mean they really have the last say. They can just take him out from the training at any time.'

The root of the problem appeared to be two conflicting views of training. For Clive and his employer, training was something you did off-the-job, separate from work. Whilst the training manager, constrained by NVQ requirements, felt most training had to be done in the workplace. 'The NVQ only works, or it works the best way, when you get a very supportive employer, where there's lots of clerical work being done by the trainee in placement and they realise that evidence has got to be collected. Because the idea of them coming in here really isn't to learn the NVQ, because they should do that in placement. They should just bring it all in to us, on the off-the-job training day, and then sit down with the tutor and put it all into the right format. So long as the tutor got it right in the first place, by going in to the employer and telling the employer exactly what they need to do and what the trainee needs to do, they should be able to work together and do it to fit that company and the pace of the company as well.'

He felt Clive was not being trained in car selling. 'When I spoke to the employer, he certainly led me to believe that Clive would be in the office quite a lot, doing the invoices and ultimately would be trained up to be a car salesman as well. Which I don't think he's done any of that at all, from what I can make out. He may train him up at some stage, but I don't think its going to be in the foreseeable future. I think they're quite happy to have him as a car valeter and odd job man. If it was a training placement and we'd found it we'd have taken him out of there.'

Clive felt the pressure from the trainers was unreasonable. He was happy to time serve until he was mature enough to sell cars. 'They said I should be in the office more and not car cleaning, which I was then. But I said to them "it is a garage and not an office". Even the car salesmen clean cars. Everybody does everything, really.'

Interviewer: 'Did you say you were working more in the office now anyway?'

Clive: 'I am now.'

Interviewer: 'Is that because of pressure from the training organisation, or would that have happened anyway?'

Clive: 'I think it would have happened eventually, but not as soon. There's only a certain amount I can do at my age. I can't go out and say to the customer "oh you've got to buy this car" 'cause they ain't gonna listen to me. 'Cause they've gotta trust you. They don't trust a little kid, like.'

If Clive did not complete his NVQ level 2, the trainers would forgo 30% of the funding. The manager thought this was likely. 'I don't envisage him completing, so we would lose 30% of the Credit. I think we are just going to have to accept that. We can keep on at him, as we will do, the tutor will go out and monitor again and tell the employer the sort of evidence we need. We are happy that it's quite clear in their minds what they should be doing. But it's a private business and clerical isn't their main concern.'

From this difficult position, things did not improve. When we returned for the final interviews, in December 1993, a further crisis had been reached and the training organisation had decided to draw things to a close. The manager said 'there hasn't been a great deal of progress. The tutor's been out there twice to see the employer and everybody's saying the right things, but the action's just not happening. If we can see that he's actually doing that type of work, OK, whether it takes us a bit of time to get the evidence together, we can see the long-term goal at the end. But what it appears that is happening there, that he isn't getting the evidence, he's not interested in collecting evidence, he doesn't get the opportunity to collect the evidence, and I don't think he's ever going to get it. But I think we've made a decision now, I sat down with the tutor, and I said "right, we won't aim for NVQ 2, we'll aim for NVQ 1", because we can actually do NVQ 1 within the training centre, all simulated, so he can actually get it. After all this time's gone by, I'm not happy just to say "OK, we'll scrub round it", because it feels as if the whole thing's been a complete waste of time. I think he needs to get at least an NVQ 1 out of it. And to that end I've asked the tutor to focus on it. By Christmas, ideally.'

For the training manager, the NVQ 1 was a solution to keep everyone happy and make the best out of a bad job. Clive did not see it like that. 'The manager comes out originally and tells us how brilliant it is, and that, until he starts on to me about how I won't get my qualification and that, so I said "well, you told me to do this course" you know "you knew what I was doing at work, and you told me this was the right course for me", I said, "and it isn't". 'Cause it isn't. 'Cause they say you've got to do filing and faxing and this and that. They teach you how to do it, and the idea is, I suppose, you go back to work and they let you do it. But because I'm not in a placement, you can't expect him to pay me £80 quid a week and just expect me to do the things that the trainers want me to do. I've got to be working for him.

'I was originally going for level 2 and then go on to level 3 and everything. And now I'm just going to end up with level 1. That's it. And hopefully I'll be finished next week. I'll be glad to get out. Bit of a rip-off, really. That's how I feel, anyway. Level 1 is very basic. I was concentrating on level 2, you see. In the end I realised I wouldn't get it, so now I've got to do level 1, and its taking me three, four weeks to do it.'

At this stage, everyone agreed that things had gone wrong. However, the trainers felt the employer and Clive were primarily responsible, whilst Clive blamed the trainers. Both sides claimed to have been misled, but that they had explained their position clearly from the start. The training manager said 'my first suggestion to the employer was that he did car mechanics, or even bodywork, because I could see him possibly doing more of that, and being more interested in that, than clerical. The employer was a bit undecided, really. We were called in originally because he had an employee who had these Training Credits. It was because this little book, which looks like a cheque book, appeared on the scene, so everybody thought "We've got to use these, whether we need them or not". So that's when we went out there to talk about options of training, which was mechanics, bodywork, or clerical. Now he said that he would never be doing mechanics or bodywork, but he said he would be getting involved in car sales, ultimately. And obviously there would be a certain amount of finances and paper-work to organise on that aspect, so it would be quite useful for him to learn that aspect of the company, along with typing and word-processing, which was mentioned at the time as well.'

This recollection of events does not entirely match what had we discovered earlier. Clive, his parents and employer all agreed the training had been decided before any of them knew Training Credits existed, and that Business had been decided upon before the training organisation had been contacted. In his final interview, Clive reiterated this. 'If I was in an office then it would be all right. I'd get my level 2 and everything. But I don't really think that its our fault, because we rung the manager up, just as an enquiry, and he came out and said, you know, "you can do this this and this".'

Interviewer: 'So you think he's sold the course to you and to your boss, when it wasn't really the right course for you?'

Clive: 'Yeah. 'Cause he knew. We was telling him what we were doing there, and he was saying "Oh we can do this and that". And my boss said "well don't get me wrong, he won't be coming in and selling cars, he have to be trained up, and it's going to take 2, 3 years, plus no one's going to buy a car off a 17 year old, 'cause they won't trust him". So, you know, the manager said it was ideal, and it wasn't. Once I was there, I couldn't get out.'

Interviewer: 'Did they explain at the start that you were going to have to do a lot of this office work on-the-job?'

Clive: 'No. They said that the idea was that I go to college one day a week, and they'd say I could do typing at the centre and all this and that at the centre, and obviously I'd have to go back to work and do some things, but the idea of the course is you do everything at work. You go to the training centre, they tell you how to do it, and then you go back to work and practice it. And I can't. We didn't have a Fax machine, we haven't got a photo-copier, how can I do all that stuff? I'm only at the centre one day a week, it's not enough time for me to do it there.'

Communications between the trainer, employer and Clive had broken down. The training tutor referred to the row between them and the employer, which Clive had described earlier. 'I did say once I wondered why he was on the course, and perhaps it might have been better if he'd gone on another course, and we had a rather irate boss ringing up, because he wasn't there when I went out to see them on a monitor visit – he's very conveniently out when I go. And I sort of went and apologised, and I said "well I'm sorry you know, but Clive's here to do the NVQ, and he needs to be doing certain things", you know, which I had already talked to him about, "he needs to be collecting what we call evidence to prove that he's actually done it." So he said "well, all he needs to do is let me know what he needs and I'll make sure that he gets it". So I went home, and I prepared a list of all the evidence that he needed to collect, and next time I went back I took this with me, explained it yet again, "and here is a list for you to use, with all the items that you should be doing, and what ones is he doing with you?" I said, "fine, he needs to collect evidence to that, to actually say that this is what he is doing". But it's not been very forthcoming. He wants Clive to get a qualification while he's working there. Well fine, but I don't know how much support he's actually getting from the man.'

From the training manager's perspective, the fact that Clive was employed by the garage had exacerbated the problem. 'The job is stopping him from being a trainee. The forces on the business make it not viable for Clive to do clerical-type work. If they've got a high turn-over of cars, as they appear to have, he's more involved in the valeting of the cars, which I think he enjoys doing more anyway, so he's not going to say to the employer "I don't want to be doing this valeting, I want to be doing paper-work". The employer's quite happy with what he's doing, and he thinks "well he's employed by the company, I can do what I like with him".'

The trainers and Clive's parents felt that Clive had contributed to the problem, because he was happier not doing the clerical work. His mother said, 'I think what he finds difficult about the scheme that he's on, is the fact that if he has to have a day off, because his boss needs him up the garage, because they're short staffed or whatever. Clive's opinion is that his job comes first. He was employed before he started all this and his job is the most important thing. So if his boss asks him not to go in on a particular day, and he goes up the garage instead, he gets the feeling that they're a bit miffed, down at the training centre, and he can't understand that. He says that "my job is more important".'

Clive could not cope with being squeezed between conflicting demands. We have already heard that he lied to the trainers to avoid pressure from them. He was also worried about pressure from his boss. The disappointment at not getting the NVQ level 2 was enough to cope with, without admitting to his boss that this had happened. 'What I was hoping to do was like go there, go to the centre one day a week, maybe perhaps for 2, 3 years, no matter how long it took, and then at the end of the 3 years I'd know most things about car sales. And then at the end of the three years, I could go and start selling cars. But it hasn't worked like that. Well, I told my boss that I'd be finished in a week, and he said "is that all of the qualification?" and I just said "yes", [laughs uneasily] 'cause, you know, [pause] I'm just going to tell him that I've got it. 'Cause, you know, [pause] I don't like the training at all, and I just want to get out now. Get my level 1 and get out.'

If the training had failed for Clive, at least he had a job. His father felt this was important. 'I think, in this day and age, to have a child employed you've got to be happy. I just wish the Government would spend more money on the employment. Creating jobs, instead of shutting them down.' But the training manager was uncertain that Clive would succeed in becoming a sales representative. 'I think the company has probably realised that Clive isn't a car sales person anyway, and that his forte is in actually valeting cars. He's good at doing that, he enjoys doing that. I think that's what they get him to do most of the time. I don't think he should be a car sales person anymore. He's not a good front person. He hates going on the 'phone. To my mind, a car sales person's got to be quite confident and outgoing. Able to put their product clearly over in a influential manner, to try to get somebody to buy the product.'

Clive's mother had reservations about car sales as a career. 'He was very fortunate that he knew he had a job when he left school. We did think we'd like him to have something behind him, because car sales is a very dodgy business anyway, and they're not exactly well respected, car salesmen, but it's what he wanted to do. I wish he'd have put something else under his belt. He's going to be sorry, when he's in his twenties, that he didn't do more. He's got a very narrow field now. He's stuck in this particular line of work. He can never improve himself anywhere else now. I'm sorry for that, I wish he'd done other things, so that he could have broadened his career prospects. But then, that's his decision.'

Clive himself had no worries about his chosen profession. However, in our final interview, he revealed that his secure job might not be as secure as he had hoped. 'The garage is up for sale now, I believe, but I'm not supposed to know this. He's on about starting again, but if say I was to lose my job or whatever, I perhaps wouldn't get another job with another garage because of the qualifications I get, but because I know them. 'Cause I know a lot of people from other garages and I could say, "well I did work for Kevin, for whatever time and you do know me". I dunno what will happen to me if he does sell. I'd probably go with him, 'cause I think he wants to start from scratch again, 'cause the fun of it is building the business. He did own a showroom and he employed loads of people in there. He had to close that down, because it wasn't doing very well, but he said "I'm going to have to make you redundant, but I've got you other jobs with other garages". So he didn't just say "sorry, goodbye". He isn't just going to let me, you know [pause] I wouldn't have thought.'

BECKY'S PROBLEMS WITH TRADITIONAL QUALIFICATIONS

Becky originally wanted to be a nursery nurse and had been offered a college place on a full-time course. When we interviewed her, in September 1992, she was working as a trainee dental surgery assistant. Becky claimed that she had changed her mind because she could not afford to take a full-time college course. 'I dunno when I decided not to do nursery nursing. When I realised, I suppose, that I had to go to college for 2 years, because of like two years without any money. I can't do it.'

Her mother suggested the change was partly because Becky did not do well in her GCSE examinations, where she only got grade C in two subjects. 'She wanted to do this NNEB [Nursery Nursing Education Board] course and then this extra training thing came up, for the dentist, so she thought she'd do that instead because it was an opportunity where she could earn herself a bit of money, rather than spend the next 2 years at college. When her results came back that weren't very good, so she couldn't do an NNEB, I said to her "if you want to go back to school and redo them, you go back to school". We're not saying "right. You've got to go out and get a job and bring some money in".'

The choice of dental surgery assistant was made together with a placement officer in a Licensed Provider organisation. He said 'when Becky came to see me she didn't really know what she wanted to. So like all trainees when they come in they don't really know they want to do, they come in and we look at them and say "well this is what I've got to offer."' He approached a local dentist and asked him if he would take Becky. The dentist confirmed this. 'The Licensed Provider persuaded me to take her on and I was slightly misled or maybe I wasn't listening or something, but that's neither here nor there. The reason you see, I had Sarah. She did vocational training or YTS or whatever you want to call it, and when my other nurse left to have a baby, I took her on, and with the Licensed Provider coming along, saying "well yes, this young lady would do blah blah blah" so I said "well yeah." It's always handy to have somebody else. At least they're going to work to your way of thinking. Becky is surplus to requirements, yeah.' Despite this, Becky was confident she might get a permanent job, if everything went well. However, she was not committed to a career as a dental assistant. 'It's just for the time being, until I find something I want, I suppose. But if I do like this then I'll carry on with it.'

The Licensed Provider acted as Becky's Approved Trainer and took responsibility for the administration of the Training Credit, through a training officer. The training was sub-contracted to a dentist who regularly trained surgery assistants. He said 'I run the course. They pay me I think it's 60% of the fee they would be getting and they have a 40% administration fee, which I accept because they have to keep tabs on it and they help me with the paper-work.'

Becky was studying for the DSA certificate, as there was no NVQ available. This required 2 years successful chairside experience and passing a written examination.To make the qualification more like an NVQ, the Approved Trainer had a list of competences to be covered at work. They kept a check on this, but the actual DSA award was based purely on examination results, following a fairly academic course. The training dentist explained what happened. 'We have regular essay work; feedback from the dentist if they're dissatisfied in a massive way – which is extremely rare, but that's very difficult to assess because personalities are often more the difficulty. And the exams are the main test. There is a practical assessment within their exam on basic techniques. But the written paper is more than 50%, so the theory side is very important. But it all ties in 'cos once they understand the theoretical most of them are pretty competent, well more than competent in their practical skills.' The training was provided on one evening a week at the local hospital.

The majority of dental surgery assistants on the course were not using Training Credits, but had been sent, as older trainees, by their employers. Training Credits had not been designed for use with this more traditional type of qualification and there were some problems, which the training dentist described. 'I misunderstood initially. I thought that our younger ones starting at 16 could have a soft option and be introduced slowly into the scheme and then in the second year go for the actual course itself, but unfortunately you only get the same amount of money for 1 year as for 2, so there was no encouragement to do that. So we decided that although the girls were too young to do it we'd put them through and hopefully they'd get good notes and be able to use them if they have to take the exam later on. It started in October and the actual course finishes it's main study at the end of July. But the complication is you're aiming for a November exam. So there's quite a break before the November exam. We fit in a revision session just before. That's so they can make sense of what they've learned, then come back to it in November and hopefully do well.'

He felt that trainees needed time to mature and gain experience in order to do well. However, from the perspective of the Approved Trainer, training had to be completed within 18 months in order to fit with the funding regime. The training officer explained that 'we've got a basic of £1250 credit for an DSA diploma. The funding really only lasts us 12 months. But we don't push for that, we want to see 18 months, because of the ruling that they've got an entitlement to training till they're aged 18 anyway. And if they achieve it within 12 months what are we going to do for them anyway unless we go on to a higher level, which is not very practical in that area. There is only so much money. You cannot afford to have a trainee in college for 3 years to do a course that should only take 18 months. So this is where the failure to achieve rates is going to be accelerated. You're going to be starting to say to young people "sorry you're not achieving. The funding's no longer available for you we're going to have to withdraw it". We haven't actually had to do that yet but we are sailing fairly close to it.'

The training dentist felt that some of the work on the DSA course was of 'A' level standard, which would make it the equivalent of an NVQ level 3, not the level 2 which most trainees began on. In the past there had been a considerable drop-out rate. 'Initially its quite an adventure, it's different, they meet up with lots of other DSAs and it's quite exciting. But when they realise what's involved in the actual study, 'cause it's not an easy course, where they're meant to be doing quite a bit of work outside of the course. By about a third into the course we get a reasonable drop-out rate – that is because they're realising by that stage that it's taking commitment as well as enjoyment.'

He explained that 'the old style dental nurse always used to reach a level of competence by working with her dentist and they were competent within their own surgery. My argument is that if anyone has to leave for any reason it is nice to feel they have got a background knowledge sufficient that they can cope in any other dental surgery. So they're competently trained in a general sense practically but also they've got theoretical knowledge to know what they're actually doing.' Becky's employer also saw both on– and off-the-job training as necessary. 'There's a minimum requirement, before you take the exam, technically speaking you should have a minimum of 2 years experience. That's what it used to be. The off-the-job training is more an academic thing. The practical side of things is done here, and she learns the theory on the course.'

In November 1993, everyone was happy with Becky's progress at work. The dental practice manager felt she had done even better than expected. 'She's come on very well. I mean young people don't always want to do exams, I think she failed her exams, I'm not sure. But actually she's coming on very well. She's very good with the patients on a one-to-one basis. And when people come into a dental surgery they're not always at their best, so yes, she copes with them very well. She's done better that I expected actually, from when I first met her.' Becky was happy at work. 'I get on really well at work. I'd like to stay, yeah.' By this time, her training officer had changed several times. The current officer had only met Becky and her boss once. She said 'I would say she's progressed as expected. Looking at the records and looking at the training plan, yes, from what I can see.'

However, as the practice manager had hinted, Becky was doing less well on the examination course. Though originally expected to take the examination that November, she was now not to be entered until the following May. Becky said 'we haven't done the exam yet. Hopefully I'll do well. I don't know. I'm doing it in May. Yeah, well there's quite a lot of us that's starting the course again, well not again, but we're carrying on to do more study about it.' Her mother was aware of the delay and believed it was to avoid having to pay for a second attempt. 'She had the option to take the exam in November, but I think she was advised not to, because obviously if she failed, we'd have to pay for the next one. So she's going to leave it until she felt confident she would pass.'

The training officer was aware of the postponement but did not see this as a problem. 'I've been told by my colleague, who I've actually taken over from, that the DSA Certificate cannot be awarded until 2 years chairside practice has been successfully completed. She's actually with us until we've given her 2 years from when she started in '92, and her anticipated achievement date for the NVQ will be September 1994. We can easily ask to extend that for perhaps 3 months, if there was a problem at all.'

Becky admitted the examination would be difficult, but never suggested to us that she feared failure. The Approved Trainer, her parents and employer seemed to believe it was only a matter of time before she passed. However, the training dentist, who was organising the preparation for the examination, was much more pessimistic. 'Becky has finished the year. She has not done well. Becky is a sweet kid, but I don't know what's the problem. She got a good dentist she works with. I don't understand. She really did badly. I mean I don't mark people down or anything like that. We mark them all the same, and her marks are generally under 20%! The majority of the girls were 40% plus, and Becky has really struggled. Some of her answers were incredible. For instance, "what is orthodontic treatment?" "Orthodontic treatment is when you root canal treat a tooth!" All the nurses should have known before they went on, orthodontics is straightening kiddies teeth. I have stressed from the beginning that Becky's been a problem. She needed a lot of help. I'm just stunned whenever I look through her papers. What I have said to her is that she would not be able to take it this November. So I said to her 6 more months, to go home and take it in a bit, I'll give her a separate test, which I don't normally do, nearer the time, and if she does well enough, we'll enter her. She's way below what I would have expected. Even with her first result, which was terrible, I really thought, after I spoke to her then, that that would have jolted her into it.'

The difference in perception between those involved was partly due to poor communication between the training dentist and the Approved Trainer. The training dentist was concerned that money had not been paid. "The Approved Trainer stopped paying for the training. We chased and chased and chased and basically, no reply, no help at all. So we just feel totally frustrated. I've sent three letters now, and we've received nothing. The last one was sent 5 weeks ago, and I haven't even had the decency of a response.' The new training officer was surprised at the lack of contact between her predecessors and the training dentist. 'Looking through the training record again it doesn't look like training dentist has been contacted at all, from us, from what I can see. So I think perhaps, closer contact with the actual tutor or tutors should have happened, but there hasn't been that working relationship. That's one thing that we are trying to overcome. Now, if need be, our reviews are done with the tutor and not with the employer.'

Like the training dentist, we found it hard to understand why Becky was doing so badly. She had two GCSEs at grade C, and understood enough to work competently in the surgery. She told us exactly what orthodontics was, without hesitation or confusion. Whatever the reason, there were doubts about her ability to complete the DSA.

Training Dentist: 'She won't make it in the spring unless she changes completely. She hasn't shown me any change, at the moment.'

Interviewer: 'Will she actually go into any of the lessons in the hospital again?'

Training Dentist: 'Well, at the moment we're not running this year's course because we've had a low number of applicants.'

The new training officer was going to see him soon after our interview, so then the problem would become clear to all, and some remedial action might hopefully be taken on Becky's behalf.

Though very happy at the surgery, Becky was still unsure if she wanted a career in dentistry. When asked how she saw herself in 9 months time, she said 'I don't know. Probably doing something completely different, but then, you never know. I don't know what I'll do.' Interestingly, the decision to give her a job with the practice where she was placed might not depend on examination success. When asked what he thought Becky would be doing in 9 months time, the training dentist said 'I think she'll probably still be nursing with her employer. But I don't think she'll have broadened her horizon with the course, which is a shame.'

Interviewer: 'She can stay anyway? She can do the job without the course?'

Training Dentist: 'Yes. Well, it's going to be more difficult. Ancillary staff for dentists are now getting to the point that they need a qualification, because our job is becoming more legally bound.'

The practice manager had indicated that Becky's future with the practice was dependent on financial circumstances, though she was unaware of the magnitude of the examination problem. 'Oh we would keep her on if we could, yes. But we don't know. It's hard to say.'

Becky's outward reaction to this uncertainty was that she wouldn't mind changing occupations and something else would turn up. Her mother was more concerned and felt that the practice owed her daughter a little more certainty. 'She's quite interested in it. She likes the job. I just hope that come spring they're going to offer her something. Because then she's back to where she started again, otherwise. If he's not going to take her on, she ought to know now, so she can actually look for something else. It's no good coming in spring time, and then he says "thank you very much and goodbye". I mean, you can't blame him for not taking her on if he can get somebody else for another two years and not have to pay a wage. He actually has been very good to her. Becky says she probably wouldn't be offered a job, unless one of the others leaves in the mean time.'

COMMENTARY

A comparison between the experiences of Becky and Clive does not allow any simplistic judgements about whether the NVQ approach is superior to what went before or a retrograde step. However, a few points can be made, which we will return to in Chapter 8. These stories support the view that no single, rigid system of training will suit all circumstances. Had Clive been offered an entirely off-the-job course in Business Studies, he would have had a better chance of success, although it has to be said that in school his track record on that type of course had not been good. Becky, on the other hand, would almost certainly have done better with an entirely competence-based course, which gave accreditation for what she was doing in the surgery, and where questions such as 'what is orthodontics?' were asked outside the artificial context of a formal examination or written essay.

In both cases, a cause of the problem was a breakdown in communication because different stakeholders had very different perceptions of what the training was about. No system can ensure that such breakdowns will not occur. However, the current obsession with using a combination of outcome-related funding and market forces to ensure quality fails to address such important issues. Ironically, the CGAP and subsequent training plans were supposed to ensure everyone in the Training Credit process shared a common understanding, at least of the goals for the training. This did not happen in either case.

These cases further illustrate the relative powerlessness of the young people in relation to other stakeholders, be they employers or training providers. The possession of a Training Credit was no help to Clive as he struggled to balance the conflicting demands placed upon him, and he found it impossible to square up his immediate desire to get on with the job he loved with a longer term ambition to get the qualification. His situation was made worse because he did not understand how the NVQ and Training Credits system worked and, right to the end, seemed certain that the problem was simply that the trainers were not doing what he felt they had promised to do. Like Elaine, both Clive and Becky coped with training difficulties by withdrawing into enjoyable work and hoping the training problems would go away. They lacked the self-confidence of Elaine, which we see as a prerequisite for the use of the Training Credits in the way which was intended. As most of the young people using Credits have in effect dropped out from school, such lack of confidence if things start to go wrong is likely. To succeed, youth training needs to provide support and encouragement to surmount problems and gain in self-esteem. Ironically, these were a more central focus of the old YTS scheme which Training Credits have replaced (Skilbeck *et al.*, 1994).

For all the young people whose stories we have told thus far, training had been problematic in some way. However, for others things were much more straightforward and, by the time our fieldwork ended, progress had been relatively smooth. We turn to these success stories next.

7

General Satisfaction and Untroubled Progress: David, Peter, Sam and Frances

Thus far we have told stories of especial interest. Laura and Helen had changed career paths during the time of the study, Elaine and Alison had used the Training Credit to exercise choice over training provision, whilst Clive and Becky had contrasting problems over training. In this chapter we focus on the remaining four young people, whose experiences were less dramatic. David, Peter, Sam and Frances share two common features. All experienced a relatively unproblematic career progression during the period of our investigation and all were broadly happy with the training and work experiences they received. To avoid repetition, we have reverted to a more conventional approach, describing patterns found within the four stories, illustrated by selected quotations. We concentrate on four issues: career intentions and finding a placement, the role of NVQs in training, career progression within and beyond training, and the significance of gender in career choice. We begin with brief pen-portraits of the young people.

David had wanted to work on a farm for as long as he remembered. His father had been a farm worker and was now an equipment driver, and his family had always kept a few animals. He got a training placement on a farm where he had previously done work experience and a part-time job, with off-the-job training provided by the local agricultural college. After 12 months of enjoyable and successful training, he was awarded his NVQ level 2. He then left the Training Credits scheme to take up a full-time place studying at the college for a National Certificate. When our fieldwork ended, he was still on track for his chosen career of farm manager.

Peter decided he wanted to work as a car mechanic after helping a friend to do up an old vehicle. He did work experience in one garage but eventually found a training place in another. He was following a 2-year programme towards a traditional City and Guilds qualification, approved as the equivalent of NVQ level 2, with off-the-job training provided by a private training organisation specialising in motor vehicle work. By our final interview, he was on course to achieve this qualification at the end of his second year and his training was likely to continue for a third year, towards an NVQ level 3 equivalent. Although Peter was a non-employed trainee, his employer expressed the intention to offer him a job once the training had been completed, though Peter was less confident of this. In effect, they were treating the Training Credits system as the first stage in an unofficial apprenticeship.

Sam had completed a year in the sixth form before getting his Training Credits. He had originally hoped to work in computing, but instead took a training place with a local engineering company where his stepfather also worked. Like Peter, he was following a traditional qualification which was an NVQ equivalent. His off-the-job training was organised by a former YTS managing agent, but sub-contracted to a local college of FE. He was on target to achieve this qualification after 2 years, when his employer would consider whether to support him to the equivalent of NVQ level 3. Like Peter, he was a non-employed trainee on an unofficial apprenticeship, and his employers intended to offer him a job once training was completed.

Frances had always wanted to work in retailing and took up a training place in a small corner shop. This did not work out, because of friction between her and her employers, and she was given a new placement in a shop selling kitchen-ware. Here she had employed status, even though the employer knew he would be unable to keep her on once the training year was up. She achieved her NVQ 2 in retailing in 1 year. Unusually for retailing, she received one day per week off-the-job training for 4 months, provided by a private training organisation. Once her NVQ 2 was completed her placement ended. Frances got a part-time job with a national retailing chain, supplemented by casual work for her former employer.

CAREER INTENTIONS AND FINDING A PLACEMENT

For all four, careers guidance had little influence in determining career intentions. However, David did value the CGAP process:

> 'They [CGAP stages] were pretty good, because they had all your thoughts down on paper and you could see what you wanted to do. The way they [careers officer] wrote it was just easy for you, to see what you wanted to do, and it helped a fair bit, actually. ... When I started seeing her [Careers Officer] I knew ... I had to go for it, like.'

For David and Frances career intentions were long standing, and neither they nor their parents could identify a point where a decision had been made.

> Interviewer: What made you want to work on a farm?
> David: Well, I don't know, really. I couldn't stand sitting behind a desk, I suppose. Got fed up with school. ... Well, dad works on this big 1,000 acre farm, ... I worked out there since I was eleven. Worked out there till I was about 14, I suppose, then went on with [the

farmer where he got a placement]. ... Its a lot better than "pen pushing", as they put it.
Don't think I could stand an indoor job now.

David's parents had tried to dissuade him from a career in farming. His
mother said:

I thought maybe that he'd have taken an office job. ... But at the end of the day, it's like
David says, if he's stuck in an office and he's not happy, there is no point in it at all. He's
an outdoor person and he's dedicated to the job. So I'd say, if you've got that much
dedication, I think he is in the right job.

Frances's parents would also have favoured a clerical career because of
her sister's successful clerical experiences and worries about the retail job
market. However, Frances herself never considered this, being firmly
committed to shop work.

Peter's interest in being a motor mechanic was more recent, but still well
established by the time the CGAP process commenced and, like the
others, was reinforced by work experience. For Sam, engineering was a
second choice:

I'm always interested in computers but the actual engineering was second choice and it
came along first so I took up that ... There'll always be stuff in computers but that can wait
for the moment.

Six months into his placement he was still talking about eventually
working with computers, though he did nothing to bring this about.
Towards the end of our study he had become used to the idea of a career in
engineering and was happy with it. He hoped to move towards the
computer controlled aspects of engineering, and was considering doing
an evening course to enhance his chances of doing this.

For all of our sample there were two main routes into training. Some,
like Helen (the first time), Clive, Elaine, David and Sam found placements
or jobs for themselves. For Sam, this happened because his stepfather
worked in the same firm. He helped get Sam the placement and
persuaded him that computing was something to learn in his spare time:

If I wasn't there, I wouldn't have made so much effort to get him into the company. I
thought he could learn a lot from it, if he learns engineering. He wants to do computers,
[but] he can do that in the evenings.

Sam's employer told us,

His stepfather is a foreman here. He [Sam] came to us on a work experience from the
school ... this was followed by working here during the holidays. He then wanted a job of
some description, I contacted [named Approved Trainer], they took up the situation from
there on, and that's why he got here.

Sam's mother saw this close family involvement as beneficial, because
they could ensure he was getting proper treatment.

We are in an unusual, fortunate position in that [husband] can almost supervise his training. Although they are in different workshops, he knows what the lad is being taught, he knows who is teaching him and he knows what standards that he is going to achieve. ... He's [husband] satisfied with the technical training and I'm satisfied that the boy is enjoying it there. I know that engineering at the company has got a future.

Sam's parents were involved in finding his off-the-job training. The employer worked through a private training provider, who should have booked Sam onto a course at the local FE college, sub-contracting the actual training. Sam's mother reported problems in getting this done.

We booked up his college course in the end because they [Approved Trainer] kept saying, "No, we're not booking him". ... Then they frightened him off. They said, "Oh we might have to send you as far as [named town]". He said, "I'm not damn well going to [other named town]"... They were very negative ... I 'phoned the college ... Then we went to the engineering site [at college] and we booked him up. The man at [the Approved Trainer's] was still saying, "We don't even know if there is going to be a course" ... But it was me ringing the college for those weeks saying, "Now look, term has started, my boy is supposed to be on day release, we have had no forms or anything". I 'phoned the man from [the Approved Trainer]: "I don't know". So I said, "The college told me they've already started".

As in several other cases, the knowledge and persistence of Sam's parents were essential in getting his training sorted out.

David's experience on the farm was important in getting a placement. In his and Sam's cases, the places were specially created for them and would probably not have existed had it not been that the young people were known. As David's employer said,

I think if it was just a matter of taking on a trainee, we wouldn't have bothered. ... Because I knew him, and I knew what sort of boy he was, you know I was quite pleased [to take him].

In such circumstances there seemed to be three factors at work. The employer valued a good worker who was already known and therefore a low risk appointment. In addition, employers valued family contacts. Finally, they did express a sense of altruism or even duty to help young people along, even if this was primarily focused on friends or the children of friends.

Others, such as Alison, Becky, Laura, Frances and Peter approached a training provider for help in finding a placement. Their experiences were mixed. Like Laura, Frances was unhappy with her first placement. She felt that she was not being fairly treated.

There were two bosses, a man and a lady who were married, and their daughter came in. I would get told to do, like, stacking the apples that way, and then when I would do it in front of another person they would say, "no, no don't do it like that, do it this way." And then when I would do it this way in front of the other person they'd say, "no I told you to do it this way." And you just sort of stand there and think "well which way am I meant to do it? Who is the boss here?"

At the same time that she decided to abandon the placement in the corner shop a different training provider, whom Frances had approached some time before, rang offering her a work placement and she took this up. The original trainer admitted that there had been serious communication problems and personality clashes with the first employer.

> We have had problems with that shop anyway. There is a problem with the lady who works there, who seems to be a little bit, what's the word, temperamental. ... She's not consistent at all.

Frances's parents felt that the two placements were very different:

> Where she was before they never gave her a break in the morning and they made her work from half past eight until six, that's a long day. ... They expect them to work for nothing, and do what they want. ... I'm just thankful now that she's found a place that she actually likes. They are not taking her for granted.

Like Laura, Frances seemed ill-equipped to deal with a difficult relationship. However she got on well in her second placement, and described coping there with a colleague whom she did not like. 'I've got a horrible person I work with ... But I've stuck her for a year ... you just don't take any notice after a while.' Unlike Laura, who appeared incapable of stepping outside a cycle of confrontation and disillusion, Frances seems to have learned from her early experience, which may not have been totally wasted.

Frances's Training Credit allowed her to change work placement without any penalty. As the training intentions and employment area had not changed, a new Credit was not issued. However, the second trainer received a reduced amount of money, as part had already been used by the first trainer.

Apart from Elaine and Clive, Frances was the only one of our sample with employed status. However, her employer only gave her that status because he was persuaded to do so by the training provider, who at that time was only allowed to place young people with employed status, and because it earned the employer an extra payment from the TEC. He never had any intention to continue her employment after the training was completed.

> Employer: She's employed status. ...
> Interviewer: As far as you're concerned, what's the difference between employed status and non-employed status?
> Employer: If she's employed status I get £100 from thingy [TEC] other than that there's really no [difference], it doesn't affect me at all.
> Interviewer: Do you think there's a difference from her point of view?
> Employer: 'I wouldn't have thought so. ... I mean, basically she comes here and she works and learns, and and she goes to college and she learns, and as far as I can see it's exactly the same whether she's on employed status or not. ...
> Interviewer: Is there a chance of you keeping Frances on after the year?
> Employer: No. Can't afford it.

Frances and her trainer both felt that her employer gave her a good training, and he claimed he had no intention to exploit her. He told us he would have kept her on if he could afford it, and that he felt the training was good value both for Frances and for him.

> She's what, about the fourth [trainee] that we've had, and apart from the one that I got rid of after 2 days they've all been good. They've all got jobs straight away, so from that point of view I think that the system works. Obviously it's a help to us in that we're getting another pair of hands that we couldn't otherwise afford. At the same time, were sending somebody out with 12 months experience, which makes them valuable to other people.

Frances's father disagreed. He felt that his daughter had been exploited and should have been given a job once the training was finished.

> I don't like the situation where when she finished her training, that was it. ... It annoys me now to think he's got another one in there. You know he can carry on doing that for ever. ... These people now realise they can get somebody for a year or 2 years for peanuts really .... All right maybe after the first one they get another one but once they've had two that should be it. They should say "look you've had two trainees now, you're taking advantage of the system". ... They should be made to take somebody on, I think. If there's a job there for 4 years like that, there's a full-time job gone.

Peter did a successful work experience at a garage (where the husband of a friend of his mother worked) which confirmed that he wanted a career as a mechanic. This employer planned to offer him a work placement once he left school. Unfortunately, due to a fire, the garage were unable to fulfil this offer. Peter then wrote to several other garages and went to one of the main training providers for the motor trade, hoping they could find him a position, but the motor trade was depressed by the recession and there were few openings. As nothing happened for a couple of months, Peter considered other occupations and was about to take a position in the leisure industry (found through family contacts) when the training provider finally got him a trial at a small garage. This proved successful, and Peter was offered and accepted a placement. Soon after this the original garage also offered a placement, having recovered from the effects of the fire. Had the offer of a trial not come through when it did, Peter might have taken up a leisure placement despite his commitment to car vehicle repairing. As with Helen when she changed to retail work, Peter's choice was nearly forced by lack of appropriate opportunity and time. For an adolescent, 2 months with no job offers seems a very long time. Once the trial period was over, Peter was taken on as an apprentice in all but name. Even though he had only trainee status, his employer intended to give him a job when the training was completed.

> If he comes up to scratch, [Peter] will be kept on, if he wants to stay on. ... I've always sort of tried to have a lad of some sort, you know, as sort of apprentice ... I do want somebody to train into a mechanic. Not just somebody for the 2 years and say "right, your 2 years is up. get out, I want another one" ... You can't beat training your own people.

THE USE OF NVQS IN TRAINING PROVISION

Like Clive, Frances and David were working for actual NVQ
qualifications whilst, like Becky, Peter and Sam were aiming for more
traditional qualifications that were judged to be NVQ equivalents. All
four were happy with the type of training they received. We talked to
several people connected with the retail trade, because Frances had two
placements and then a job and Laura also had one retail placement. All felt
NVQs were appropriate for this occupational area. As one of Frances's
trainers said:

> I think the NVQs are wonderful. They are far far better particularly in retail than anything
> that we have had before. ... And I know the employers feel exactly the same. 'Cos they
> would much rather have somebody that they know can physically do a job. It has much
> more relevance to the employer.

In retailing, 1 year was felt to be the normal time span for the
achievement of an NVQ 2.

Frances was unusual in that her trainers supplemented on-the-job
training with regular off-the-job provision, including sessions to help
build confidence and sessions to give a better overview so that trainees
could see that there might be more ways of doing things than the way it
was done in one shop. They covered procedures that did not happen in
many small shops and topics like retail law which some shopkeepers
might have neither time nor knowledge to discuss with a trainee.

> Some organisations don't do any training, some do workshop training where if the
> employer outlines a specific unit they will get a group of people who also feel they need
> extra input on that unit, and do that. ... what I actually did was looked at the knowledge,
> the essential knowledge that they actually require. Now what we have found from the
> placements is, through no fault of their own, they are just too busy sometimes to give the
> underpinning knowledge. ... Therefore what we've actually done is put together a
> programme that takes them through all the essential knowledge elements of all the units
> that they are going to be doing. And it takes approximately 4 months coming in one day
> a week. ... what we are trying to do is give them the essential knowledge input before they
> bang into the assessments, so they have the knowledge and then can apply it.

Frances appreciated this off-the-job training: 'It is good 'cos it does help
'cos when I've been in the shop ... you think, "oh I know that". And you learn
things in the college that you would never think of at the shop.' At the end of
our study, she said she would have liked more of the off-the-job provision,
having realised the value when moving from one employer to another.

> Probably [I'd have liked to] go to college a bit more. Instead of like it being a 4 month,
> maybe it being longer, 'cos then you learn more about different things. Maybe like having
> computer systems in it ... it teaches you about different stores.... Like now I'm in a
> completely different store.... Most of the people there knew they weren't going to stay on
> at their placements.... It would help you go on to another store.

Her employer also felt it was beneficial for her to meet other trainees and share experiences. Her parents were satisfied with the trainers saying that they felt they were more 'for the trainees' than other trainers they had come across under YTS. They valued the support Frances had been given by the trainers at work, and the help and encouragement they gave her in applying for jobs as her training neared its end.

Frances's trainers felt NVQ level 3 was inappropriate for young trainees, because it contained a supervisory element, and 17 year olds were too inexperienced to do supervisory work.

> In theory she could move on to level 3 and get a Training Credit for it. Although I have to say that ... the jump between 2 and 3 is ridiculous. ... It makes a little bit of a mockery of the system in a way, because NCVQ [say] "oh yes you can go from level 2 to level 3, it all works, it's a natural progression." ... But what they forget to tell you is that you need at least 2 years experience in between.

Consequently, Frances did not immediately follow up her NVQ level 2 with level 3 training.

Frances's subsequent employer decided to stop using NVQs soon after Frances was appointed. The picture is complicated. Frances was given a part-time job by a branch of a national retail chain. The branch personnel manager claimed that Frances was appointed partly because she possessed her NVQ 2. However, this chain ran their own retail training for employees, based on NVQ plus other content applied to their own particular circumstances, and spread this training over at least 2 years. After Frances started with them, they made a national decision to abandon NVQs, preferring exclusive use of their own training system. The local manager explained that recruits with NVQs achieved elsewhere did not necessarily have the depth of experience or competence that they expected of their own trainees. They felt that NVQs were an insufficient safeguard of training quality – an issue we return to in the next chapter.

In agriculture, NVQs were welcomed by David and his employer. David liked the fact that if he got something wrong he could redo it later.

> We get assessed on these things. And if you get 'em wrong, you got to do 'em again, in a few weeks time, to see if you can still remember it. Because they tell you what you got wrong, then they'll say "right. You've got your assessment, get it right this time." ... You keep going till you get it right. ... I did get one thing wrong the other day. And you keep remembering what you forgot, then, because it keeps nagging at you, why you missed it. Then when they ask you, you think "oh I'll 'ave 'em this time", and get it right. It works very well.

His employer, who had been trained as an NVQ assessor, felt the competence elements were appropriate and was happy to assess David's work against them on the farm.

> Now you've got a complete book, as it were, to ... assess these [trainees] on tasks which they're doing. ... And if, when you're drenching bullocks one day, there's one section which you don't think he's quite up to, well you don't tick that. You leave it until the next time.

... I think that this [NVQs] is, to me, is what is needed.

His trainer, at the agricultural college, also liked NVQs but felt the need to supplement them with formal teaching.

> Trainer: I'm not saying I'm not in favour of NVQs. There's a lot which I like. It's far better, in some ways that the City and Guilds but the depth and the level of background knowledge [is what] they actually want, so we have to give it to them.
> Interviewer: The "they" being?
> Trainer: The students, their providers [farmers], their parents. They do want the lectures. They want to be told about the insides and the outsides of animals and how to grow crops.
> Interviewer: Is it that they feel they need that knowledge and theory, or is it simply that they think that's what education is?
> Trainer: I think they feel they need it. ... There is this feeling of need. "We want you to teach him something we cannot do on the farm".

Peter and Sam were both on traditional craft courses. They, their employers and their trainers were all happy with this, and no one could see any benefit in moving over to NVQs. Peter's employer did not know a lot about the off-the-job training, which he preferred to leave to the trainers. But he expected what Peter learned there to complement what he learned at work, to provide theoretical background, and to teach Peter to do different jobs on different types of car which he did not meet at work. This would be important if Peter changed jobs. His trainer also believed that it was important to broaden the experience Peter was getting at his workplace.

> I think the off-the-job training gives Peter a lot broader knowledge of the more technical aspects. Quite a few of the practical things that he'll do in work will be very repetitive ... Citroen cars have got characteristics all of their own ... so a lot of his work revolves around Citroens. The bulk of the work will be servicing. What we do here is give him a broader knowledge of the subject inclusive of what he would also do in company.

Sam's trainer perceived a similar relationship with the engineering firm, for the training at college provided theoretical background and experience of other areas of engineering not available at work, work being limited to what he described as the 'rough end' of engineering.

Peter was less enthusiastic about the theory, and could not see the relevance of all of it.

> There's a lot of stuff I won't need to know and I still don't understand ... It's mainly electrics, I don't come in contact with electrics that often yet ... I don't mind it. Again, I've just got to be left to play with it and I'll figure it out. ... At college they was teaching us Ohm's law and all this ... when it gets down to it you just want to trace back a feed you just smack a meter on it and that's it. You find it somehow. ... Some of it you don't need.

Both trainers were strongly opposed to the imminent change to NVQs, arguing that this might result in falling standards. Peter's trainer felt that work now done at what was supposedly the equivalent of level 2 would in future not come in until level 3:

> The NVQ for this industry is a joke. ... It's not until you come onto level 3 that you become a bit more technical. ... We've already undertaken that if it stays in its present format we'd have to look to level 3 right away ... because of syllabus content. Otherwise we're not going to be delivering what the employers expect.

Concern was also expressed about the credibility of NVQs with employers, who knew and liked the traditional qualifications. In contrast to agriculture and retail, it is noticeable that, in both these cases, 2 years was the norm to achieve NVQ 2 equivalence.

Peter's trainer felt the Training Credits system was an improvement on what went before, because training could be continued for more than 2 years.

> One of the benefits that was derived ... is get them a Training Credit to cover the cost of their 3rd year training ... as long as they achieve level 2 ... we can put a case for them to go on to NVQ 3.

All four young people were receiving more than the basic NVQ training entitlement. Frances had off-the-job training which was not generally seen as necessary for retailing. Peter was following an NVQ equivalent training programme which the training provider claimed contained much more theory than was specified. Sam was studying for two qualifications.

> Training Provider: It's basically City and Guilds 201 [that Sam's doing] which is what we call the foundation course in engineering. ... We've had to revamp because unfortunately City and Guilds 201 is not NVQd [recognised as an NVQ equivalent]. The ENTRA, which is the old Engineering Industrial Training Board Certificate which has been renamed or revamped, they do offer an NVQ level 2. ... He'll get through NVQ 2 via the ENTRA scheme. The 201 is [done] in parallel .... although it's [NVQ] been around quite a while it has not really filtered through into engineering mainly because the academic qualification which City and Guilds offer.

David was given extra theory by the College. All the training providers were doing more than they needed to do to get full funding under the Training Credits scheme. We return to the the adequacy of NVQs in the next chapter.

CAREER CONTINUITY AND PROGRESSION

All four young people had had a fairly smooth and successful career progression up to the point where our fieldwork ended. Peter and Sam were both part way through an ongoing training programme, leading to the equivalent of NVQ 2 and probably beyond. Both hoped to continue working for their existing employer once training was completed, though Peter did have vague ambitions to leave garage work and become an RAC (Royal Automobile Club) mechanic eventually. Their employers regarded them as apprentices and consistently claimed that they intended to take them on as employees once the training had been completed. In both cases this derived from a mixture of self-interest and obligation. They felt that they had invested in training and that the future success of the firm depended on a steady stream of trained workers. They also felt that taking on a trainee obliged them to offer employment, unless the trainee was unsuitable or other factors made it impossible.

For Peter, the future appeared to have become uncertain after his employer took on a second trainee. Once more, it was local networks that were responsible. As the employer said:

> A new trainee's just started. ... I know his dad like, and I know the lad's keen. I normally wouldn't have taken another one on until next year ... I've had him in on odd days, and his dad's in the trade anyway. And you're half way there if you know spanner sizes and how much not to do. So I thought, oh well!

Even before this, Peter had been worried that he was not quite good enough to be kept on after his training was finished, though he hoped things would work out all right.

> *Interviewer:* Do you think he'll keep you at the end?
> *Peter:* If I speed up a bit, yes ... he expects everything to be done yesterday like. ... He was spoilt with Mal [the garage mechanic]. When Mal started went there ... he knew a lot more than I did. Mal had been stripping engines down since he was about 12 I think. Because Mal learned to do it so quick he [the employer] expects everybody else to as well. ... The last couple of weeks we haven't had the work in and I've actually sped up a bit and he says, "Calm down, Peter, take your time, you've got all day".

Peter was worried that the new lad was faster than him and that for this reason, and because the employer knew the lad's father, if it came to a choice between the two of them, Peter would be the one who was unlucky.

> There's a bit of rivalry now between me and the other boy [Robert] that's just started. ... His dad's a mechanic and he's been working on cars for like the last 4 or 5 years, doing major things like heads off and all sorts. Things I wouldn't dream of doing when I first started. ... 'Cos Robert couldn't find a job, I think ... he [employer] just made a job for [a friend's] son ... Me and Mal didn't think we were busy enough. Well we're not. Like because there's four of us there working, we're finished by 2 o'clock each day. ... We used to get on a lot better but ... silly things are going on in the garage now. ... Where before we used to get on with our job, then once the job's done we'd have a laugh. But now there's a lot of stupidity going on. ... I like the lad, I get on all right with him, I do socialise with him outside of work. ... He can get away with a lot more than I ever could. Like he'll stand around a lot and do nothing, where if I was stood around the boss would shout at me. ... Like now I don't think I've got a chance in hell of being kept on. ... Since he's took Robert that has become a worry. ...
> Various jobs I look and think, "Oh, I'm looking forward to doing that ... I'm really going to have a go at doing that, first one of those I've ever done, I think I'll make a good job of that." And the boss says, "oh Robert's doing that."....
> I think Fridays are the best day when he's at college. We get on like we used to, everybody's not on edge.

In a similar way to Clive, Peter felt that a future that had once seemed secure was now no longer so. His employer gave no indication to us that he had changed his mind about keeping Peter on. However, given the self-doubt and tension in Peter's attitude to work, it was possible that he could now enter the sort of downward, negative spiral that we have seen in Laura's story.

David's progression had been very different. Having successfully completed a year's training and gained his NVQ 2 in agriculture, he applied for and was accepted on to a full-time college course, at the same college where he had done his off-the-job training. This had been his intention right at the start of the Training Credits programme. Supported by his parents, he wanted to develop a career as a farm manager rather than remain a farm worker. To do that he would have to succeed not only at the National Certificate in Agriculture course he was doing when our fieldwork ended, but also at the more advanced National Diploma course that could follow it. As our fieldwork finished, David felt things were going well on the Certificate course: 'Yeah. Not too bad. I get quite good marks. 50–60%, that sort of thing. ... I definitely want to go and do the Diploma, because I haven't got a farm to go back to. So I've got to try and go as hard as I can.'

Despite the fact that his parents were both working in relatively low paid jobs, they were spending a lot of money to support David in his course. The fees were paid by the Local Authority, but they were paying for his residential accommodation at the college, which was only a few miles from home. David was financially worse off than he had been as a trainee. He had no training allowance and, though he was still doing casual work at weekends on the farm, he did not have time to earn as much as he had in the previous year.

If everything went well, David hoped to get a farm management job 'up country', because farms were too small to provide that sort of opening in the area where he lived. If he succeeded in transferring to the Diploma course, he would need a farm placement for a year. He was thinking of doing this abroad.

Well, a few of us have been talking about Canada or Australia. And if we can't get that, we'll go up country. We're not going to stay in [county]. We're going to try to go on the Canadian corn belt.

David knew he he might not become a successful farm manager.

Interviewer: How likely do you think it is that you will manage to do all that?

David: Well, 50–50 I suppose really. ... I thought so long about it. I know what I wanna do. I'm just going to go for it ... Hopefully I'll get there.

For David's parents, his progress was remarkable. His last year at school had gone wrong, and his mother had been afraid that things could have gone from bad to worse.

> [I was worried about] where he was going. Because he'd been playing truant from school. ... He didn't get into any serious trouble, but it could have led to that. You don't know. It was petty little things, but at the end of the day you've still got the worry there.

David's story is a success for Training Credits as well as for him. The scheme gave him a fresh start on a worthwhile career and he seemed to be making the best of the opportunities presented.

Progression for Frances was different again. She had successfully competed her NVQ 2 in retailing and her full-time placement came to an end. She searched for full-time retail work but all she could find was a part-time placement with a national retail chain, supplemented by casual work for her previous employer. When our fieldwork finished she was happy with her place of work, but hoping to convert her part-time job into full-time. She and her boyfriend wanted to set up house, and she saw a larger income as important in making this happen.

> I'm going to ask them there if I can have a full-time job... . Well there's a girl who's pregnant and she's leaving in January. ... If we are going in for this house I'm going to say, "is there a chance of either getting permanent hours a week even if it isn't full-time or getting a full-time job?"

We have already described the changing views of this employer towards NVQs. For Frances this created some ambiguity. Those employees trained to NVQ 2 level in house were automatically awarded a pay rise. Despite already having the qualification, Frances did not receive this and felt unfairly treated.

> I'm going to find out this month to see if I've got my raise [for having NVQ 2] or not. If I haven't I'm going to find out why not. ... I was talking to a lady who I work with the other day ... and I said, "oh, I'm a level 2." And she was laughing at me at first. She said, "Well you haven't got a badge like the rest of them." I said, "well ... I didn't do it here". I said, "I got my certificate and everything." And just as I was saying it my boss came through the door ... and said, "oh, that isn't right here", or something. "It's not the same as ours." So whether I've got to be up to their standard? But ... like all their certificates go on the wall, when they've got their level 1s and level 2s ... and they're exactly the same certificates as mine, all done by City and Guilds ... so why should mine be any different from theirs? ... One girl there she's been there six years and she isn't a level 1 yet! ... Maybe they're afraid that I'm jumping the gun. ... Even if they put my money up to a bit below theirs I don't mind. ... They're getting like a level 2 person for an under 18 [year old]'s money.

Her employer explained that they were not prepared to trust the NVQ until they had checked Frances's performance for themselves:

> [Because of] the fact that she had achieved it [her NVQ] somewhere else we would have to make sure that she was to [our] standard. ... In order for us to assess Frances, she's got really a probationary period as far as the level one's concerned. I mean with our existing employees those that reach level one and level two they actually get paid ... because of the additional responsibility they'll be given literally because of the work involved in achieving the NVQs. Now in Frances's case what would happen is that she,

once she's proved to us that she can achieve set criteria as far as [we] are concerned, then we would pay her automatically. So at the moment she's on basically level zero pay as far as we're concerned even though she's achieved the NVQ.

However, the employer intended that Frances should be credited as worthy of the level 2 she already possessed and hoped she would prove capable enough to train to level 3 or beyond.

Interviewer: What would you see her position as being in about 9 months time?
Employer: Well she would have achieved level 2 hopefully by our standards, and certainly be well established as part of the team within the store ...
Interviewer: 5 years?
Employer: Well the company are developing level 3 and level 4 at the moment anyway, so within 5 years ... certainly if she shows potential for management.

When the firm decided to abandon the use of NVQs it was unclear whether Frances's NVQ 2 would be used to accredit her progress thus far or if she would revert to the beginning, as if she had learned nothing from her previous year. Frances was ambitious and intended to go for the level 3, once she had a little more experience: 'I'm going to ask them if they do a level 3. I'm going to wait till I'm 18 but see if the store do a level 3 and maybe I can go into management.'

GENDER STEREOTYPING AND GENDER DIFFERENCES

There is a growing literature that stresses the importance of gender in the complex transition to work processes that are the subject of this book (Griffin, 1985; Gaskell, 1992). Our study confirmed many of these earlier findings. All the young people we followed, in the end, chose occupations that fell within traditional gender-stereotypical roles. The only exception was Helen, but she reverted to type once she was made redundant from her car spraying placement, a 'cooling out' of ambition towards male jobs that Griffin (1985) shows to be quite common. Whatever else can be claimed for the new Training Credits system, it appears to have done little to promote equality of opportunity.

Gaskell (1992) maintains that young women are more likely than young men to find unfulfilling jobs. Within our data a slightly different picture emerges, but with such a small sample it may be coincidental. In the stories in this book, those of the young women are more extreme. At a positive end, it was two women, Elaine and Alison, who exerted most control over their situations. However, it was also a young woman, Laura, who had the most difficult and traumatic time. Of the four 'straightforward' stories in this chapter, it is Frances who faced the most difficulties and whose experiences could be possibly described as exploitation. In contrast, the males had more mundane, straightforward experiences. We would not wish to over-emphasise this observation, however, for they also faced uncertain futures and troubles may confront them at any time.

Gaskell (1992: 79) also claims that, unlike young men, young women see a job or career in the context of the family and domestic labour. 'This belief that work outside the home will be secondary to work inside the home is critical to an understanding of how these young women plan their lives, and "voluntarily" choose paths that will tend to reproduce their secondary status at work'. Our research design did not focus on issues of family or domestic labour directly. However, our interview schedules were open-ended and we did ask general questions about hopes for the future and about changes in circumstances, expecting to get responses from some young women about boyfriends, families, marriage and motherhood. Laura came closest to the pattern Gaskell describes. She tended to think about employment and domestic issues simultaneously. In June 1993 we asked,'so where do you see yourself in a few years time then?' Laura replied 'I haven't got a clue, hopefully married. Get out of it all then.' When we repeated the question 6 months later, the response was slightly different: 'I'd like to have improved my job by then. Probably have a house by then. Be even slimmer. No, I'd like to have a better job, maybe be a secretary or something. I don't know if I'll be with anybody, you know boyfriend or anything. It doesn't really bother me. I don't want to be married. I'm definitely not going to be married in 5 years time. And I'm not going to have any children in 5 years time not after seeing my sister.'

By the end of our fieldwork, Frances also linked the need for a full-time job to her plans for setting up house with her boyfriend, and saw her future in terms of both work and family.

> *Interviewer:* What do you hope to be doing in 5 years time?
>
> *Frances:* Hopefully still at [same store], because I do like it there and the girls are nice. With a house. I don't think I want any children by then. Probably married by then. ... I hope to stay at [this store] as long as I can, if not I would like another store. I liked [the small shop where I did my training], but, like a friend of Mum's said, you would never work your way up there. You're always a sales assistant.

This contrasts with her response to the same question, earlier in our study, when she refuted her father's suggestion that marriage was her ambition.

> *Interviewer:* So what do you hope you might be doing in a four or five years time?
>
> *Mother:* In charge.
>
> *Father:* Married, got a house, gone.
>
> *Frances:* That's what you want, not what I want! ... I would like to stay with retail ... at the moment I think just staying as I am, trying maybe to build my hours up. ... I would like to be a department manager if I could, not necessarily there. But I would like to work my way up.

One interpretation of this change in emphasis is that family and marriage figured in her reported plans only once they had become a concrete possibility. As the move to live with her boyfriend became realistic, it impinged much more closely on her equally real decisions about her job. However, issues of domesticity did not appear to dominate these decisions, and she always saw progress in her career as important.

The last extract graphically illustrates the pressure on young women to consider a domestic career, and it is extremely unlikely that any young man would have been subjected to the same banter. Alison had a similar dialogue with her mother.

> *Mother* [Joking]: But you're not worried about that are you, 'cos you're going to find a wealthy farmer.
>
> *Alison* [Joking]: That's all I'm up there for really ...
>
> *Interviewer:* Seriously though, what do you see yourself doing in about 5 years time?
>
> *Alison:* Hopefully working on some sort of yard. ... Depending on the sort of experience I get in different areas which sort of yard I work on really ... Find that sort of yard and hopefully some sort of instructor's job on that yard ... I'm going to take my instructor's exams so that I'll be able to teach ... Start my own yard, [joking] mum's going to pay for it! ...
>
> *Mother:* The ideal is to be self-employed really isn't it ... If she hasn't found a wealthy farmer in the meantime!

However, the other young women in our sample made little reference to marriage or domestic work when describing their future plans. This does not necessarily mean that they were not thinking about such issues. However, it does suggest that domesticity may not be the dominant consideration for some. If we think of (young) people as having, amongst others, a paid career identity and a domestic, family life identity, the relevant question becomes the degree to which these are separate or overlap. Our tentative conclusion is that they are more likely to overlap for young women than for young men, but that the degree of overlap varies within the female population. Elaine's responses about her future might be seen, by some, as stereotypically male:

> *Interviewer:* How do you see yourself in 9 months time?
>
> *Elaine:* [Jokingly]: Rich, with a Jaguar XJ6! I enjoy working in the Council, so I'd like to stay in there, but obviously the aim is to get as high as possible ...
>
> *Interviewer:* How about in 5 years?
>
> *Elaine:* Haven't thought that far at all.

Throughout this and previous chapters, we have examined closely the experiences of our young subjects and some of the the other stakeholders that they interacted with. We have used these stories to make occasional comments about the effectiveness of the Training Credits scheme. In the next chapter, we broaden out the implications of our study for VET policy in a more general sense. To do this, we step back from the detail of individual experiences to critique some of the underlying principles behind that policy.

8

Markets, Vouchers and Training Policy

In Chapter 1 we traced the emergence and characteristics of a new paradigm for VET policy in Britain, of which Training Credits are the most complete embodiment. Key elements of that paradigm include:
- the creation of customer-driven markets for VET
- individual commitment to and responsibility for learning
- provision of 'neutral' careers guidance
- compulsory use of NVQs, based on competence
- use of NTETS and other output targets
- payment by recruitment, retention and results
- the inspection and formal approval of VET providers.

In this chapter we critically examine this new paradigm. We argue that current approaches do not work in the ways which were intended, because they are based on an over-simplified view of the social world. We further argue that the current paradigm obscures and largely ignores wider purposes and consequences of VET policy, which should also be addressed. We begin by exploring some of the theoretical assumptions that underlie the new paradigm.

TECHNICISM AND TECHNICAL RATIONALITY IN THE NEW VET PARADIGM

Behind this individualist, market paradigm is a belief in instrumental or technical rationality. This term derives from the work of Habermas (1972), and is analysed further by Grundy (1987), Held (1980) and Gibson (1986). In essence:

> instrumental rationality represents the preoccupation with means in preference to *ends*. It is concerned with method and efficiency rather than with *purposes*. ... It is the divorce of fact from value, and the preference, in that divorce, for fact.
>
> (Gibson, 1986:7, original emphasis)

Such technical rationalism assumes that people can be managed as if they behaved like machines. Education and training are seen as production, using the metaphor of the assembly line, with inputs, processes and outputs. Quality and efficiency dominate the discourse.

A belief in rational choice analysis is a complementary part of the technicist approach. As Hindess (1988:1) says, 'models of maximising behaviour are widely used in economics, and rational choice analysis can be understood as extending that economic approach to other areas of human behaviour'. For example, Elster (1986) claims that analysing personal actions on the assumption that choices are rational normally provides the best explanation of human activity. The CGAP procedures in the scheme investigated were based on such thinking. That model of action planning presupposed that young people should reach decisions in a systematic way, moving logically from a consideration of their own strengths and achievements through to a decision about what they want to do and then on to explore how to achieve that aim, including identifying training needs. Some writers assume that all people consider long-term career goals and chart a path towards them:

> We assume that, knowing their capacities and other personal characteristics, individuals form an estimate of expected earnings resulting from each education, training and labour market option, and, taking into account their taste for each, choose the stream which offers the greatest net utility.
>
> (Bennett *et al.*, 1992:13)

Such a model sees career development as what Kidd (1984:25) calls 'a process involving a matching of self and occupation'. Both she and Law (1981) criticise this congruence model as at best oversimplified. In the scheme under investigation, this *technically rational* model of career choice (Table 8.1) was reinforced by the instrumental way in which guidance sessions had to be provided (Hodkinson and Sparkes, 1993, 1995a). Interviews had to fit a timed sequence through the school year, concentrating on part 2 interviews before looking at part 3. This meant that guidance provision often failed to fit in with the perceived time priorities of the young people.

The Training Credits system was based on the assumption that decision-making was a technical process to be utilised, which was separated from personal development rather than embedded within it. Improving decision-making was seen as providing more and better information and helping young people to consider that information logically. Decisions were made deliberately, within what Giddens (1984) calls discursive consciousness, that is, they could be verbalised and explained by the decision maker. No one suggests that young people's decision making is entirely technically rational in these ways. Rather, the assumptions are that technical rationality is the ideal to be striven for, that anything less is dysfunctional and that, despite shortfalls due to human fallibility, assumptions of technical rationality give the best explanations of behaviour and the best predictions of future actions.

Table 8.1 Technical and pragmatic decision making

Technical rationality	Pragmatic rationality
Decision-making consists of applying rational skills to objective information derived from the labour market.	Decision-making is part of the development of habitus. Information is both subjective objective, deriving from habitus as well as being external to it.
Decision-making is an individual activity, though individuals can be helped or hindered.	Decision-making is social and a culturally embedded activity.
Decision-making takes place within discursive consciousness.	Decision-making takes place within both practical and discursive consciousness.
Decision-making is directed at long term goals, though ideas often change before the goal is reached.	Decision-making might be directed at a long term goal but there are other possibilities. It might be an extension of the recent past or a response to serendipitious opportunities.
Decision-making follows a planned linear sequence, e.g. (i) discover your own strengths, weaknesses and interests, (ii) weigh up possible choices, (iv) choose what to do.	Decision-making does not follow a linear sequence. Stages can be in any order and timed, occurring as chances are perceived. It does not always result in choice.
Decision-making should aim to be totally rational. Though this is never achieved, anything less is dysfunctional.	Decision-making is always boundedly rational, being partly governed by emotions and embedded in habitus.
Decision-making is based on maximising personal benefits, often seen in financial terms.	Decisions may be made for a wide range of reasons, not all part of discursive consciousness. Maximising benefits may be part of this for some people.
Decision-making is only improved by making it more rational and/or providing better information.	Decision-making can be enhanced by various means, including maximising discursive, rational thought and giving information.

Our stories demonstrate that the actual decision making by young people was not technically rational. We coined the parallel concept of *pragmatically rational* choices, to make sense of what we found. Table 8.1 illustrates some of the differences between technical and pragmatic decision making. The pragmatically rational decision making we observed was grounded in the culture and identities of the young people we interviewed. Their decisions were bounded by *horizons for action*. These were determined by the external job or educational opportunities in interaction with personal perceptions of what was possible, desirable or appropriate. Those perceptions, in turn, were derived from their culture and life histories. In this way, job opportunities were always both objective and subjective.

Thus, Helen considered a stereotypically male job, spraying cars, because she had worked on cars with her father. Other typically male jobs lay outside her horizons for action and were never considered. Furthermore, young people did not simply 'choose' jobs from those available. For some, like Helen and Clive, they were created through local networks and contacts, a pattern replicated in other studies (Moore, 1988; Lee *et al.*, 1990; Rikowski, 1992). Yet the young people's pragmatic choices were rational, not irrational. They considered evidence about jobs and careers that was valid in their terms, drawing on personal experience (part-time jobs or work experience) or on the testimony of an insider they knew and whose judgement they respected (parent, neighbour, relative or friend). Above all, the career decision was integral to their sense of identity. It was both an extension of how they already saw themselves and a central part in the process of refining or reforming who they actually were. We have seen how Helen's identity was transformed, from car sprayer to shop assistant, as the result of her forced job change. David, on the other hand, always saw himself as a farmer, an identity he never consciously chose. His love of farming grew through his cumulative experiences, but was no less real because he had never articulated precisely why he felt that way. We revisit this model of career decision making from a theoretical perspective in the next chapter.

The notion of market efficiency is another dubious theoretical plank of the new VET paradigm. Drawing on New Right thinking of the 1980s, it is now often taken as a truism that markets are the best way to allocate scarce resources in any area. Thus Davies (1992) advocated the artificial creation of markets in social areas, like education, where none existed. Both Le Grand and Bartlett (1993) and Bennett *et al.* (1994) report on the workings of the 'quasi-markets' being introduced in health, education and training. Like us, they report major flaws in current systems. Le Grand and Bartlett regard such quasi-markets as unproven. Bennett *et al.* are more enthusiastic, but both suggest that much more needs to be done to give such markets a chance to succeed. Our findings suggest that such market approaches are based on mistaken oversimplifications of social reality. They ignore issues of status, power and struggle, and assume that technically rational choice is a key component of behaviour.

Very few of the young people or their employers acted as customers for training in the way the scheme planning assumed would happen. There were practical reasons for this, some of which may have been specific to the particular scheme and context under investigation. Perceptions of the recession meant that young people were unlikely to turn a placement down because of poor training opportunities, which might be a consequence of the unfortunate timing of the pilot scheme. As Unwin (1993) suggests, Credits were designed for youth labour shortage and introduced in a glut. In this particular scheme the Training Credit was only used once, immediately a placement was gained, so it had little symbolic value. In some other schemes the credit was used periodically throughout the training period by the young person.

Other factors were more likely to be universal. The lack of knowledge and confidence and the relative powerlessness of many young people, together with the pragmatically rational ways in which they made career decisions, meant that many did not shop around for placements or training. The use of local networks to find placements often combined with such decision-making to restrict 'choice' to simply saying yes or no to a particular opportunity. The effectiveness of local links between employer and trainer, which were functional for both, meant that employers were unlikely to shop around amongst trainers, preferring to stick with an organisation they knew. The marginality of small employers in the Training Credits process meant that many of them neither understood it nor had the time or interest to find out about it (Hodkinson and Sparkes, 1994). Even when choices were made they were unlikely to be made on criteria of training quality. Neither small employers nor young people had a very clear idea of what training quality was, beyond a simplistic belief that X training organisation 'knows what sort of young people I need and does a good job'.

The third theoretical strand within the VET paradigm relates to the measurement of quality and outcome-related funding. This is part of a new managerialism in education and training, deriving from an attempt to introduce industrial management techniques, through an emasculated form of Total Quality Management (TQM). Central to TQM is the constant search to improve quality and increase consistency and efficiency against measurable performance indicators. Such measurement is believed to be vital, so that managers can differentiate between essential spending, which affects quality, and inessential spending, which does not. It is assumed that quality can be raised and costs cut simultaneously. Other parts of a TQM approach include the direct involvement of the whole workforce in the search for improvement, thus replacing Taylorist bureaucratic hierarchies with fewer layers of management and flexible teams, where responsibility and decision-making are shared. The assumption is that procedures like TQM can be used to raise the quality of education and training, whilst avoiding additional spending or whilst making further cuts. Our research suggests that this is a dangerous illusion. In education or training, quality essentially involves the process of learning and the social interactions that are associated with it. As Skilbeck et al. (1994) suggest, the most important elements of VET are not easily measured anyway. Current policy trends over-look these self-evident truths and confuse real quality in education and training with the measurement of qualification achievement and NTETS. Such performance indicators may be increased whilst important aspects of quality remain unaffected or even fall as, for example, when Alison and her employer felt that she had not been adequately trained in horse breeding and feeding, but she got her NVQ level 2 anyway.

In Chapter 2, we saw that the introduction of Training Credits was also technically rational. We return, at the end of this chapter, to examine this technically rational, individualist paradigm for VET as a whole. Before that we turn to some specific aspects of VET as experienced in the scheme, to point up some lessons derived from the experiences of our interviewees.

CAREERS EDUCATION AND GUIDANCE

There was a contrast between the experiences of careers teachers and careers officers in the scheme. Our interviews confirmed other findings (Sims and Stoney, 1993) that Training Credits generally produced status enhancement for careers officers. Their work was seen as central to the procedures and extra funding was provided. On the other hand, careers teachers felt alienated and marginalised. Though there are other factors, the technically rational model of decision making and guidance within the project design was one cause of this difference, in two ways.

On the one hand, it was felt that careers officers could give 'neutral' guidance. Careers teachers could be less independent and were more likely to follow the line required by the school. As we have seen, one careers officer reported being pressured by the school as some key staff felt that she was pushing Training Credits at the expense of their own vocational courses. On the other hand, an implicit view of guidance as 'giving accurate information and advice on how to decide', turned a complex process into a simple technical problem, requiring short-term interventions in a series of guidance interviews. This view was reinforced by a hope that appropriate guidance would enable a large proportion of young people to reach a 'correct' decision, against which their training provision could be planned, as the final part of the CGAP was completed.

Careers education was seen as background support.

We argued, early in the study (Hodkinson *et al.*, 1992), that the enhanced status for the careers service through Training Credits might have been bought at too high a price. This was because the careers services had to accept the technically rational decision making model, with its emphasis on CGAP completion. In so doing, they left unchallenged unrealistic assumptions about what high-quality guidance could achieve – that young people could be helped to make a decision and stick to it, and that the detail on the CGAP would be valuable for the design of training plans by Approved Trainers.

The guidance process described by careers officers was much more complex than that. Though most felt that the completion of the CGAP was a useful guide to young people, it often lacked precision. For some young people it was necessary to leave several options open, as they did not really know what they wanted to do. One officer described leaving part 3 until a placement was found, because only then could relevant detail about training needs be included. Another argued that it was impossible to identify training needs until the young person had some experience of the job. Several young people described changes of mind, so that a CGAP that seemed relevant at the time was felt to be valueless soon after.

By the time our study was completed, the TEC had become disillusioned by the frequency with which young people began one training programme only to change later to something different, and by repeated complaints by Approved Trainers that the CGAP details were valueless to them. In October 1994 a senior official stated that their current policy was to cut back on careers guidance and enhance careers education instead. He hoped that greater investment in careers education earlier in the educational process would reduce the number of career changes and result in more correct decisions.

Our analysis suggests that a balance of both careers education and guidance will be beneficial to young people, but that the hope for unchanging decisions about career and training routes prior to the issue of a Training Credits remains unrealistic. Better provision will not convert a pragmatic decision making process into a technical one. Careers education and guidance have to be envisaged as enhancing the ways in which decisions are actually made.

If careers education and guidance are to be effective, any justification of their value must be independent of the actual decisions made by young people. As Watts (1991:244) says, 'guidance services should be evaluated not in terms of the outcomes of their clients' decisions but in terms of the processes through which the clients make their decisions'. The danger with the Training Credits approach is that these processes are rendered invisible by the focus on the utility of the CGAP documents and decisions produced. There are parallels with issues of training quality, to which we return below.

None of this is means that action planning is inevitably technically rational or that any form of Careers Guidance Action Planning is inappropriate. Many careers officer and careers teachers believed the forward-looking focus and the recording of action points to be beneficial, and many young people valued the interviews which had resulted in those plans. Watts (1992) identifies seven different types of action plan, with varying degrees of tightness of focus. Our findings suggest that any plans produced could usefully be seen as tentative and exploratory rather than definitive and that, in many cases, several possible ways forward should be flagged. Watts (1994) points out that action planning skills have to be learned by young people, which is a further argument for the provision of appropriate careers education. It may be the case that drawing up an action plan is inappropriate in some sessions, where an unfocused discussion of career options or the consequences of possible career decisions is all the young person needs or can value at that time. It follows that a change of mind that took place after a plan was drawn up does not necessarily mean that the guidance given lacked value. Nor does it mean that the guidance interview either could have or should have foreseen the coming change.

Giving careers guidance at the wrong time is not always helpful. For Clive, the interviews with a careers officer were too late, as he had already muddled his way to finding a training programme. For others they were too early. But it is impossible to determine in advance when the time is right, and simply relying on the young people to come when they need help does not always work – often those most in need do not seek help, possibly because they do not know they need it. This points to one of the strengths of the Training Credits scheme under investigation. There was no rigid limit on how many interviews a young person could have and this entitlement to support continued after they had left school and embarked on the Training Credits programme. No system can fund unlimited numbers of sessions, but the tempting technical approach to ration all young people to identical numbers of interviews should be resisted, as should its corollary of defining 'efficiency' and 'cost effectiveness' as the minimum number of sessions needed to produce a specified outcome.

NVQS AND ON- OR OFF-THE-JOB TRAINING

For many young people, the NVQ approach has been beneficial. David liked the fact that if he did something wrong he only had to be re-tested on that bit, rather than redo the whole activity. His employer was pleased with the competence elements and the system of assessment, which he felt confident about using on the farm. Similarly, Frances and her second employer felt that NVQs were appropriate for retail work. Becky might well have been better off under the NVQ approach, which would have valued and recognised her undoubted dental surgery expertise, rather than assuming that her problems with written examinations accurately reflected her supposed inability to understand even a basic fact such as the nature of orthodontics.

There are suggestions in our data that NVQ approaches may be less suitable in some occupational areas (engineering) than others, and less suitable for some young people than for others. For Clive, the problem lay in the need for extensive on-the-job experience that his employer could not provide. Clive found it difficult to understand how training built around NVQs would work. He retained a belief that the trainers he was working with should have produced a programme to give him all the training he needed, off-the-job. They felt unable to do this, because they could not accurately simulate the sorts of working conditions under which NCVQ required his assessment to take place. It does not seem unreasonable for an employer and trainee to want entirely 'off-the-job' training, but this is not part of the current NVQ system.

The inevitable concentration of training on-the-job, which follows from NVQ assessment procedures, created other problems. Some of the young people described gaps in their training programmes, because the situation where they were working did not offer the experience needed. Furthermore, the emphasis on work-based training inevitably gives employers a central role. Yet this was precisely the sort of involvement that many of the small employers we spoke to did not want. It also meant that the training of some young people was inadequate, partly because of unhelpful employer actions. Clive's case has already been alluded to, but Alison's first employer was not prepared to train her in areas beyond the stables' normal activity, and Helen's first employer knew nothing of NVQs and terminated her training by making her redundant.

The concentration of learning in specific workplaces opens up another problem. Many employers talked of the importance of working in their own idiosyncratic ways. This raises three obvious questions:

1. Is such idiosyncratic training appropriate for those young people who will not be kept on in the same firm but will look for jobs elsewhere?

2. If all trainees should be brought into contact with excellent practice, however excellence is defined, can this be realistically done in most workplaces?

3. Can training in current practices prepare the adaptable and flexible workforce that policy makers identify as essential for our future prosperity?

Our interviews suggest that the answer to all of these might be 'no'. It follows that substantial elements of off-the-job training may be beneficial in many cases. This may be more necessary when a trainee is located with a small employer, even though small employers are often reluctant to release young people from the workplace.

Many of the Approved Trainers felt that NVQs were not enough on their own. The agricultural college provided additional theory on David's farming course, whilst Peter's tutor, on a traditional mechanic's course, was highly sceptical about the adequacy of NVQs. Such views reinforce other research, which suggests that NVQs give inadequate coverage of theory and core skills. For example, Steedman and Hawkins (1994) suggest that, in the building trades, mathematical content has been greatly reduced in the transition from a traditional City and Guilds qualification to an NVQ, and that this widens the skills gap between British trainees and their counterparts in France and Germany. Similar comments have been made about the use of competence-based approaches in the caring professions (Hodkinson and Issitt, 1995). At the time of writing, a new pattern of 'modern apprenticeships' is being piloted in Britain. This programme, which is aimed as providing high-level training to young school leavers, entails a deliberate combination of NVQ, to at least level 3, with additional content. This may be a way forward for all levels of training. If NVQ approaches are not to be abandoned altogether, they need to move much further away from the reductionist, mechanistic and behaviourist approaches that have been so heavily criticised by Hyland (1994), amongst others [7]. It may also be sensible to consider using Training Credits for qualifications other than NVQs. In November 1994, the TEC concerned was considering the use of General National Vocational Qualifications (GNVQs) within the Training Credit scheme, so that future Clives and Beckys might be given choices of different qualifications and training approaches.

TRAINING QUALITY

Within the new VET paradigm quality is emphasised but seldom defined. It is taken for granted and assumed to be measurable and uncontested. Yet Gleeson and Hodkinson (1995) argue that what is understood by educational quality varies according to the beliefs of the individual. For example, within the Training Credits scheme it is unclear whether 'quality' is that which customers are prepared to buy, that which employers or the economy need (not necessarily the same things), that which leads to a recognised qualification, or some supposedly unproblematic combination of the four.

With the current emphasis on measured achievement, educational or training quality is, in practice, defined by outcomes such as the achievement of a recognised qualification. Under the drive to increase performance against NTETS, the qualification becomes the main determinant of quality. Especially with NVQs, it is argued that any programme that leads to the successful achievement of the qualification must, *ipso facto*, be quality provision. We challenge that assumption and argue that the nature of the learning experience itself is an important part of quality, which cannot be guaranteed by the achievement of a qualification. Alison's experiences illustrate the point.

We wish to draw out, from the experiences reported earlier, some elements of quality training that appear to us to be largely unaddressed by the new controls of markets, choice, performance-related funding and NVQ qualification. In doing so, we focus on training as an ongoing process. There are very good reasons for this. There is a growing body of literature about learning which recognises that it is a socio-cultural process. Brown *et al.* (1989) argue that in learning, a combination of the learning context, the activity engaged in and the concept (or skill) being studied are interrelated. Effective learning depends on the mutual reinforcement of all three. Driver *et al.* (1994) talk of the importance of enculturation in learning to be a scientist. This model of enculturation, or the gradual absorption of experience as an integral part of learning, is drawn from studies in work-based vocational contexts. Resnick (1987) argues that the ways in which we learn in everyday life differ in significant ways from the formal approaches in schools and other learning institutions. This is one justification for locating the bulk of Training Credits experience on-the-job. Helen was becoming a shop assistant by absorbing the culture of the record shop. Laura failed to become a nursery nurse because she found aspects of the work culture alienating and left. It follows that the quality of the learning experience itself should not be overlooked.

The new VET paradigm in Britain does not deny the importance of a high-quality learning process, but assumes that this will inevitably result from the effective manipulation of output controls, but these outputs do not directly measure process quality. One illustration of the problems caused relates to time wasting. It almost universally accepted that the old apprenticeship schemes were full of 'time wasting' when, for example, trainees spent most of the first year making tea and sweeping up. Such a view ignores the possibility that young people were actually absorbing the culture of work in a useful way, which supported the technical skills they went on to develop. Whether this is true or not, that old system has been replaced by one based on time saving. Programmes leading to NVQ do not specify any entitlement to training time and funding is paid partly on completion. The result is that trainers reported pressures to push young people through quickly. Despite this, many of the young people still describe time wasting. In some cases, as with Alison, this went on while gaps in the training they felt they really needed were not addressed.

Time saving is not the opposite of time wasting, as a simplistic, technically rational view of training efficiency suggests.

Smithers (1993) and Steedman and Hawkins (1994) highlight a second problem. In the NVQ system most assessment is done by employers or training providers in the workplace. The result is the farcical situation whereby trainers are responsible for doing the assessments, the results of which will determine whether or when their firm gets a substantial proportion of its funding. Steedman found college lecturers reporting pressure to pass weak students, and some of our interviewees said the same. One manager claimed that:

> Training Credits are looking at NVQs as outcomes and putting cash values on outcomes which makes it very very difficult for trainers to resist the pressures put upon them by their managers to achieve the outcomes. ... There's bound to be some pressure to pass them ... and where there's a marginal case where the people who are assessing and teaching would prefer to see someone have a bit more practice, you could say 'yes, OK, they "can do"'.

In such ways, the technically rational view of training as a simple system, where the process is controlled through measuring outputs, is fundamentally flawed. As Brown and Evans (1994) claim, both processes and outcomes should receive explicit attention. To do this, a clearer idea of what makes a quality learning process is needed, together with a policy structure that encourages the development of those features. Our research allows tentative suggestions about what some elements of a quality process might be.

Learning experience needs to be coherent. Lee *et al.* (1990) criticised unstructured work experience on the YTS, and the use of NVQs on this scheme seems to have done little to change that. NVQs are designed so that assessment can be done in an *ad hoc* manner, ticking off elements of competence as they naturally occur. Attempts by Approved Trainers to follow NVQ principles of flexibility and choice resulted in some young people receiving disjointed off-the-job training. Mechanisms should be devised to encourage Approved Trainers and employers to plan for structured, coherent experiences.

We agree with Steedman and Hawkins (1994) when they argue that all trainees should be entitled to specified amounts of off-the-job training, to address those issues not well developed in a specific workplace. It follows that the on- and off-the-job components of training need to be co-ordinated and integrated. In large firms which are responsible for both on- and off-the-job elements, this will be difficult enough. It will be even harder when small employers have to co-operate with separate training providers. The current system, which relies on negotiation in a supplier/purchaser market, did not achieve this, as Elaine's experiences demonstrate. In many cases, both the employer and the Approved Trainer had legitimate needs that were more important, to them, than achieving a coherent training programme for a young person. Alison was caught between an employer whose main concern had to be running a commercial riding stables successfully, and a trainer who had to ensure that groups in college remained large enough to be viable. Unless scheme regulation require a coherent programme, such experiences are likely to be quite common (Hodkinson and Hodkinson, 1995). For Clive, tensions between employer and trainer resulted in his failure to reach an NVQ level 2.

It is difficult to see how a coherent training process can be achieved when the structure is designed so that a small employer takes the lead. For any small firm, giving quality training must always take second place to the commercial objectives of survival and profitable trading. For this reason we remain sceptical about suggestions that we should give employers the power to choose and purchase training. Those young people with employed status were, ironically, more vulnerable than those who were simply trainees, because the Approved Trainer had little power to influence what happened in the workplace or even to ensure regular release for off-the-job training. Brown and Evans (1994) argue that only large employers should be engaged in youth training. Whilst having some sympathy with their analysis, this seems to us to be unrealistic. In many areas small employers provide a high proportion of jobs for young people, and many of our subjects would have been denied placements and training which they valued, had such a policy been in place. However, control of the training process should be located elsewhere, with the training providers and/or the TEC. This could be done through a return to older YTS-type approaches, where training process controls and entitlements were a condition of acceptance on the scheme.

Above all, a quality training process will be built around good relationships between learner, trainer and employer. Such a relationship depends, to a significant degree, on the quality of trainers being used on the scheme. Hargreaves (1994: ix) reminds us that 'teachers don't merely deliver the curriculum. They develop, define it and reinterpret it too. It is what teachers think, what teachers believe and what teachers do ... that ultimately shapes the kind of learning young people get'. The unofficial National Commission on Education (1993: 43) put it more directly: 'high-quality learning depends above all on the knowledge, skill effort and example of teachers and trainers'. Yet in this scheme the Approved Trainer personnel felt alienated, and there was no central provision for staff development of trainers. Instead, there was a belief that market forces, training regulations and funding controls would compel or encourage the training firms to provide quality training. Any staff development was the responsibility of the Approved Trainer, not the TEC. Despite this, several TEC officials complained that trainers did not understand the system and were still trying to behave as if older procedures applied.

THE USE OF VOUCHERS

Though our analysis has been predominantly negative about the system of which Training Credits were a central part, we would not wish to dismiss the idea of vouchers entirely. There is evidence from other studies (Sims and Stoney, 1993) that the use of credits had raised awareness of many young people about their entitlements to careers guidance and training. We have shown how credits helped Elaine to get training and to choose what qualification to aim for. The system brought one other major advantage to several young people, even though a TEC official acknowledged it was unintended. When a young person, like Laura or Helen, changed from one training programme to another, they remained entitled to a full credit for the second, third or even more subsequent training programmes, provided they changed occupational areas. This is an improvement on what was done before.

Vouchers or credits are inherently neither good nor bad. However, there is a central problem about their use for which a solution has not yet been found. Paradoxically, this central weakness is seen by advocates of a voucher system as a strength. The problem is that it is very difficult to conceive of a voucher system that is not inherently tied up with a form of payment by results. If young people have vouchers, then the income of any provider must largely come from the effectiveness of their recruitment. As soon as that happens, provider institutions and their staff are forced to place institutional needs in front of those of individual young people. Thus, Clive was recruited for an NVQ level 2 in Business Administration, even though his job was largely unrelated. For the training provider, Clive's recruitment was necessary income. Alison was fitted in to college groups for courses different from her own, because the college could not afford uneconomic groups but would lose income if she had been turned away.

Current managerial responses to such problems make the situation worse. They emphasise payment by results through systems of funding that reward trainee retention, course completion and the successful achievement of the qualification. Though this is supposed to discourage the recruitment of 'unsuitable' young people and encourage the tailoring of courses to meet individual needs, the results are sometimes the opposite. Most young trainees are less confident and less resourceful than the training providers. Consequently, their needs often become distorted as institutions try to balance their own funding imperatives against the diverse interests of the trainees. Far from empowering young people, when vouchers are used like this the funding regimes make it more difficult for any provider to put the trainee's needs first, if and when these clash with the needs of the organisation itself.

There remain two alternatives for vouchers. One way would be to abandon the pretence that they are to empower the young person and investigate, in ways that lie way beyond the scope of this study, whether or not they are an efficient and/or effective method of funding a training system where the needs of others, be they the Government, TECs, employers or the providers are paramount. For example, giving vouchers to employers raises a host of possibilities, though our study casts doubt on the advisability of doing that with small employers. The second alternative is to explore the possibilities of using vouchers in a system where aspects of payment by results are minimised and the potentially negative effects of such approaches are ameliorated. Whilst this may be possible, we are aware of no voucher scheme where it has been tried and are unclear about what form it might take.

Because such an approach has not been tried, the introduction of vouchers and markets in Britain did not address central issues of inequality in access to jobs or training places, rather, it distracted attention from them. Local networking to find jobs raises some such issues. Wellington (1994:314) summarises the argument well: 'discrimination is often hidden by the use of informal contacts and word-of-mouth recruitment, which clearly disadvantages those who cannot or do not use informal channels'. It is often implied that the solution to such discrimination is to move all recruitment over to a more technical selection process, with advertisements, interviews and competitive selection. However, the small employers in our study showed no intention of recruiting in this way, and it is difficult to perceive of any means of encouraging them to do so. In dealing with the problem of some people's lack of access to local networks, an alternative approach seems more likely to bring partial success, by providing a broker service to network with employers on young people's behalf, rather than rely on spurious notions of technical rationality backed up by a voucher. Ironically, such a system existed within the unofficial workings of the scheme, but was seen, by the TEC, as a weakness to be eliminated and was radically diminished during the period of our study. For many of the employers operated a second networking system with local training providers. They knew and trusted the trainers, who in turn, knew where the good training placements were and what sorts of trainee would be likely to succeed with each employer. In effect, the training provider gave sponsored access to the local networks to those young people who did not have access already through family contacts. This happened to Becky, when she was placed in the dentist's surgery, and with Laura, in the nursery school. Peter got his garage placement this way, when his own contacts failed because of the fire, and Frances got both her shop placements like this.

But the obsession with setting up a training market threatened to disrupt this system and, by the end of our study, all placements were supposed to be found by an independent placement service, to break cozy relationships between training providers and employers. Lawrence (1994) reminds us that such placement was once the central role of predecessors of the modern careers service. In the scheme investigated, two dual services were developed for subsequent cohorts to ours. A careers service gave the now conventional 'neutral guidance' and a separate placement service found training opportunities for young people. As our sample did not use this service, we no direct evidence about how effectively it worked.

BEYOND TECHNICAL RATIONALITY

The common thread behind all these criticisms and policy suggestions is the inadequacy of a technicist approach to policy, planning, management and innovation. Judged in its own terms it does not work in the ways claimed by protagonists. The basic reason for this failure is the misunderstanding of social reality upon which it is based. Unrealistic beliefs about the ways in which career decisions are made, about the impact and supposedly benign nature of markets and funding controls and about the managerial control of people have all been described.

Part of the problem is a fallacious view that a wide range of different interests and purposes can be combined in an unproblematic way. For example, this Training Credits scheme assumed that the interests of employers and young people would be close enough that negotiation could always produce a training package both were happy with. Trainers would also be happy, because they would be rewarded for meeting customers' needs. As we have seen, the reality was of differing interests and intentions, resolved through struggle as well as agreement, utilising differing and unequal resources. At national level there is a parallel belief that the interests of individuals, employers and the national economy could be similarly combined (DfEE, 1996). Yet small employers wanted idiosyncratic training to meet their specific needs, whilst national policy objectives are for broader based competence development, relevant across occupational areas. Further, the policy paradigm assumes that if the needs of the economy and employers are met, somehow the needs of a wider society will also be fulfilled and that long-standing problems of marginalisation, alienation, inequality and social disadvantage can also be addressed through a technically rational, individualist, market policy focus.

At the time of writing, the term 'Learning Society' has become dominant in the discourse in Britain (DfEE, 1996), in the ways in which 'enterprise' was in the late 1980s (Coffield, 1990). Once more, the assumption of the dominant paradigm is that market forces, an individualist commitment to and responsibility for learning, the development of 'learning organisations' and the development of the new managerialism can and should all contribute to the development of a Learning Society that is in the interests of employers and economic prosperity. It is no coincidence that the supposedly independent government research agency, the ESRC, should have launched a £2 million research initiative with the title 'the Learning Society: *knowledge and skills for employment*" (our emphasis). However, as Ranson (1994:106) argues, this sort of economic rationalism (or rationalisation) is not the only possible conception of a Learning Society. He presents a radically different version, based on principles of a duality of citizenship 'as both individual and member of the whole, the public; ... as autonomous persons who bear responsibilities within the public domain'. He goes on to explore the conditions for a 'learning self' as part of a moral, participative democratic community. His view of public good is much wider than the economic instrumentalism of current VET policy.

In analysing the evolving management of education and educational policy in Britain since the Second World War, Ranson mounts a detailed and erudite challenge to current market ideologies, concluding that they preserve inequalities and serve the vested interests of those already in power. He goes on to argue that the market deflects attention away from a series of real problems which it fails to address, let alone solve:

> Markets cannot resolve the problems we face. ... Those problems derive from ... the restructuring of work; environmental erosion; the fragmentation of society. They raise questions about what it is to be a person, what is the nature of the community, what kind of polity we need to secure the future well-being of all ... markets can only exacerbate these problems: they ensure that we stand no chance of solving them and are unlikely to be legitimated by the majority of people who will be defeated and excluded by markets. (Ranson, 1944: 99)

Regardless of whether one accepts this trenchant attack, and none of our evidence has caused us to question it, VET policy in Britain needs to be refocused upon a wider agenda. Policy makers need to address a raft of long-standing issues that have not gone away because the paradigm of individualism, markets and technical rationality does not recognise them. They include:

- the wider needs of society in a social democracy
- global issues of inter-dependence
- deep-rooted inequalities in society, based on class, ethnicity, gender, sexual orientation and other factors
- mass (youth) unemployment

- conflicts of interest between individuals, groups and institutions
- the accelerating rate of social change, beyond and including changes in work and employment.

Testing the Ranson critique will be quite easy. If he is wrong, and if the new paradigm does not bring the weaknesses and unfairness that we and he describe then, within the next few years, the following will happen in Britain:

1. Those small employers, who employ an increasing proportion of the British labour force, will take training seriously, invest in it, and play a leading role in developing high-quality training programmes.

2. Currently disadvantaged groups in society will find they are more able to get high-quality training and the jobs that are assumed to go with it.

3. The status of VET in the public perception will rise, so that vocational courses and programmes will be seen to be of 'equivalent status' to academic alternatives.

4. Young people will find themselves able to choose jobs and training that they want and that they can succeed at.

It is our contention that all of these are extremely unlikely, and we cannot afford to wait, in the hope that all will come right in the end.

THE SEDUCTIVE APPEAL OF TECHNICISM

We explore some of the deeper theoretical problems with current policy in the final chapter, examining aspects of the cultural complexity of the transition to work that are ignored in the current technicist approach. Before then, we wish to examine briefly why the current policy paradigm has acquired such wide support. It is obvious why such approaches appeal to employers and the CBI, for the new paradigm takes what is essentially an industrial metaphor for educational and training management. The constant focus on individual trainees deflects attention from the changes needed in industrial employment, the youth labour market and British financial systems (Finegold and Soskice, 1991; Brown and Evans, 1994; Hutton, 1995; Avis et al., 1996) which, if addressed, would challenge employer freedom. For the government, the paradigm offers the illusion of a simple policy solution, which is consistent with broader market and tax-cutting policy objectives. It fits within one of the dominant Conservative ideological positions which emphasises that employers know best and should be empowered by the removal of 'state interference'. It deflects attention from deeper societal causes of problems such as unemployment, effectively blaming the victims for their own difficulties – be they individual young people, single training organisations or single TECs. Further, Gleeson (1993) suggests that the creation of a market in the educational context was primarily concerned with emasculating Local Education Authorities and, ironically, centralising control over the curriculum and teachers, rather than with creating a genuinely effective education system. As we have seen, Ranson (1994) argues that markets inevitably favour the interests of the most powerful groups in society, so that they appeal to a political party which represents existing white middle- and upper-class value positions.

In different ways, technically rational models of management and choice appeal to other politicians and Trades Unionists as well as to senior managers of many political persuasions, such as college principals, senior careers officers, TEC chief officers or Civil Servants. This is because they offer the illusion of control and of managerial solutions. If people really did behave predictably like machines, complex social processes could be as easily managed as a computerised production line. But the new individualist, market paradigm for education and training is a seductive, dangerous rhetorical illusion. Successful policy, that is genuinely aimed at raising educational and training standards for all and/or at empowering disadvantaged young people, must be built on better understanding of real social processes and contexts, in all their confusing complexity.

Given this claim that current VET policies are based on a dangerous over-simplification of the social and cultural realities which they are intended to regulate, in the next chapter we conclude by addressing this cultural complexity directly. To do this we draw extensively on the stories already told, and combine them into a theoretical account of decision making in the transition to work. We return to and amplify the model of careership outlined in the prologue. In exploring and explaining these theoretical ideas, we range beyond the policy debate of this chapter, important though that is. Our findings, we argue, have a wider relevance for thinking about the nature of the transition to work, and for clarifying the apparent incompatibility between research findings which emphasise determined career trajectories for young people and policy assumptions based on choice and free will.

9

Career Decision Making and Culture in the Transition from School to Work

In Chapter 1 we outlined a paradox within the current literature on the transition from school to work. On the one hand, much research describes long-standing patterns of inequality, influenced by class, ethnicity and gender. On the other hand, much policy making is now driven by assumptions of free choice and individual responsibility. The stories described in this book strongly suggest that both perspectives contain an element of truth, though we would give more credibility to the former than the latter.

In this book we explore a middle position, examining the ways in which the young people we studied interacted with others and with the context and culture in which they found themselves. From this we have constructed a model of the transition to work that is different from others in the literature. This advances understanding of some elements of the transition that are dealt with less effectively elsewhere. In constructing this model we have ranged beyond our data into what Wolcott (1994:36) calls 'interpretation'. This he describes as 'a threshold in thinking and writing at which the researcher transcends factual data and cautiously analyses and begins to probe into what is to be made of them'.

Pragmatically rational decision making was described in the previous chapter. This must be seen as having three inter-locked dimensions, which are shown in Figure 9.1. Firstly, that decision making process is part of a wider choice of lifestyle and is strongly influenced by the social context and culture of the person making the decision. Secondly, that decision making must be seen as part of the ongoing life course. Finally, the decision making is part of the interaction with other stakeholders, which means that a pragmatic decision can only be understood as part of the actions of others, as well as those of the person supposedly making the choice. Once we have analysed each of these three dimensions, we finish this chapter by summarising the ways in which social structure and culture permeate all parts of the model, explaining how the socially structured patterns of career choice, which so much research has revealed, are perpetuated. This is balanced by a summary of the ways in which individuals do have some freedom to influence their own lives. It is this scope for some individual freedom that makes the efforts of teachers,

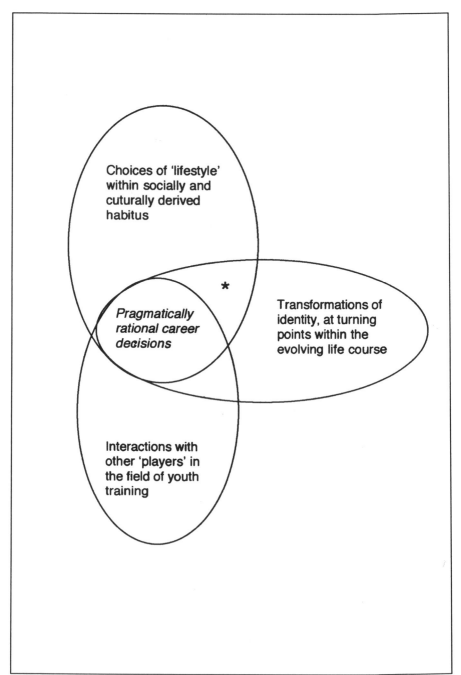

Figure 9.1 The dimensions of career decision making. *In reality, this overlap between lifestyles and the life course is total. They are separated here for analytical clarity

careers officers and others, on behalf of young pupils and clients, so worth while. However, if we are serious about doing something to ameliorate existing inequalities, individual help alone is not enough. We also have to address more intransigent problems at a cultural and structural level. We begin examining our model from the dimension of the life course.

ROUTINES AND TURNING POINTS

One problem with much current writing is that the transition from school to work tends to be seen as an isolated point in a person's life. Thus, even such thoughtful work as that of Brown (1987) or Okano (1993) focuses exclusively on that stage in a person's career. We feel that it is more helpful to see the transition to work, and any decisions make about it, as but one important stage in the whole life course. One problem of not doing so is the sometimes implicit assumption that, beyond the transition point, the future career trajectory is knowable and often known – that, once the transition to work is complete, adult working life is firmly set into predictable patterns. Strauss (1962) suggests that we often describe this predictability according to one of two metaphors. The first is the career ladder. From this point of view, early decisions around the transition to work are the lower rungs of the ladder. As our lives develop we gradually climb, in a direction that is clear and predictable to a knowledgeable outsider. Though plans and directions can change, these are seen as occasional aberrations when a person changes track, stepping from one ladder to another. The use of the phrase 'career trajectory' (e.g. in Banks *et al.*, 1992) implies this metaphor, whilst a technically rational view of decision making assumes that the decision maker can predict the direction of the 'ladder' they are choosing.

The other metaphor for career development, according to Strauss, is that of cooking an egg. Whether we poach it, fry it, boil it or scramble it, it will always be recognisably an egg. This metaphor is seen in studies which emphasise the segmented nature of career progression due to factors such as class, gender or ethnicity. Working-class males, let us say, can develop in a variety of ways, but their central 'working-class maleness' will always allow the expert outsider to predict the range of opportunities and types of trajectory that they will follow. Though such patterns are a reality in many societies, it is a fallacy to apply models based on the explanation of patterns in large populations to the interpretation of the actions of single individuals.

At the individual level, Strauss (1962) claims that neither the ladder nor the egg metaphor for career development gives an appropriate explanation, for 'neither metaphor captures the open-ended, tentative, exploratory, hypothetical, problematical, devious, changeable, and only partly unified character of human courses of action' (p. 65).

He goes on to talk about career development as a series of 'turning points': '... these points in development occur when an individual has to take stock, to re-evaluate, revise, resee, and rejudge' (p. 71). Strauss claims that turning points are found in all parts of our lives, including job or career. In many careers there is a predetermined structure to these turning points, some of which involve formalised status-passage. However, even within organisations where official structures resemble ladder-like trajectories, many individuals fail to match the predetermined norms. He describes problems of pacing and timing, and of mismatch between personal motivations and official structures.

In other life course or life history studies, similar notions of turning points are often used. Denzin (1989) calls them 'epiphanies'. Working in Finland, Antikainen *et al.* (1995) talk about life-changing learning events, whilst Alheit (1994), writing about youth unemployment in Germany, talks of 'biographical discontinuity'. The central idea is the same. At a turning point, which may be of short duration or extend over a period of time, and which may be recognised at the time or only with hindsight, a person goes through a transformation of identity. The stories presented earlier can be understood in this way, and turning points are when the young people make significant, pragmatically rational, career decisions.

Within these stories we identified three different types of turning point, classified by cause. Firstly, they can be structural. The presence and timing of such turning points are largely determined by structural patterns of life course that are built in to the society where the person lives. Two examples are fixed ages for retirement and the ending of compulsory education. All young people in England and Wales are forced to consider their futures at the age of 16+. They have to decide whether to leave full-time education or not, what type of course to follow and/or what type of job they want to get. The move from compulsory schooling need not always involve a transformation of identity and is not a significant turning point for everyone. However, even those who decide to continue in full-time education face change. Both school sixth forms and FE colleges make much of the differences between post- and pre-16 student identities. A significant feature of structural turning points is that they occur at predictable times in the life course.

Another type of turning point occurs when young people encounter external factors beyond their control, which force a reconsideration of their future. Often such forced turning points are unexpected and they can be traumatic. Helen was forced into a turning point when her garage employer made her redundant. Though she tried to continue as a car body sprayer for a few weeks, she was eventually forced to take a very different job in a record shop. If we look beyond the transition to work, bereavement, acute physical injury, an external change in the conditions of work as well as redundancy are all examples of situations that can result in a forced turning point and changed identity for the individual concerned. Other turning points are largely self-initiated. Laura chose to give up her training placement in a nursery school and her involvement in the Training Credits scheme, and become someone rather different. More generally, such decisions as to get married, to set up home alone, to retire early or to change career are sometimes self-initiated. Many turning points do not fall neatly into one of these three categories, being caused by a combination of factors. If Becky fails to pass her dentistry examinations, she might change career through a combination of a structural cause (the ending of her training entitlement) and forced external circumstances (if her employer refuses to keep her on). All the experiences of our sample could be classified by one or other of these three types of turning point, either singly or in combination, though we are not claiming that there can be no others.

Turning points are not always predictable, either in timing or effect. Take the example of David. Throughout our study, his career had continued along a linear path, close to that which might be predicted by the ladder metaphor. His relatively minor transformations of identity had been entirely structural, as he changed from school pupil to trainee farm worker, and from trainee farm worker to full-time agricultural student. However, we have no way of knowing how long his career will continue uninterrupted. He might fail future examinations, or decide he is fed up with full-time study. He might fail to get a job that he likes in farming and move into something else. Neither he nor the most expert outsider can possibly know.

All conceptual models possess limitations, and the notion of 'turning points' is no exception. There are two pitfalls for those adopting too rigid a view of the concept. Firstly, the identification and nature of a turning point is partly a consequence of scale and distance. Thus, we have described Helen as going though two turning points, from school pupil to apprentice car body sprayer and from that to shop assistant. However, if she looks back on her life from, say, retirement age, both may be seen as part of one larger turning point, the whole of which was not visible at the time of our study. It may be that patterns of turning points and routines appear at any scale, but those that seem significant for the life course as a whole may be different from those that are of importance within a small segment of it. Secondly, it is likely that the impact of turning points on personal identity vary in nature. For example, Alheit (1994) suggests that the loss of work may be different in kind from the death of a close relative.

Turning points are interspersed by periods of routine. By 'routine' we mean the periods of our lives when nothing dramatic happens. One, we would claim mistaken, view of the Straussian model of turning points is that during routine periods transformation does not happen. We believe that things are more subtle than that. From our data it appears that turning points are inseparable from the routines that follow and precede them. The experiences of our sample revealed three different types of routine.

Firstly, some routines are confirmatory. That is, they reinforce a career decision already made so that the new identity develops broadly in the way in which the subject hoped and intended. David's experiences as student and trainee all confirmed his identity as a prospective farm manager, whilst all Alison's experiences confirmed her identity working with horses. Such confirmatory routines are part of the ongoing development of identity and, in such cases, the divide between routine and turning point becomes largely arbitrary. Whilst a routine continues to be confirmatory, self-initiated turning points are unlikely, except in the circumstance where a transformation is sought within the established career path, such as Alison's decision to continue her training at a different stables.

The second type of routine is contradictory. This time the person's experiences undermine the original decision, as he or she becomes dissatisfied and either begins to regret the original change or decides that the current experience is no longer adequate or appropriate. Laura went through two contradictory routines, firstly in a shop and later in a nursery school. In both cases, after a short confirmatory period, her experiences made her less and less satisfied with her lot. The result of such contradictory routines is to undermine the transformed identity acquired at the previous turning point. The result can be either a self-initiated further turning point, as in Laura's case, or the development of coping strategies, such as a focus on home or leisure interests, to deflect attention away from dissatisfaction with work. Elaine and Clive focused on the workplace, to cope with their contradictory experiences in off-the-job training. The same model can be applied to other forms of identity development, so that one way of understanding marriage is through the idea of confirming or contradictory routines following the original turning point of marriage or choosing to live together.

Finally, some routines are socialising. By this we mean that they confirm an identity that was not originally desired. Helen wanted to be a car body sprayer. When she first took the placement in a record shop she saw it as a stopgap and still intended to recommence her car spraying career as soon as the opportunity arose. However, by the end of our study she had become socialised into seeing herself as a shop assistant, intending to continue car spraying only as a hobby. In a similar way, Sam was being gradually socialised away from a career in computing as his engineering training progressed. Bates (1990) describes similar processes as a group of young women were socialised into the roles of carers for the elderly, and their original ambitions to work with children were cooled out.

When using this model of career development, based on routines and turning points, the term 'career trajectory' is inappropriate, because of its deterministic overtones. As an alternative, we prefer the notion of *careership*, though not in the sense intended by the CBI (1993). Careership conveys the idea that a career, i.e. the development of identity, is formed by the individual, constrained and/or enabled by the historical, socio-cultural and economic contexts within which that individual lives.

LIFESTYLES, CAREERSHIP AND IDENTITY

Thus far we have tried to place working career progression into the wider context of the life course. Now we turn to another dimension of career decision making, lifestyles and identities. In this book we have concentrated on the training experiences and working careers of the young people, but their lives are about much more than this. They are members of families, have friends, engage in leisure activities etc. Though, for research purposes, it was advantageous to retain a sharp focus, as Jones and Wallace (1992) emphasise, all these different facets of a person's existence inter-weave and impinge upon each other. The ways in which pragmatic career decision making is influenced, by this social context and culture, lie at the heart of our analysis.

For Giddens (1991), the self develops at least partly through a person's choices of lifestyle, of which we see choice of career as a part. For him, this is an increasingly important feature of what he calls 'late modernity':

> In the post-traditional order of modernity, and against the backdrop of new forms of mediated experience, self-identity becomes a reflexively organised behaviour. The reflexive project of the self, which consists in the sustaining of coherent, yet continuously revised, biographical narratives, takes place ... . In modern social life, the notion of lifestyle takes on a particular significance. The more tradition loses hold, ... the more individuals are forced to negotiate lifestyle choices among a diversity of options.
>
> (Giddens, 1991: 5)

It is difficult to do justice to the complexity of Giddens's position briefly. Our view, which may not be exactly his, is that 'lifestyle choices' are made in two over-lapping ways. One is through what he calls 'discursive consciousness' (1984) – that is, the reasons can be expressed and discussed with others. The other is intuitively, through what he calls 'practical consciousness' (1984). Practical consciousness is similar to the tacit knowledge described by Polanyi (1958) – we know something without being able to explain it. In the latter sense, some 'choices' of lifestyle, which includes a working career, are not conscious, discursive choices in the way in which choice is often understood in everyday language.

We would also interpret 'reflexivity' in two ways. The self changes reflexively as lifestyle choices are made. Also, actions of one individual are in a reflexive relationship with the culture and society within which that person lives, so that change in culture affects the individual and change in an individual contributes to change or continuity in the culture. Giddens is clear that choice for some is much more restricted than it is for others, due to cultural and structural inequalities:

> Modernity, one should not forget, produces *difference, exclusion* and *marginalisation*, ... Yet it would be a major error to suppose that the phenomena analysed in the book are confined in their impact to those in more privileged circumstances. 'Lifestyle' refers also to decisions taken and courses of action followed under conditions of severe material constraint.
>
> (Giddens, 1991:6, original emphasis)

For Bourdieu, individual action, belief and therefore choice must always be culturally and socially situated, for we are all born into a social setting. We cannot, therefore, act or think other than as a person of a particular gender, race, class, nation, etc., living in a particular period of time. The 'dispositions' that make up individual subjective perceptions are located within objective 'positions' or social structures. Within these social structures Bourdieu gives pre-eminence to social class but, at least to the extent that we use his ideas here, they might equally apply to gender or ethnicity. Despite giving primacy to social 'positions', like Giddens, he sees a reflexive relationship between them and dispositions. For Bourdieu, a key concept in understanding this relationship is 'habitus'. This concept encapsulates the ways in which a person's schematic beliefs, ideas and preferences are individually subjective but also inevitably permeated by the objective social structures and cultural or sub-cultural traditions in which that person lives. David was a white, working-class male, who lived and breathed farming because of his upbringing. This conditioned and became part of his developing habitus. Bourdieu describes habitus as:

> the strategy-generating principle enabling agents to cope with unforeseen and ever-changing situations ... a system of lasting and transposable dispositions which, integrating past experiences, functions at every moment as a matrix of perceptions, appreciations and actions and makes possible the achievement of infinitely diversified tasks.
>
> (1977: 72, 95; cited in Bourdieu and Wacquant,1992:18)

It is 'that system of dispositions which acts as a mediation between structures and practice' (Bourdieu, 1977: 487). Habitus involves more than perceptions or beliefs, for Bourdieu sees it as deriving from and being part of the whole person, including the body. David's habitus developed partly through the physical labour on the farm, which he enjoyed so much.

Within the limited focus of our analysis of careership, these aspects of Giddens's and Bourdieu's theorising appear complementary. The habitus of an individual acts as the means through which the lifestyle is pragmatically chosen, and it modifies as the lifestyle develops. Lifestyle and habitus are inseparably interrelated – one is the manifestation of the other. They evolve, partly through choice and partly through changing circumstances, as life progresses. They are constrained and enabled by the social and cultural conditions within which a person lives, which are, in turn, influenced by the actions of that individual. This process can be illustrated by and can help explain the career decisions made by the young people in our study, in the context of the routines and turning points of their careership. Before making this link explicit, we briefly explain why we find existing theories of career decision making inadequate.

THEORIES OF CAREER DECISION MAKING

Within the careers guidance field there are a range of theoretical views of decision making, summarised by Osipow (1990) and McNeill (1990). There is a lack of agreement about which of three predominant theories is of greatest utility, though Osipow (1990) claims they all contain strong similarities. The first is 'trait theory', which concentrates on matching personal qualities (traits) with different jobs. The second is a developmental theory, which concentrates on an evolutionary view of decision making, suggesting that there are stages of prior development that have to be progressed through before a 'proper' decision can be made. Finally, there is the 'social learning' theory, which emphasises the interrelated social and psychological factors involved in decision making, but through a now outdated version of behaviourism. None of these capture the complexity of the pragmatic process we have already illustrated and described.

There are two bodies of work which seriously question all these models. Roberts (1968, 1975) questions their focus on aspiration and choice, arguing that career decisions are mainly about 'opportunity structures'. Following Roberts, Law (1981) advocates a community interaction theory, which contains elements of both a psychological and sociological approach, overlapping both opportunity structures and personal development. However, he never fully articulates his idea. Baumgardner (1977, 1982) and Miller (1983) attack from a different direction, arguing that planned career decision making is a myth and that, in reality, 'happenstance' is a dominant characteristic. However, 'most of our current theories of career development were shaped in the 50s and 60s in an expanding economy' (Osipow, 1977:23), and there has been relatively little new thinking. Boreham and Arthur (1993) and Taylor (1992) examine the factors which influence career decision making, but do not directly address the ways in which decisions are made.

Aspects of pragmatic decision making, described in the previous chapter, have been identified before. Baumgardner (1977) upset the American guidance community by describing vocational planning as 'the great swindle'. He dismissed both what he calls the 'rational' and 'impulsive' ends of a decision-making continuum, arguing, very like us, that it always involves both. We have chosen not to use his terminology of 'non-rationality', for the decisions of our subjects contained rational elements, in what we have called a pragmatic way. Drawing on Baumgardner's work, Miller (1983) describes career decision making as governed by 'happenstance' (serendipity). However, he also underplays the rationality of pragmatic responses to such opportunities.

In explaining pragmatic rationality, it is necessary to refer back to habitus. The career decisions of the young people we interviewed can only be understood in terms of their own life histories, wherein habitus had evolved through interaction with significant others within the social structure and culture in which the subject has lived and is living. We are using 'culture' to describe the socially constructed and historically derived common base of knowledge, values and norms for action that people grow into and come to take as a natural way of life. In relation to such a view of culture, Clarke et al. (1981: 52–53) claim 'a culture includes the "maps of meanings" which makes things intelligible to its members. ... Culture is the way the social relations of a group are structured and shaped; but it is also the way those shapes are experienced, understood and interpreted'. We use habitus in a similar way, though we prefer horizons for action (see below) to 'maps of meanings'.

As we have shown, Giddens (1984) suggests we know through 'practical consciousness' and 'discursive consciousness'. The latter is grounded in the former. Both contribute to the development of habitus. Both types of consciousness can be seen as developing through schemata (Rumelhart, 1980; Howard, 1987). We all develop conceptual structures (schemata), which we use to filter information. Schemata both limit and enable understanding, by relating new information to existing understandings. Thus, we could say, Laura considered a range of jobs that are culturally associated with working-class females. This was partly because she had a schematic view of what sorts of jobs she could and wanted to do, developed through her own, working-class, female background. That background enabled her to choose these possible careers, but prevented her from considering others – such as being a plumber or a solicitor.

Work on situated cognition (Brown et al., 1989) suggests that what is learned is related to the context in which learning takes place and the activities being undertaken whilst it takes place. What is learned, therefore, is the outcome of an interaction between schemata, activity and situation, which results in a further development of habitus. This happens in periods of routine. Differences between the activities and situations of individuals contribute to variations of habitus between members of the same sub-culture, so that not all working-class females will choose the same jobs or even types of job. Helen could choose to work in a garage, because many details of her culture and life history were different from those of other young women in the study. Individuals make their own selections from the culture, both discursively and intuitively, as they choose their lifestyles. Though difficult to change fundamentally (Chinn and Brewer, 1993), the schemata which are part of habitus modify incrementally as new information is absorbed and new experiences or situations encountered, during periods of routine. Haugaard (1992) suggests that when schemata are challenged by accumulated or powerful anomalous experiences they may transform and transfers of knowledge between practical and discursive consciousness are likely. Thus a person's habitus can occasionally change radically, at what we have called a turning point.

The transformation at a turning point is grounded in previous experience. That is, the new present is created out of the past. However, Baert (1992) suggests that, when our view of the world changes, we reconstruct the past in our minds, to fit our current perceptions. That is, the past is retrospectively recreated out of the present, as what he calls 'the past for now'. Helen did this when, towards the end of our study, she described her previous attempt to become a professional car body sprayer as foolish. Laura also did it when she eventually dismissed Training Credits as irrelevant to her previous needs, claiming she would advise others to avoid them. Baert's notion of 'the past for now' adds an important dimension to the ways in which habitus can change, for it shows that though we evolve out of our past, it does not always keep us prisoner.

Differences in habitus influence the ways in which career choices are made as well as which options are considered. Willis (1977), argued that male working-class culture was more about collective solidarity than individual choice. There is evidence that young women from Moslem families are more likely to see career choice as being made by the family and in family interests, rather than by and for the individual (Siann and Knox, 1992). We have already summarised Gaskell's (1992) view that women are more likely than men to make decisions through the filter of domestic identity.

HORIZONS FOR ACTION AND SEGMENTED CAREER CHOICE

Young people make career decisions within their horizons for action, which incorporate externally located opportunities in the labour market as well as the dispositions of habitus. Perceptions of what might be available and what might be appropriate influence decisions, so that opportunities are simultaneously subjective and objective. Horizons for action are both enabling and restricting. Furthermore, opportunities are not just 'out there', waiting to be chosen. They can be created, for example as young people or their parents use local contacts to find a training placement. Through the habitus, horizons for action are often based on interpretations of the present made in the light of past experiences, as young people and their parents try to make sense of current labour market opportunities through experiences of past situations that no longer apply (Brown, 1987). In our study, many parents tried to make sense of Training Credits through their understanding of the previous YTS system.

The horizon for action for any individual is limited to a segment of the education and labour market, for no one considers the whole range of possible opportunities. We see such segments as changing and over-lapping, rather than mutually exclusive discrete boxes. In explaining the causes of such segmentation, Ashton *et al.* (1987) and Lee *et al.* (1990) focus on the labour market. Because of segmentation within it, young people only consider a limited range of jobs or careers. On the other hand, for many sociologists, divisions in personal perception derive directly from discrete sub-cultures, for example based on class, gender and ethnicity, which affect the types of job different groups are prepared to consider.

The concept of horizons for action explains segmentation by combining these employment structural and sub-cultural dimensions. The reason that Alison, for example, chose the typically female occupation of working with horses, is partly because the labour market is segmented and partly because her schematic perceptions of a suitable job, derived from her habitus in a working-class, female and horse-related culture, presented working with horses as a possible, desirable and suitable career. It is the interaction of the subjectivity of choice within a social sub-culture with the objectivity of job availability within a stratified and segmented labour market that helps explain the choice she and others made. Horizons for action enable the choice of some careers but prevent the choice of others. Either Clive or Sam might have had the skills, intelligence and personal qualities to work as a nanny with young children. But had this been the case, and we are not claiming that it was, their culturally grounded horizons for action meant that, as working-class lads, they would not have considered such a stereotypically female occupation as a possible choice. It would lie outside their horizons of action.

Tait (1993: 41), writing about youth, claims that sub-cultural theories are inadequate, because they are 'essentially normative, since it is through the construction and demarcation of pathologies (such as "streetkids") that social, legal, psychological and medical norms of normality are extrapolated'. In other words, the place of the individual is lost in talk of artificially created and damaging stereotypically homogeneous groups.

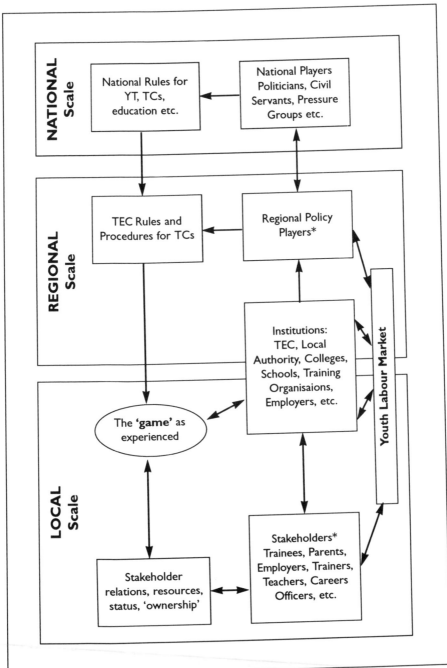

Figure 9.2 The Training Credits Field. The whole lies within and interacts with the historical, cultural, social and economic context. *Some of these people may be the same

Rather, he argues, segmentation arises out of government driven mechanisms of social formation. This happens when 'a diverse group of individuals are positioned as a discreet entity, seemingly with specific codes of behaviour and ways of relating to the outside world' (Tait, 1993: 41). These categories increasingly colour the way in which we see and interpret society, and are reinforced by sub-cultural analyses, which help create the very divisions they claim to identify. Such divisions render invisible personal attributes or dispositions which do not fit the stereotypes. Brown (1987) and Okano (1993) put it differently, claiming that variations within groups are as important as differences between them, and that such within-group differences are rendered invisible by many sub-cultural studies, which treat, say, all white working-class males as the same. However, neither Brown nor Okano deny the importance of those larger, class-based sub-cultural groupings, and neither do we.

Frykholm and Nitzler (1993) argue that patterns of schooling in Sweden contribute to what we call segmentation of horizons for action, in ways that appear to us to accommodate some elements of both Tait's analysis and sub-cultural theories, despite their apparent incompatibility. Frykholm and Nitzler argue that different vocational courses are characterised by what they call different *notions*. In our terms, 'notions' are over-arching schemata, shared by course tutors, students and others, which become part of the habitus of those on the course. These notions, for example of appropriate ways of studying and of appropriate future careers, develop differently on different vocational tracks, through the mutual reinforcement of expectations of teachers, pupils and, we presume, parents, employers and other members of society. These separate tracks can be seen as being created by official processes of curriculum division, but draw on and reinforce the sub-culturally derived habituses of people involved [8]. Such a view is consistent with horizons for action and the interactive, reflexive processes which contribute to their development. What Frykholm and Nitzler describe is one example of what we call a routine, as young people are confirmed or socialised into a particular educational identity, influencing and influenced by their habituses and horizons for action.

Thus far we have concentrated on careership and career choices from the perspective of the individual person. However, even a cursory glance through the stories in this book will show that choices were both constrained and enabled by interactions with other stakeholders. It is necessary now to widen our focus and examine these interactions, which form the third dimension of career decision making, shown in Figure 9.1.

THE TRAINING CREDITS FIELD AND THE 'GAME' OF YOUTH TRAINING

To examine such interactions it is helpful to use Bourdieu's concept of *field* (Bourdieu, 1984, 1993). Although he sometimes talks of a field as a market, more often he uses the analogy of a game. In the Training Credit 'game' stakeholders are players but different players are striving to achieve different ends. For example, a young person may want training that leads to an enjoyable job, an employer may want to use a trainee as part of running a profitable business, whilst a training provider may want to ensure viable groups on a training programme. Though there are official rules, 'it is the state of the relations of force between players that defines the structure of the field' (Bourdieu, in Bourdieu and Wacquant, 1992: 99).

Figure 9.2 summarises the Training Credit field. It is embedded in a wider context of historical, cultural, social and economic factors which have been omitted for simplicity. There are three levels of 'play'. At the national level, 'rules' are drawn up and periodically changed which affect the other levels. Training Credit regulations, legislation and orders for educational institutions, the careers service, TECs and youth employment are all important, as are the restrictions on social security payments to those under 18 (Jones and Wallace, 1992). The regional level is determined by TEC boundaries. The rules for Training Credits were drawn up separately by each TEC, influenced by pressure groups in the context of national regulations. Both individuals and institutions are important, but our research did not examine the role of institutions, so we can merely acknowledge their significance.

Our fieldwork focused on the local level, in the stakeholder networks we followed. The data suggest that the way in which Training Credits worked on the ground depended on a complex pattern of stakeholder relations and their various reactions to the official regulations, filtered down from the national and regional levels and experienced in the local context.

Each stakeholder (see Chapter 2) holds resources of different types. The value of these resources is specific to the situation in the 'game' and resources that are positive in one situation could be negative or neutral in others (Okano, 1993). The local contacts of parents were often positive resources for young people, which were used to get a placement. Helen, Clive and Sam were taken on because employers knew their families. Elaine's parents were instrumental in persuading her to take a job with a large employer, which they felt gave better training and job security. Such resources are constraining as well as enabling, for other opportunities were not explored because they lay beyond the perceived horizons for action.

Many of the other stakeholders had more resources than the young people. Careers officers had professional status and detailed knowledge of VET systems and the local labour market. Employers could hire and fire, determine whether or not time could be taken for off-the-job training and specify that training would be done with a favoured training organisation. Trainers had a detailed knowledge of the Training Credit system, second only to TEC officials. They had considerable control over access to placements because of their links with employers.

Young people also have resources and sometimes the Training Credit facilitated their use. However, possession of a credit made little difference to the existing resource balance. Elaine chose her training after discussions with her employer, who allowed her to select a programme that would not have been his choice. Though her choice was facilitated by the credit, it was the employer's decision not to exercise power that allowed her to choose, together with her self-confidence. Laura lacked confidence and some social skills. She did well when given pastoral support on transition training. In the subsequent placement things went wrong, partly because the same level of pastoral support could not be provided and the Training Credit was no substitute. She did, however, demonstrate the power to withdraw from the scheme.

These players, through their perceptions and interactions, define the rules of the Training Credits game in practice. Thus, relations between trainer, employer, trainee and parent negated the intended customer market for training. It is the playing of the game, with its complex interactions, negotiations and conflicts based on unequal resources, that determines the actual career destination of the young people. The dispositions within habitus and the pragmatically rational choices of young people are part of this wider, more complex process. It is through the game, as well as through the evolving habitus of individuals, that structural inequalities are produced and reproduced.

CAREERSHIP, STRUCTURAL INEQUALITIES AND SOCIAL CHANGE

The current policy obsession with expanding the skills and qualifications of *individuals* so that employers have a skilled workforce to compete in international markets, means that issues of social inequality have been sidelined. But the evidence of deep-seated inequalities in the youth labour market in Britain, linked to structural divisions of class, gender and ethnicity, is overwhelming and was summarised in Chapter 1. Though we have been critical of these studies for an implicit determinism, our work does nothing to challenge the patterns described and is wholly congruent with them. Our model of careership presents a view of the mechanisms by which such inequalities are perpetuated, whilst recognising scope for individual choice and social change.

Social structure permeates the transition to work in several different ways. Though beyond the scope of this study, the process of schooling may be different for different sub-cultural groupings (Willis, 1977; Brown, 1987; Gaskell, 1992; Okano, 1993). Through the development of habitus, individual perceptions and career choices and even the way in which decisions are made are inseparable from their culture, which in turn is related to social structure. Structural/cultural factors influence the resources that are available to young people and their allies in the Training Credits field. Structural/cultural factors permeate the networks young people can access, which may help find a job or a training place. Finally, structural/cultural factors influence the perceptions of other stakeholders, such as employers and training providers, whose views of what might be an appropriate opening for X and what sort of young person is suitable for position Y derive from their own habituses. The whole of the transition to work is permeated by structural and cultural factors. Consequently, the belief in largely free individual choice, upon which much current policy is based, is, therefore, a myth that is either breathtakingly naive or sinister.

However, though structural influences are all-pervading, individuals can and do make differing choices. Habitus differs from individual to individual within any given sub-group, because the detail of their life histories and the social situations in which they are located differ. Furthermore, their situations and habituses provide a range of options within horizons for action – horizons that are wider for some than for others. We have described young people as 'choosing' jobs or training places from the range of opportunities within their horizons for action, which in turn are created by a combination of subjective perception and objective availability

Within the training field, young people and their allies are not without resources, though some have more than others. They can negotiate, they can struggle for what they want and sometimes they succeed. Furthermore, as Okano (1993) points out, resources vary according to context. Helen's love of cars and painting was a positive resource in getting a garage placement, but a negative resource when she openly declared it whilst trying to get shop work the first time. In other circumstances, such as when she tried for shop placements without mentioning these interests and ambitions, they were completely unimportant. Through using their resources, many of our sample of young people were happy with their lot, and several were in careers they had positively sought. They were neither 'cultural dopes' nor victims.

The relationship between social structure and social change is one of the perennial unsolved and possibly unsolvable questions facing sociology. We are not claiming to have succeeded in providing an answer, and we have little to say about how individual actions can contribute to structural change. However, we would claim to have gone some way to answering those critics of Bourdieu who claim that his use of habitus is inherently deterministic (Jenkins, 1992).

We have argued that individual change can take place within all-pervading social structures in the following ways. Firstly, though socio-culturally derived, habitus gradually evolves during periods of routine. Though one variant is to confirm existing dispositions, the other two allow for change, through what we have called contradiction or socialisation. Secondly, habitus can be transformed at personal turning points, so that the individual emerges in ways that are partly unpredictable. Part of this transformation process involves the recreation of the past, thus reinforcing the new rather than old dispositions (Baert, 1992). Thirdly, we have demonstrated that routines and turning points are causally inter-linked, so that (i) a turning point may originate in a contradictory routine, in a structural point in the life course or in a significant external event;and (ii) that a turning point leads to either a confirming, socialising or contradictory routine in its turn.

Our analysis has implications for policy directed towards lessening inequalities in the labour market, but we have only space to touch on them briefly. The mechanisms for choice and change that we have identified provide hope that things can be done to help members of disadvantaged groups, given that rare combination of understanding, will and resources. But the the current technicist policies are at best a dangerous distraction from such an objective, despite the seductive rhetoric about empowerment through vouchers in markets. It may be helpful to explore ways of enhancing the actions and strengthening the resources of disadvantaged young people in the existing processes that they adopt. We should concentrate on enhancing pragmatically rational decision making, rather than trying vainly to substitute an unrealistic technical alternative. As Miller (1983) suggests, careers guidance should alert young people to what he calls the 'happenstance' of job finding and young people should be helped in the networking process. There should be further investigation of ways to increase the resources available to young people from socially disadvantaged groups in the training field.

Above all, we must recognise that inequalities will not be lessened by paying attention primarily to the young people themselves. Changes are needed to job availability, employer recruitment patterns, workplace cultures and labour market structures. As Ashton (1993:21) writes, 'whether young people obtain a job, and what kind of job they obtain, depends not so much on their efforts as the decisions of the business elite and the success of governments in delivering high levels of economic performance'. Current training and labour market policies in Britain seem to ignore this important truth, and the current acceptance of permanently high levels of 'structural' unemployment with steady increases in part-time and short-term contract working (ED 1994), do not bode well for the immediate future.

Epilogue:
The Problem with Endings

'It is difficult to know where to end, when to stop reflecting on the clues uncovered in the last story, when to stop pointing out one more contradictory juxtaposition in the situation and the selves portrayed, and when to stop writing.'

(Ellis, 1995:162)

We, like Ellis, are having trouble with ending. Not least of these problems is the artificial neatness and abstractness of the previous chapter. In presenting our theoretical thinking, for the sake of clarity we have been forced into a careful packaging of ideas that may unintentionally imply a completeness and closure that we do not feel and that does less than justice to the richness, contradiction and complexity of the stories which we presented earlier.

In some ways, we would have liked to let the stories 'speak for themselves', but to do that would have been at least partly disingenuous. In constructing those stories we have used tiny extracts of 196 taped interviews. In order to make the stories readable, we have pruned down and edited a vast mass of available data. In doing that we have inevitably chosen to highlight some things more than others. As is the case in all such research, the resulting text is a construction, arising from our own interpretations of what was said to us. Chapter 8 and especially 9, therefore, serve a dual purpose in the book. They share with you, as reader, the current extent of our own thinking and analysis around some of the issues raised by the stories, in the hope that we have contributed some new ways of seeing old problems. Secondly, they allow you to understand the conceptual frameworks which influenced our story editing, causing us to concentrate on some issues whilst ignoring others.

One of our purposes in writing this epilogue is to remind ourselves and others that our work has an ongoing, if irregular, spiral structure. The data feeds our developing thinking which in turn changes the ways in which we see the data. Each time the spiral comes round, the picture we hold of the issues considered moves and changes. This presents another 'ending' problem, for that spiralling will continue once this manuscript has been printed. In this book we can only present a snapshot, fixed in two times – 1992–93 when our fieldwork was done, and 1995 when the bulk of the manuscript was written.

Another way of looking at the problem of endings, is to contrast the dialectical spiral of the research and writing process with the inevitably linear structure of a book. In turning one into the other we faced several possible choices. A common solution would have been to blend the stories and the analysis as the text advanced. We chose not to do this, for we believe that, had we done so, the narrative strength of the stories and the conceptual clarity of our thinking could both have been compromised. Furthermore, to a greater extent than was the case anyway, the stories would have become subservient to the theoretical development, rendering the complexity of the lives of our subjects less and less visible. Once we had decided to largely separate stories from analysis, we faced the problem of sequencing. The analysis only makes sense once the stories are known, but the stories can only be understood once the analysis has been appreciated. We chose to present the stories first because we hoped, by so doing, to allow them to stand partly on their own, to allow you to engage more directly with the lives they were based upon. Perhaps naively, we would now hope that, having read our analysis, you will find it worthwhile to revisit some or all of the stories and will thus see them and our conceptual constructions in a different light.

Writing the lives of others is always difficult. Richardson (1990:39) describes some of the problems better than we could:

'Deciding how to present voices and lives is a continuous problem for qualitative writers. Because we use the voices and experiences of the people we study, both for their own sake and as evidence of our credibility, we are constantly making writerly decisions about who gets to say what and how often in the text, and who the narrator talks about, how and how often. How do you write the voices and lives of interviewees and informants so that both literary and scientific writing criteria are met? This is not an either/or problem. Qualitative books are often critiqued as bad science, not because they necessarily are, but because the literary decisions regarding the presentation of lives is busily undermining the work's credibility.'

In trying to balance these two things we have gone for a mixed style of presentation. As was explained in the prologue, in the longer stories we minimised our authorial presence and incorporated quotations into continuous prose. This style was adopted in the hope that the narrative would flow, and allow you to engage with the lived experiences of our subjects, and make your own interpretations and evaluations from your own unique vantage points (Barone, 1995). However, we remain uncomfortable about writing ourselves out of these stories. As Sparkes (1995:165) writes:

'an author needs to be written into, and not out of, the text. This is an important issue because, although many qualitative researchers seem happy to write narratives that situate the subjects of inquiry in culturally and historically specific locations, these researchers seem less assured about recognising that they as authors also write from specific historical and cultural locations, and are infused by the social categories to which they belong.'

To remind readers of our authorial presence, as well as to do justice to what Richardson would call our 'science', we have deliberately mixed writing styles, hopefully managing to avoid irritating discontinuities. Thus, in chapters other than 2, 3 and 4 we used indented quotations, and raised the presence of the authors in the text. We have also used the pronoun 'we' on frequent occasions, rather than the once universal distortion of presenting what are our views and constructs as somehow definitive and value free, through the use of the third person and passive tenses. In the prologue and this epilogue, we changed style once more, using what Van Maanen (1988) calls a confessional tale, revealing some of the authorial processes and decision making which many writers prefer to conceal. We have not done this in an attempt to justify those decisions, but to reveal to you what they were, so you are in a better position to judge what effect they have had on the text.

Of all the stakeholder groups we had interviewed, we gave primacy to the voices and lives of the trainees. In doing so we merely reproduced the bias in the original research design (see Chapter 1), for other stakeholders were selected because they were involved with the sample trainees and not vice versa. But there was more to the decision than this. Despite the abundance of literature about young people's transitions from school to work, in almost all of them, the voices of those young people are either amalgamated into collective stories or told largely in the words of the researcher. We wanted, within the authorial constraints already discussed, to give voice to this largely silent group of relatively disadvantaged youth, where the rhetoric of empowerment through vouchers was so much at odds with their total lack of involvement in any of the planning and decision making for the Training Credits scheme. However, as Sparkes (1995) once more makes clear, 'giving voice' to such groups is neither easy nor straightforward:

'If all stories were given the same valence, credibility, and weight, the politics of the text would seem democratic and egalitarian. However, the incorporation of so many voices would threaten to vitiate the impact of any specific voice, and the story of the event would threaten to consume the individual story. In this situation ... the potential benefits of polyphonic interpretation give way before a *commodified cacophony* in which the reader ends up only with a kind of tourist experience.'

(p. 167, original emphasis)

Our hope is that, by strongly editing the stories, we have avoided such a cacophony. In deciding which stories to emphasise, we looked at issues of interest to us. It is no coincidence that Laura and Helen, given a full chapter each, went through the most dramatic and hopefully gripping experiences of all our subjects. They also best exemplify our careership model in its multi-faceted entirety. Elaine, Alison, Clive and Becky we chose as representing dramatic episodes which, in turn, illustrate key facets of the ideas we were developing. The remaining four were given less detail, because their training careers had been less dramatic than the rest.

In ending this ending to the book, we would like to raise a few questions which are for others to answer. We hope that, in Richardson's words, we have satisfactorily balanced science with narrative. Have we? Our intention was to draw readers into our stories, so that they could share something of the triumphs and tears of the young people we spoke to. Did we manage to involve you? Did those stories give insight into the lives of these young people as they went through a key period in their lives? Has our theoretical analysis added to the understanding of career decision making, the transition to work, education and training markets and the relationship between individual agency and structural/cultural contexts? Perhaps above all, have we stimulated you to rethink some of the issues raised, even if only through what appear to be flaws and/or omissions in our writing? It is against questions such as these that we would hope the quality of this book will ultimately be judged.

Appendix: Glossary of Acronyms

BHS	British Horse Society
BTEC	Business and Technician Education Council
CBI	Confederation of British Industry
CGAP	Careers Guidance Action Plan
CV	Curriculum Vitae
DSA	Dental Surgery Assistant
ESRC	Economic and Social Research Council
FE	Further Education
GCSE	General Certificate of Secondary Education
GNVQ	General National Vocational Qualification
HGV	Heavy Goods vehicle
ILEX	Institute of Legal Executives
LEA	Local Education Authority
MSC	Manpower Services Commission
NNEB	Nursery Nursing Education Board
NTETS	National Targets for Education and Training
NTI	New Training Initiative
NVQ	National Vocational Qualification
RAC	Royal Automobile Club
RSA	Royal Society of Arts
TEC	Training and Enterprise Council
TEED	Training, Enterprise and Employment Directorate
TQM	Total Quality Management
TUC	Trades Union Congress
VET	Vocational Education and Training
YT	Youth Training
YTS	Youth Training Scheme

Notes

1. A glossary of acronyms used is given in the appendix.
2. Since our fieldwork was completed, the Employment Department has been merged with the Department for Education, into the new Department for Education and Employment. TEED no longer exists, having been swallowed up by the new organisational structures of the new, merged Department.
3. In the summer of 1993, part-way through our study, the name was changed from Training Credits to Youth Credits. To increase the confusion, each TEC chose its own name for the initiative, whilst in Scotland it is universally called Skill Seekers. We have retained the term Training Credits here, because that is what our interviewees called the scheme, and the name still has widespread currency.
4. Year 11 is the final year of compulsory schooling, in Britain. By the end of Year 11, most pupils are 16 years of age.
5. In this section, the type of pupil quoted is indicated by a symbol in brackets. f = female, m = male, 6 = sixth former (either Year 12 or Year 13).
6. Since we interviewed, the careers service and most schools targeted more careers guidance into the sixth form.
7. Considerable changes to the NVQ system were proposed in the Beaumont Report (Beaumont, 1996), just as this book was going to press. Some of the problems discussed here may be ameliorated if those reforms are introduced. This is not the place to discuss those recommendations in detail, but a preliminary reading suggests that they do not go far enough.
8. The various chapters in Bates and Riseborough (1993) illustrate graphically the different notions held in different parts of post-16 education and training in Britain, though none of the authors use the term 'notion'. Like Frykholm and Nitzler, these authors do not devote much attention to individual differences within groups holding to a group notion.

References

Ainley, P. and Corney, M. (1990) *Training for the Future: The Rise and Fall of the Manpower Services Commission*. London: Cassell.

Alheit, P. (1994) *Taking the Knocks: Youth Unemployment and Biography – A Qualitative Analysis*. London: Cassell.

Antikainen, A., Houtsonen, J., Huotelin, H. and Kaupilla, J. (1995) *In Search of the Meaning of Education. Life Histories of Learning in Finland*. Joensuu: Joensuu University Press.

Ashton, D. (1993) 'Understanding Change in Youth Labour Markets: A Conceptual Framework', *British Journal of Education and Work*, 6 (3), 5–23.

Ashton, D.N. and Field, D. (1976) *Young Workers*. London: Hutchinson.

Ashton, D.N., Maguire, M.J. and Spilsbury, M. (1987) 'Labour Market Segregation and the Structure of the Youth Labour Market'. In Brown, P. and Ashton, D.N. (eds) *Education, Unemployment and Labour Markets*. Lewes: Falmer Press.

Atkinson, J.S. and Meager, N. (1991) 'Changing Working Patterns: How Companies Achieve Flexibility to Meet New Needs'. In Esland, G. (ed.) *Education, Training and Employment. Volume 1: Educated Labour – the Changing Basis of Industrial Demand*. Wokingham: Addison-Wesley.

Avis, J., Bloomer, M., Esland, G., Gleeson, D. and Hodkinson, P. (1996) *Knowledge and Nationhood: Education, Politics and Work*. London: Cassell (in press).

Baert, P. (1992) *Time, Self and Social Being*. Aldershot: Avebury.

Ball, C. (1991) *Learning Pays: The Role of Post-compulsory Education and Training*. London: Royal Society of Arts.

Banks, M., Bates, I., Breakwell, G., Bynner, J., Elmer, N., Jamieson, L. and Roberts, K. (1992) *Careers and Identities: Adolescent Attitudes to Employment, Training and Education, their Home Life, Leisure and Politics*. Milton Keynes: Open University Press.

Barone, T. (1995) 'Persuasive writings, vigilant readings, and reconstructed characters: the paradox of trust in educational storytelling.' In Hatch, A. and Wisniewski, R. (eds) *Life History and Narrative*. Lewes: Falmer Press.

Bates, I. (1990) 'No Bleeding, Whining Minnies', *British Journal of Education and Work*, 3 (2), 91–110.

Bates, I. (1993) 'A Job which is 'Right for Me?' In Bates, I. and Riseborough, G. (eds) *Youth and Inequality*. Buckingham: Open University Press.

Bates, I. and Riseborough, G. (1993) (eds) *Youth and Inequality*. Buckingham: Open University Press.

Baumgardner, S.R. (1977) 'Vocational Planning: the Great Swindle', *Personnel and Guidance Journal*, 5 (6), 17–22.

Baumgardner, S.R. (1982) 'Coping with Disillusionment, Abstract Images and Uncertainty in Career Decision Making', *Personnel and Guidance Journal*, 6(1), 213–217.

Beaumont, G. (1996) *Review of 100 NVQs and SVQs*. London: NCVQ.

Bennett, R.J., Glennester, H. and Nevison, D. (1992) *Learning Should Pay*. Poole: BP Educational Service.

Bennett, R.J., Wicks, P. and McCoshan, A. (1994) *Local Empowerment and Business Services: Britain's Experiment with Training and Enterprise Councils*. London: UCL Press.

Blackman, S. (1987) 'The Labour Market in School: New Vocationalism and Issues of

Socially Ascribed Discrimination'. In Brown, P and Ashton, D.N. (eds) *Education, Unemployment and Labour Markets*. Lewes: Falmer Press.

Boreham, N.C. and Arthur, T.A.A. (1993) *Information Requirements in Occupational Decision Making*. Research Series, No.8. London: Employment Department.

Bourdieu, P. (1977) 'Cultural Reproduction and Social Reproduction'. In Karabel, J. and Halsey, A.H. (eds) *Power and Ideology in Education*. Oxford: Oxford University Press.

Bourdieu, P. (1984) *Distinction: A Social Critique of the Judgment of Taste*. London: Routledge and Keegan Paul.

Bourdieu, P. (1993) *Sociology in Question*. London: Sage.

Bourdieu, P. and Wacquant, L.J.D. (1992) *An Invitation to Reflexive Sociology*. Cambridge: Polity Press.

Brown, A. and Evans, K. (1994) 'Changing the Training Culture: Lessons from Anglo-German Comparisons of Vocational Education and Training', *British Journal of Education and Work*, 7 (2), 5–16.

Brown, J.S., Collins, A. and Duguid, P. (1989) 'Situated Cognition and the Culture of Learning', *Educational Researcher*, 18 (1), 32–42.

Brown, P. (1987) *Schooling and Ordinary Kids: Inequality, Unemployment and the New Vocationalism*. London: Tavistock Publications.

Brown, P. and Lauder, H. (1992) 'Education, Economy and Society: an introduction to a new agenda'. In Brown, P. and Lauder, H. (eds) *Education for Economic Survival*. London: Routledge.

Bynner, J. and Roberts, K. (1991) (eds) *Youth and Work: Transition to Employment in England and Germany*. London: Anglo-German Foundation.

CBI (1989) *Towards a Skills Revolution*. Report of the Vocational Education and Training Task Force. London: Confederation of British Industry.

CBI (1993) *Routes for Success – Careership: A Strategy for all 16–19 Year Old Learning*. London: Confederation of British Industry.

Chinn, C.A. and Brewer, W.F. (1993) 'The Role of anomalous Data in Knowledge Acquisition: A Theoretical Framework and Implications for Science Instruction', *Review of Educational Research, 63* (1), 1–49.

Clarke, J., Hall, S., Jefferson, T. and Roberts, B. (1981) 'Subcultures, cultures and class'. In Bennet, T., Martin, G., Mercer, C. and Wallacott, J. (eds) *Culture, Ideology and Social Process*. London: Batsford.

Coffield, F. (1990) 'From the decade of the enterprise culture to the decade of the TECs', *British Journal of Education and Work*, 4 (1), 59–78.

Coopers & Lybrand Deloitte (1992) *Training Credits Evaluation: National Coordinator's Report of the 11 Case Studies*. London: Employment Department Mimeo.

Cross, M. and Wrench, J. (1991) 'Racial Inequality on YTS: Careers Service or Disservice?' *British Journal of Education and Work*, 4 (3), 5–24.

Davies, H. (1992) *Fighting Leviathan: Building Social Markets that Work*. London: The Social Market Foundation.

Denzin, N. (1989) *Interpretive Biography*, Qualitative Research Methods Series, 17. London: Sage.

DfEE (1996) *Lifetime Learning : A Consultation Document*. Sheffield: Department for Education and Employment.

Driver, R., Asoko, H., Leach, J., Mortimer, E. and Scott, P. (1994) 'Constructing Scientific Knowledge in the Classroom', *Educational Researcher, 23* (7), 4–12.

ED (Employment Department) (1990) *Training Credits for Young People: A Prospectus*. Sheffield: Employment Department.

ED (1992) *Progress: Training Credits, A Report on the First Twelve Months.* Sheffield: Employment Department.

ED (1993) *Assessing the Effects of First Phase Training Credits,* Quality assurance Study No 15. Sheffield: Employment Department.

ED (1994) *Labour Market and Skill Trends, 1995/6.* Nottingham: Skills Enterprise Network, Employment Department.

ED/DES (1981) *A New Training Initiative: A Programme for Action.* London: HMSO.

ED/DES (1991) *Education and Training for the 21st Century.* London: HMSO.

Ellis, C. (1995) 'On the other side of the fence: seeing black and white in a small town', *Qualitative Inquiry,* 1 (2), 147–167.

Elster, J. (1986) *Rational Choice.* Oxford: Blackwell.

Evans, B. (1992) *The Politics of The Training Market: from Manpower Services Commission to Training and Enterprise Councils.* London: Routledge.

Field, J. (1995) 'Reality Testing in the workplace. Are NVQs Employment Led?' In Hodkinson, P. and Issitt, M. (eds) *The Challenge of Competence: Professionalism in Vocational Education and Training.* London: Cassell.

Finegold, D. (1991) 'Institutional Incentives and Skill Creation: Preconditions for a High Skill Equilibrium'. In Ryan, P. (ed.) *International Comparisons of Vocational Education and Training for Intermediate Skills.* Lewes: Falmer Press.

Finegold, D. and Soskice, D. (1991) 'The Failure of Training in Britain: analysis and prescription'. In Esland, G. (ed.) *Education, Training and Employment, Volume 1: Educated Labour – The Changing Basis of Industrial Demand.* Wokingham: Addison-Wesley.

Frykholm, C. and Nitzler, R. (1993) 'Working life as pedagogical discourse: empirical studies of vocational and career education based on theories of Bourdieu and Bernstein', *Journal of Curriculum Studies,* 25 (5), 433–444.

Fullan, M. (1991) *The New Meaning of Educational Change.* London: Cassell.

Furlong, A. (1992) *Growing Up in a Classless Society? School to Work Transitions.* Edinburgh: Edinburgh University Press.

Gaskell, J. (1992) *Gender Matters from School to Work.* Buckingham: Open University Press.

Gibson, R. (1986) *Critical Theory and Education.* London: Hodder and Stoughton.

Giddens, A. (1984) *The Constitution of Society: Outline of the Theory of Structuration.* Cambridge: Polity Press.

Giddens, A. (1991) *Modernity and Self-Identity: Self and Society in the Late Modern Age.* Cambridge: Polity Press.

Gleeson, D. (1993) 'Legislating for change: Missed Opportunities in the Further and Higher Education Act', *British Journal of Education and Work,* 6 (2), 29–40.

Gleeson, D. and Hodkinson, P. (1995) 'Ideology and Curriculum Policy: GNVQ and Mass Post-Compulsory Education in England and Wales', *British Journal of Education and Work,* 8 (3), 5–19.

Green, A. and Steedman, H. (1993) *Educational Provision, Educational Attainment and the Needs of Industry: A Review of the Research for Germany, France, Japan, the USA and Britain.* Report No. 5. London: National Institute of Economic and Social Research.

Griffin, C. (1985) *Typical Girls? Young Women from School to the Job Market.* London: Routledge.

Grundy, S. (1987) *Curriculum: Product or Praxis.* Lewes: Falmer Press.

Habermas, J. (1972) *Knowledge and Human Interests,* 2nd edn. London: Heinemann.

Hargreaves, A. (1994) *Changing Teachers, Changing Times: Teachers' Work and Culture in The Postmodern Age.* London: Cassell.

Hargreaves, D.H. (1967) *Social Relations in a Secondary School*. London: Routledge and Keegan Paul.

Harris, S. (1992) 'A Career on the Margins? The position of careers teachers in schools', *British Journal of Sociology of Education*, **13** (2),163–176.

Harvey, D. (1989) *The Condition of Postmodernity: And Enquiry into the Origins of Cultural Change*. Oxford: Basil Blackwell.

Haugaard, M. (1992) *Structures, Restructuration and Social Power*. Aldershot: Avebury.

Held, D. (1980) *Introduction to Critical Theory: Horkheimer to Habermas*. Cambridge: Polity Press.

Hindess, B. (1988) *Choice, Rationality, and Social Theory*. London: Unwin Hyman.

Hodkinson, P. and Issitt, M. (1995) (eds) *The Challenge of Competence: Professionalism through Vocational Education and Training*. London: Cassell.

Hodkinson, P. and Hodkinson, H. (1995) 'Markets, Outcomes and VET Quality: some lessons from a Youth Credits Pilot Scheme'. *Vocational Aspects of Education*, **47(3)**, 209-225.

Hodkinson, P. and Sparkes, A.C. (1993) 'Young People's Choices and Careers Guidance Action Planning: A Case Study of Training Credits in Action', *British Journal of Guidance and Counselling*, **21** (3), 246–261.

Hodkinson, P. and Sparkes, A.C. (1994) 'The Myth of the Market: the negotiation of training in a youth credits pilot scheme', *British Journal of Education and Work*, **7** **(3),** 2–20.

Hodkinson, P. and Sparkes, A.C. (1995a) 'Taking Credits: A Case Study of the Guidance Process into a Training Credits Scheme', *Research Papers in Education*, **10** **(1),** 75-99.

Hodkinson, P. and Sparkes, A.C. (1995b) 'Markets and Vouchers: the Inadequacy of Individualist Policies for Vocational Education and Training in England and Wales', *Journal of Educational Policy*, **10** (2), 189–207.

Hodkinson, P., Sparkes, A.C. and Hodkinson, H. (1992) *Careers Officers and Training Credits*, Working Paper No 1, Training Credits in Action project. Crewe:Education Department, Crewe; and Alsager Faculty, Manchester Metropolitan University.

Hord, S. (1987) *Evaluating Educational Innovation*. London: Croom Helm.

House, E. (1979) 'Technology versus Craft: a Ten Year Perspective on Innovation', *Journal of Curriculum Studies*, **1,** 1–15.

Howard, R.W. (1987) *Concepts and Schemata: An Introduction*, London: Cassell.

Hutton, W. (1995) *The State We are In*. London: Jonathan Cape.

Hyland, T. (1994) *Competence, Education and NVQs: Dissenting Perspectives*. London: Cassell.

Jenkins, R. (1992) *Pierre Bourdieu*. London: Routledge.

Jessup, G. (1991) *Outcomes: NVQs and the Emerging Model of Education and Training*. Lewes: Falmer Press.

Jones, G. and Wallace, C. (1992) *Youth, Family and Citizenship*. Buckingham: Open University Press.

Jones, K. and Hatcher, R. (1994) 'Educational Progress and Economic Change: Notes on Some Recent Proposals', *British Journal of Educational Studies*, **42** (3), 245–260.

Kidd, J.M. (1984) 'Young People's Perceptions of their Occupational Decision-Making', *British Journal of Guidance and Counselling*, **12** (1), 25–38.

Kuhn ,T.S. (1970) *The Structure of Scientific Revolutions*, 2nd. edn. London: University of Chicago Press.

Law, B. (1981) 'Community Interaction: a 'Mid-Range' Focus for Theories of Career Development in Young Adults', *British Journal of Guidance and Counselling*, **9** **(2),**

142–158.

Lawrence, D. (1992) 'The Careers Officer: a marginalised member of the education family', *School Organisation*, **12 (1)**, 99–111.

Lawrence, D. (1994) 'The Careers Service: Threatened by Youth Unemployment – Saved by Youth Training', *British Journal of Education and Work*, **7 (2)**, 63–76.

Lee, D., Marsden, D., Rickman, P. and Duncombe, J. (1990) *Scheming for Youth: A Study of YTS in the Enterprise Culture*. Milton Keynes: Open University Press.

Le Grand, J. and Bartlett, W. (1993) (eds) *Quasi-Markets and Social Policy*. Basingstoke: Macmillan.

MacDonald, R. and Coffield, F. (1993) 'Young People and Training Credits: and early exploration', *British Journal of Education and Work*, **6 (1)**, 5–22.

McNeill, J.K. (1990) *A Question of Choice*, MEd. Dissertation, University of Sheffield.

Maguire, M. (1995) 'The Youth Labour Market in the 1990s'. Paper Presented at the Conference, *Young People and the Labour Market*, Institute of Employment Research, University of Warwick, 14th February.

Marsh, C. (1988) 'Unemployment in Britain'. In D. Gallie (ed.) *Employment in Britain*. Oxford: Basil Blackwell.

Miller, M. (1983) 'The Role of Happenstance in Career Choice', *Vocational Guidance Quarterly*, **32 (1)**, 16–20.

Moore, R. (1988) 'Education, employment and recruitment'. In Dale, R., Ferguson, R. and Robinson, A. (eds) *Frameworks for Teaching*. London: Hodder and Stoughton.

MSC/DES (1986) *Review of Vocational Qualifications in England and Wales*. A Report by the Working Group to Review Vocational Qualifications. London: HMSO.

Murray, R. (1991) 'Fordism and Post-Fordism'. In Esland, G. (ed.) *Education, Training and Employment. Volume 1: Educated Labour – the Changing Basis of Industrial Demand*. Wokingham: Addison-Wesley.

National Commission on Education (1993) *Learning to Succeed: A Radical Look at Education Today and A Strategy for the Future*. London: Heinemann.

Nicholls, A. (1983) *Managing Educational Innovations*. London: George Allen & Unwin.

Okano, K. (1993) *School to Work Transition in Japan*. Clevedon: Multi-Lingual Matters.

Osipow, S. (1977) 'The Great Expose Swindle: A Reader's Reaction' *Personnel and Guidance Journal*, **5 (6)**, 22–24.

Osipow, S. (1990) 'Convergence in Theories of Career Choice and Development: Review and Project', *Journal of Vocational Behaviour*, **36 (2)**, 122–131.

Petersen, A.C. and Mortimer, J.T. (eds) (1994) *Youth Unemployment and Society*. Cambridge: Cambridge University Press.

Piore, M.J. and Sabel, C.F. (1984) *The Second Industrial Divide – Possibilities for Prosperity*. New York: Basic Books.

Polanyi, M. (1958) *Personal Knowledge*. London: Routledge and Kegan Paul.

Raffe, D. (1992) *Participation of 16–18 year olds in Education and Training*. Briefing Paper No 3. London: National Commission on Education.

Ranson, S. (1994) *Towards the Learning Society*. London: Cassell.

Reich, R. (1991) *The Work of Nations*. London: Simon and Schuster.

Resnick, L.B. (1987) 'Learning in School and Out', *Educational Researcher*, **16 (9)**, 13–20.

Richardson, L. (1990) *Writing Strategies: Reaching Diverse Audiences*. London: Sage.

Rikowski, G. (1992) 'Work Experience Schemes and Part-time Jobs in a Recruitment Context', *British Journal of Education and Work*, **5 (1)**, 19–46.

Roberts, K. (1968) 'The Entry into Employment: an Approach Towards a General Theory', *Sociological Review*, **1 (6)**, 165–184.

Roberts, K. (1975) 'The Developmental Theory of Occupational Choice: A Critique and an Alternative'. In Esland, G., Salaman, G. and Speakman, M. (eds) *People and Work*. Edinburgh: Holmes McDougall with Open University Press.

Roberts, K. (1991) 'Mass Unemployment Returns'. In Esland, G. (ed.) *Education, Training and Employment. Volume 1: Educated Labour – the Changing Basis of Industrial Demand*. Wokingham: Addison-Wesley.

Roberts, K. (1993) 'Career Trajectories and the Mirage of Increased Social Mobility'. In Bates, I. and Riseborough, G. (eds) *Youth and Inequality*. Buckingham: Open University Press.

Roberts, K. and Parsell, G. (1992) 'The Stratification of Youth Training', *British Journal of Education and Work*, **5** (1), 65–83.

Rudduck, J. (1986) *Understanding Curriculum Change*. Sheffield: USDE Papers in Education.

Rudduck, J. (1991) *Innovation and Change*. Milton Keynes: Open University Press.

Rumelhart, D.E. (1980) 'Schemata: the building blocks of cognition'. In Spiro, R. *et al.* (eds) *Theoretical Issues in Reading Comprehension*. Hillsdale, New Jersey: Lawrence Earlbaum.

Ryan, P. (ed.) (1991) *International Comparisons of Vocational Education and Training for Intermediate Skills*. Lewes: Falmer Press.

Sarason, S.B. (1982) *The Culture of School and the Problem of Change*, 2nd edn. Boston: Allyn and Bacon.

Siann, G. and Knox, A. (1992) 'Influences on Career Choice: the Responses of Ethnic-Minority and Ethnic-Majority Girls', *British Journal of Guidance and Counselling*, **20** (2), 193–204.

Sims, D. and Stoney, S. (1993) *Evaluation of the Second Year of Training Credits*. Slough: NFER.

Skilbeck, M., Connell, H., Lowe, N. and Tait, K. (1994) *The Vocational Quest: New Directions in Education and Training*. London: Routledge.

Smith, J. (1989) *The Nature of Social and Educational Inquiry: Empiricism versus Interpretation*. Norwood: New Jersey: Ablex.

Smithers, A. (1993) *All Our Futures: Britain's Education Revolution*. London: Channel 4 Television.

Sparkes, A.C. (1989) 'Towards an Understanding of the Personal Costs and Rewards Involved in Teacher Initiated Innovations' *Educational Management and Administration*, **17**, 100–108.

Sparkes, A.C. (1995) 'Writing People: Reflections on the Dual Crisis of Representation and Legitimation in Qualitative Inquiry', *Quest*, **47**, 158–95.

Sparkes, A.C. and Hodkinson, P. (1996) 'The Paradoxical Position of Careers Teachers in relation to the Training Credits Initiative as an Innovation', *The Curriculum Journal* (in press).

Springhall, J. (1993) 'Entering the World of Work: the Transition from Youth to Adulthood in Modern European Society', *Paedagogica Historica*, **29** (1), 33–52.

Steedman, H. and Hawkins, J. (1994) 'Shifting Foundations: the Impact of NVQs on Youth Training for the Building Trades', *National Institute Economic Review*, **August**, 93–102.

Strauss, A. (1962) 'Transformations of Identity'. In A.M. Rose (ed.) *Human Behaviour and Social Processes: An Interactionist Approach*. London: Routledge and Keegan Paul.

Tait, G. (1993) 'Youth, Personhood and 'Practices of the Self': some new directions for youth research', *Australia and New Zealand Journal of Sociology*, **29** (1), 40–54.

Taylor, M.J. (1992) 'Post-16 options: young people's awareness, attitudes, intentions and influences on their choice', *Research Papers in Education*, **7** (3), 301–335.

Unwin, L. (1993) 'Training Credits: the pilot doomed to succeed'. In Richardson, W., Woolhouse, J. and Finegold, D. (eds) *The Reform of Education and Training in England and Wales*. London: Longman.

Van Maanen, J. (1988) *Tales of the Field: On Writing Ethnography*. Chicago: University of Chicago Press.

Wallace, C., Boyle, F., Cheal, B. and Dunkerley, D. (1993) 'The Employment and Training of Young People in Rural South West England', *British Journal of Education and Work*, 6 (3), 25–44.

Watts, A.G. (1991) 'The Impact of the 'New Right': Policy Challenges Confronting Careers Guidance in England and Wales', *British Journal of Guidance and Counselling*, 19 (3), 230–245.

Watts, A.G. (1992) 'Individual Action Planning: Issues and Strategies', *British Journal of Education and Work*, 5 (1), 47–62.

Watts, A.G. (1994) 'Developing Individual Action-Planning Skills', *British Journal of Education and Work*, 7 (2), 51–62.

Wellington, J. (1994) 'How far should the post-16 curriculum be determined by the needs of employers?' *Curriculum Journal*, 5 (3), 307–322.

White Paper (1994) *Competitiveness: Helping Business to Win*. London: HMSO.

White Paper (1995) *Forging Ahead*. London: HMSO.

Willis, P. (1977) *Learning to Labour: How Working Class Kids Get Working Class Jobs*. Farnborough: Saxon House.

Wolcott, H.F. (1994) *Transforming Qualitative Data: Description, Analysis and Interpretation*. London: Sage.

Young, M. (1993) 'A Curriculum for the 21st Century? Towards a new basis for overcoming academic/vocational divisions', *British Journal of Educational Studies*, 41 (3), 203–222.

Index